# THE QuarkXPress IDEABOOK

Over 300 ready-to-use QuarkXPress "PrePages" for marketing your products, your services, and your organization.

The goal is honesty, clarity, and style.

# THE QuarkXPress IDEABOOK

Over 300 ready-to-use QuarkXPress "PrePages" for marketing your products, your services, and your organization.

BY **CHUCK GREEN**

The QuarkXPress Ideabook
Over 300 ready-to-use QuarkXPress "PrePages" for marketing
your products, your services, and your organization.



ISBN 0-9669587-6-4



This book is available for special purchase in bulk by organizations and institutions, at special discounts. Please direct your inquiries to the Logic Arts Corporation, 804-266-7996.

See the The QuarkXPress Ideabook/PrePage License Agreement in the back of this book.



*Other books by Chuck Green*

The PageMaker Ideabook

The QuarkXPress Ideabook

Design it Yourself: Graphic Workshop

Design it Yourself: Newsletters

Design it Yourself: Logos, Letterheads, & Business Cards

Clip Art Crazy

The Desktop Publisher's Idea Book

www.ideabook.com

# Preface

Design is everywhere. We celebrate carefully conceived and executed design in the symmetry of great buildings, within the layouts and messages of dynamic print, and in the spirit of remarkable artwork. To those of us who believe, there is design in everything.

My small thread in the ever-growing fabric of ideas began as *The Desktop Publisher's Idea Book* published by Random House. It is a collection of 100 out-of-the-ordinary design projects: the kind of stuff you use your hardware and software tools to produce after you've used them to design the stuff you bought them to produce. In addition to sparking the imagination, I think what made the *Idea Book* popular was that it provides all the detail you need to reproduce the projects: the dimensions of pages, the placement of illustrations and artwork, the size and configuration of fonts, and so on.

The next logical step was to expand the collection and provide actual program-specific computer files.

That was accomplished by way of *PrePage for Adobe PageMaker*, a product that included templates for most of the projects in the *Idea Book* with the addition of 200-plus others for a total of 300 files.

This is step three: a combination of the *Idea Book* and 315 project files. But it is far more than the sum of the two. Roughly one-third of the projects are entirely new. It includes some of the most requested document types, and features many of the projects I created for my most recent books on newsletters, logos, letterheads, and business cards.

The tried and true projects have all been edited and updated—many significantly. My goal was to weed out anything that was not truly useful—there are no designs for the sake of designs. In fact, I ended up with 15 more projects than the 300 I planned because there were new ones I simply could not cut.

The final piece of the puzzle is that the templates are now available for three different software programs: PageMaker, InDesign, and QuarkXPress. If you would like to purchase a set of files for one of the other programs, they are available from ideabook.com.

Finally, I would like to acknowledge a few folks who helped along the way. They are: Tom Graney, Deborah Green, Jim Green, and Elisabeth Sipkes.

Chuck Green

# Contents

**Register your copy of The QuarkXPress Ideabook and WIN!**
Page 255

# Introduction

There has been a massive, fundamental shift in the craft of graphic design. A few short years ago, the primary barrier to producing print communication was the tools—today, the only barrier is your imagination.

Think about it. As recently, as the 1980s, the machinery and gear necessary to create what you and I now produce from our desktop would have cost tens-of-thousands, even hundreds-of-thousands of dollars to assemble. There were separate machines for producing headline type and body text, darkrooms for shooting, developing, and printing photographs and illustrations, not to mention all manner of special systems and skills necessary to assemble the pieces and to prepare final artwork for a printing press. Twenty years before that, individual access to mass printing and publishing was simply unheard of.

Today, virtually anyone with the expertise and a modest investment in software and hardware can become a publisher. We can translate our ideas into words and pictures and, with the advent of worldwide delivery, distribute the results to every corner of the planet. All for a tiny fraction of what it once cost in effort, resources, and time.

But, what is so interesting to me is this: though we are in the throes of a revolution, an overwhelming majority of print documents still follow standardized formats used for a surprisingly limited range of applications. In some ways, the toolbox has expanded further than our ideas about how to use it.

*The QuarkXPress Ideabook* is an exercise for expanding that thinking. It is designed to help you reexamine the design and function of everyday documents, explore ways to maximize their effectiveness, and to step out and invent new applications and solutions.

For the standards—brochures, newsletters, forms, and such—the *Ideabook* provides hundreds of pre-designed, laid-out pages (I call them PrePages) that allow you to start a project with most of the work already done. But you will also find other projects you may not have considered—unusual solutions for direct mail, packaging, and labeling, and other out-of-the-ordinary projects such as a brochure in the form of a paper airplane, a series of clock faces, and a postcard newsletter.

A professionally presented message is a proven method for distinguishing yourself, your product or service, and your organization from the crowd. Whether you're a new computer user with no design experience or an experienced pro with hundreds of projects under your belt, *The QuarkXPress Ideabook* will put the power of print to work for you.

## What do you need?

To use the PrePage files you must have QuarkXPress (version 4.1 and higher) installed on your computer. It is important to understand that the files in the Ideabook CD-ROM are QuarkXPress files, there is no separate software program. Therefore, you only need the same hardware/software configuration you normally use with the QuarkXPress program itself.

Before diving in, you should be familiar with QuarkXPress program basics. There are no complex special skills needed to use the files. If you have questions about working with QuarkXPress refer to the QuarkXPress User Guide—it provides excellent, comprehensive instructions for working with files such as those supplied on the *Ideabook* CD-ROM.

## What's inside?

It's not enough to see what can be done; you have to understand how to get from the idea to the published piece. In Chapter 1 you'll learn just that: a simple step-by-step method for establishing a goal, composing a message, and producing a winning design.

Chapter 2 fills in the necessary details. You'll find tips on working with type, clip art and photography, finding and working with illustrators, photographers, and printers, and how to choose paper types, finishes, and weights.

Chapter 3 contains a step-by-step guide for opening and editing the files in QuarkXPress for the first time.

And Chapters 4 through 22 describe, catalog, and index the 300-plus project files.

## A different kind of design book

Most design books show you examples created by designers for their clients with the idea that you'll apply the same principles to your own work. The unwritten rule is that you don't copy the designs or contents exactly. But the projects in *The QuarkXPress Ideabook* were created exclusively for you to integrate into your own work. Use the files as is or add your own personal touches.

## Continue the discussion at www.ideabook.com

I love ideas. Thinking of new ways of doing things. Looking at problems from different angles. Digging for treasure in cultivated earth.

Whether I'm writing a book, designing a brochure, or building a web site—the process is the same—I look at the obvious solutions and try to take them a step further. Am I always successful? Not hardly. What may be a new wrinkle to me may well be old hat to you.

Which leads me to the purpose of my web site—www.ideabook.com. It's a place to continue the discussion. A place to trade ideas. A place for you to learn a little more about me and, hopefully, for me to hear about you. Between the two of us, we may even get the next visitor to pause for a second or two and pay us the ultimate compliment: "Hey, why didn't I think of that?"

If you have ideas and tips you'd like to share, or comments and suggestions about the Ideabook, come by and have a look around.

*Chuck Green*

*www.ideabook.com*
*chuckgreen@ideabook.com*

Chapter 1

# Turning Ideas Into Results

Robert Frost said "An idea is a feat of association." An accomplished designer learns to gather ideas while looking at the work of others. You mentally file away the design, how the writer crafted the message, which fonts were used, how major points were illustrated, and details about how the final piece was produced and printed.

Later, you craft your own documents by blending, not copying, the best of these ideas with your own knowledge and experience, and use their influence to develop ideas of your own.

The goal of *The QuarkXPress Ideabook* is to advance that process. With this book and the accompanying files, you can start a project with most of the work already done—use it exactly as it is or use the layout as a foundation to develop, build, and inspire your own design.

## The basics of project production

If you're not already familiar with taking a project from beginning to end, you can simplify the process by looking at production as a series of steps. These are not hard and fast rules that apply to every type of project, but they are the basis of most.

### 1. SET YOUR GOAL

No matter what kind of product, service, or idea you're promoting, begin each project by establishing a clear goal. Ask yourself what you must achieve to consider your effort a success: an inquiry, a documented change in the reader's thinking, a purchase? Decide up front who your audience is and find out everything you can about them; research where you are likely to find them, what their tastes are, what other types of information they respond to, and so on.

### 2. COMPOSE YOUR MESSAGE

The message is king. Even the best design, the most dramatic illustration, and the most expensive printing can't save the wrong message.

Most effective marketing materials communicate the same main messages: "This is what we can do for you." "This is the problem our product solves for you." "This is how you will look or feel once you've take the action described." They don't waste space trying to convince you how great their organization is or boast about how many features their product has. Why? Because you and I don't buy features and facts, we buy outcomes. You could educate your readers and let them make up their own minds, but why would you pass up a prime opportunity to lay out the outcome for them?

A reader-centered message is just as important to a simple form as it is to the most sophisticated brochure—if you can't promise a little enjoyment or ease a little pain, few readers will take notice.

### 3. CHOOSE THE MEDIUM

Next, choose the vehicle for the message. Which type of layout works best: a brochure, a flyer, a self-mailer, a promotional item? Sometimes, as with a business card, the medium is obvious. Other times, your message may work in a whole range of layouts.

### 4. SELECT A DESIGN

Once you have a winning message, organize your design around it. Decide which *Ideabook* layout best targets your audience and open the file in QuarkXPress. Take a close look at how the elements are arranged. What is often difficult for a new designer to grasp is how important little adjustments and additions make. A good design often requires hours of experimenting—of moving, adding, or subtracting elements, playing with different typefaces, finding just the right artwork to illustrate your message, and so on. The difference between a design that works and one that doesn't is often hidden in these details.

### 5. ILLUSTRATE YOUR MESSAGE

The purpose of an illustration or photograph is to emphasize your words or to show what you can't say. That doesn't mean that you can't use graphics merely to set the tone or draw attention, but whenever possible, make the illustration do some work. Show your product in action, picture people getting their problems solved, communicate the excitement and energy of your idea.

### 6. PREPARE YOUR ARTWORK

Set up the document for the printer you will use to output it. Import your text and apply styles, insert additional pages (if necessary), place your images, then take some time to move the pieces around and add your own personal touches.

When you think you're finished, print out and mock up the finished piece—tape together back to back pages, fold where there will be folds, and trim the piece to size. The computer screen can be deceptive—a mock-up is the best way to get a clear idea of how the finished piece will look and feel.

### 7. CHECK THE ARTWORK AND TEXT FOR ERRORS

Let the finished artwork sit for a day or two, then review it from the reader's perspective. Does the main message ring true? Does the design ease the flow of information? Have you supplied all of the information necessary for the reader to take action?

Check for typographical errors. Double-check spelling and grammar, and triple-check your phone number, address, and other contact information. Once you're certain you've uncovered every possible problem, have someone else proof it—they're sure to find at least one or two more mistakes. Make the corrections and repeat the process.

### 8. GAUGE READER REACTION

If you are new to the process, ask a few people who do not know your product, service, or idea to tell you what the piece communicates to them. Don't give them a lengthy setup about what you are trying to accomplish (you don't have that luxury when it is distributed), just ask them to read it over and to answer your questions afterward. You need a thick skin to be a designer. Some people will get the message and appreciate the look and feel of a piece, it may leave others cold—shoot for consensus and be open to changes.

### 9. PRINT OR PUBLISH YOUR PROJECT

Print multiple copies of your finished artwork from your computer or take it to a commercial or specialty printer to have it reproduced in quantity.

Chapter 2

# Adding the Professional Touches

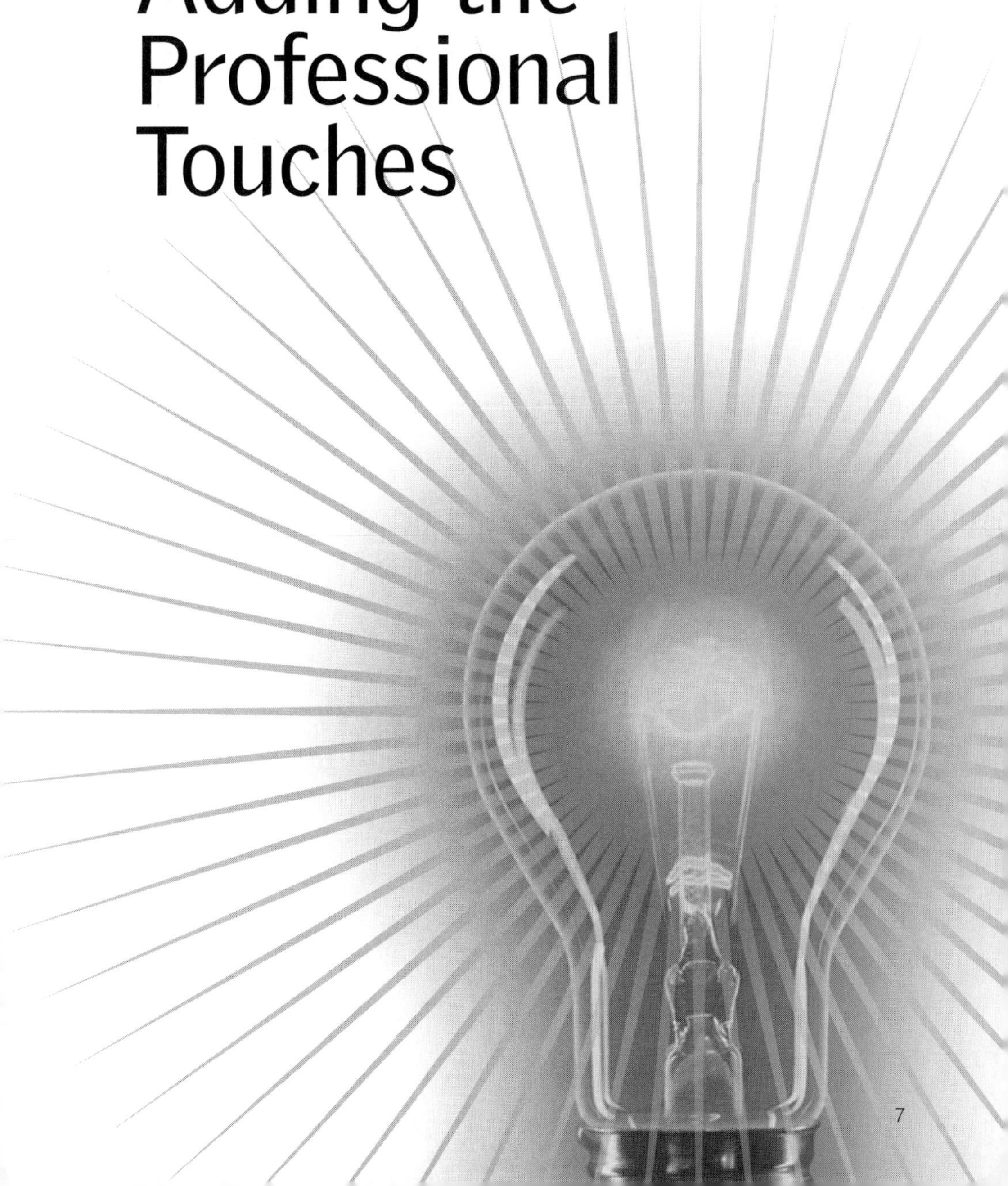

You don't need to be a creative genius to produce top-quality work with your computer system. With a carefully chosen collection of fonts, clip art, photographs, and the services of outside experts, great things are possible.

The following are tips for finding and working with the products and people that will make your documents a cut above the rest.

### Selecting typefaces

Typefaces have a profound effect on the design of your documents. Each has a personality of its own. There are three basic categories of type: display, serif, and sans serif.

| | |
|---|---|
| Display<br>Example font: Giza Seven Seven | **Place your text in this position. To achieve the same look, choose a** |
| Sans Serif<br>Example font: Franklin Gothic Book Cond | Place your text in this position. To achieve the same look, choose a similar font and duplicate the size, spacing, and alignment settings. To match the overall page design, duplicate the positioning of each element and its proportion to the other elements on the page. The difference |
| Serif<br>Example font: Garamond | Place your text in this position. To achieve the same look, choose a similar font and duplicate the size, spacing, and alignment settings. To match the overall page design, duplicate the positioning of each element and its proportion to the other elements on the page. The |

The easiest way to describe *display fonts* is to define how they are *not* used. Typically, they are not used for body text. Display fonts are designed primarily for headlines, subheads, titles, and other short text blocks sized 20 points or larger.

Most of the projects herein use *serif fonts* for the body of text (serif fonts have "feet" at the tops and bottoms of the characters). Although these fonts also work well as headlines and subheads, they are designed primarily for body text.

Serif fonts, in general, are said to be more readable than sans serif (without serifs) or display fonts. Theories why range from speculation that the "feet" lead your eye from one character to the next, to the belief that you are simply accustomed to reading serif text in books, magazines, and newspapers.

*Sans serif fonts* are also used for body text and display purposes but they are generally considered slightly more difficult to read than serif fonts. Sans serif fonts are particularly good for captions, very small text (6 point and under), and for creating the titles and subheads that break up the body text.

As you will see, you don't need hundreds of different typefaces to recreate the *Ideabook* projects, nor do you need the exact *same* fonts. You can use fonts that are roughly the same or substitute the fonts you have available.

On the facing page are the names of most of the typefaces used in the *Ideabook* files, and to the right, the names of fonts you could use in their place. The fact is, all 315 projects could easily be recreated with one serif, one sans serif, and two or three display typefaces.

Why not include the fonts used in the original files? Cost. One or two high-quality fonts cost more than this book and CD-ROM. In fact, it is not unusual for a designer to pay upwards of $200 for variations of a single typeface. See a font you particularly like? All the fonts used are available from various foundrys through myfonts.com.

If you were going to invest in just two fonts buy these versatile text fonts: Franklin Gothic Book Condensed (sans serif ) and Minion Regular (serif); one or the other is used in just about every project in the book.

| Don't have this font? | Substitute this font... |
|---|---|
| Charlemagne<br>HONESTY, CLARIT | Bernhard Modern<br>Castellar<br>Trajan |
| Copperplate Gothic 33bc<br>HONESTY, CLARIT | ITC Motter Corpus<br>ITC Ozwald<br>Madrone |
| Fette Fraktur<br>Honesty, Clarity, | Goudy Text Lombardic<br>Monotype Script Bold<br>Willhelm |
| Franklin Gothic Book<br>Honesty, Clarity, an | Eras Light<br>Formata Light<br>Helvetica Light |
| Franklin Gothic Book Condensed<br>Honesty, Clarity, and St | Helvetica Condensed<br>Monotype Grotesque Light Cond |
| Franklin Gothic Condensed<br>Honesty, Clarity, and | Helvetica Cond Black<br>Tempo Heavy Cond<br>Trade Gothic Cond Bold |
| Franklin Gothic Heavy<br>Honesty, Clarity, | Frutigar 95 Ultra Black<br>Futura Extra Bold<br>Helvetica Black |
| Impact<br>Honesty, Clarity, and S | Eurostile 2 Bold Cond<br>Helvetica Inserat<br>Placard Bold Cond |
| Minion Regular<br>Honesty, Clarity, anc | Caslon Reg<br>Garamond Reg<br>Times New Roman |
| Raleigh Gothic<br>Honesty, Clarity, and Style HONESTY, CL | Bodega Sans Light<br>Industria<br>Universe Ultra Cond |
| Shelley Allegro Script<br>Honesty, Clarity, and | Bickham Script<br>Boulevard<br>Poppl-Residenz |
| Times New Roman<br>Honesty, Clarity, anc | Caslon<br>Garamond<br>Minion |
| Willow<br>Honesty, Clarity, and Style HONESTY, CLARITY, a | Birch<br>Bodega Sans Light<br>Racer |

## Choosing clip art

If you doubt the value of high-quality illustrations, price a custom one. Even a simple black and white image by a proficient artist will typically cost at least $100. Color work by recognized illustrators begins in the thousands. By comparison, good clip art is a bargain.

As any designer will tell you, the main criteria for choosing an image are a sound concept and a stylish execution. What it costs and what form it is in are only important if an illustration says what you want to say, the way that you want to say it.

### CHOOSING A CONCEPT

A good illustration is much more than mere ornamentation. At a minimum, it should grab attention and draw your reader into the message. At its best, it will express something words cannot.

The clip art images that are the easiest to execute, and therefore the most common, are objects: something material such as a bouquet of flowers. By putting the bouquet in the context of a flyer for a florist, you visually communicate the topic.

More interesting and less common are images that illustrate ideas or tell a story—such as the act of giving the flowers. These images are more interesting because they contribute meaning to your message, and they are less common because they are more difficult to conceive and are useful in fewer situations.

Once you begin to notice the subtleties of the visual language, you'll be better equipped to choose concepts that more precisely illustrate your message. Some examples:

A CLICHÉ has a widely understood meaning. In this case, a skull and crossbones represents a danger to life.

An ICON is an image that suggests its meaning. The opened padlock represents the state of being unlocked.

A METAPHOR suggests a likeness between two ideas. Here, a half full/half empty glass of water is analogous to one's attitude about life.

A SIGN is a shorthand device that stands for something else. The @ sign, for example, represents "at."

A VISUAL PUN uses one or more symbols to create two or more possible meanings. In this illustration, the sharks' fins represent the concepts of money and caution.

A SYMBOL is a visible image of something invisible. Here, an hourglass represents time.

Borders, rules, ornaments, and backgrounds typically are decorative elements used to break up space and enhance the overall design of the page.

Illustrations (opposite) Skull and Lock: © Image Club Graphics Inc. eyewire.com; Glass: © CMCD Inc. visualsymbols.com; @: Adobe Minion font. © Adobe Systems Inc. adobe.com; Shark: © Art Parts. ronandjoe.com; Hourglass: © Dubl-Click Software Inc. dublclick.com

## CHOOSING A STYLE

If concept is what you say, style is how you phrase it. There are as many illustrative styles as there are illustrators. In fact, it is not uncommon for one artist to use several different styles.

These light bulbs give you some idea of that diversity.

Illustrations (left to right): © NVtech. nvtech.com; © MVB. mvbfonts.com; © Art Parts. ronandjoe.com; © Image Club Graphics Inc. eyewire.com; © Chuck Green; © Image Club Graphics Inc. eyewire.com

While one artist simplifies the image to a series of basic shapes, another captures the contours and shading to achieve a completely different look and feel.

Style must be built on a strong foundation. It is said that to be a good abstract painter, you must first master realism. Although all good illustrators have not necessarily mastered realism, they understand basics such as the proportions of the human figure and the use of light, shade, and perspective. If you find it difficult to nail down if inconsistencies in a drawing are part of an artist's style or simply poor execution, move on to another source.

And old is not necessarily bad. Like wide lapels and bell-bottom pants, illustrative styles come and go. It's not unusual to find artwork from past decades incorporated into the work of a leading-edge design studio or advertising agency.

If you have space within your design to isolate one image from the next, you can often use more than one style. If the piece is small, or images are close, it's better to use a single style throughout.

## THE CLIP ART CHECKLIST

Beyond concept and style, judging a drawing is subjective—you either like it or you don't. But before you make your final selection, consider these issues.

INTEGRITY. Isolate the image from others around it. Twenty different images grouped together on the same page take on a personality of their own. To get a realistic view, cover the surrounding images and see if the artwork survives on its own.

SIZE. View the image close to the size you will use it. Lots of images look terrific as tiny specks on a catalog page and not so terrific blown up to two or three inches across. Likewise, some images work better larger than smaller.

SHAPE. Consider the shape of the overall image. A long horizontal image may not work well on a short vertical brochure cover. Non-uniform shapes may require white space you simply can't spare.

## Using royalty-free and stock photography

The photographic equivalent of clip art is royalty-free photography. These are collections of photographs on CD-ROM that you pay for one time and are free to use, in most cases, anyway you like. Like clip art, the subject matter is necessarily generic but the categories are growing by leaps and bounds. You'll find city skylines, food, business people, families, money, backgrounds, antiquities—you name it.

The term "stock" illustrations and photographs ordinarily means that the material is governed by a more restrictive agreement. The royalty you pay to use a stock image is most often based on criteria such as the type of project, the size of the potential audience, and/or the number of copies you plan to print.

Though they typically cost more, the top stock houses have libraries of hundreds of thousands, even millions of photographs from which to choose. Subject matter includes photographs staged for advertising and a mind-boggling array of historic subjects, movie stills, and news photos.

Today, virtually all the major royalty-free and stock providers allow you to search for and purchase images online. Some even offer research services to help you find what you're looking for. You describe the subject matter you're looking for and a representative of the provider searches its files for images that meet your criteria.

## Commissioning custom illustrations and photographs

Electronic clip art and stock photography are just the tip of the illustration iceberg. There are huge numbers of illustrations and photographs commissioned each year for individual projects. After all, an image that speaks directly to your audience can pay off in a big way. It makes the publication uniquely yours.

If you have never commissioned an illustration or a photograph, the process can seem a bit intimidating, but it's really quite simple.

The first step is to find an artist whose style fits the project. Illustration styles range from near photographic realism to abstract symbolism. The techniques include digital drawing and painting, pen and ink, scratch board, 3D sculptures, airbrush, pencils, and many different types of painting.

Photography styles also run the gamut. A skilled photographer uses props, effects, and lighting to make each image one-of-a-kind.

Portfolio sites are an excellent way to make contacts. The artists or their agents buy space in these directories to present their best work. You'll find international, national, and regional portfolios all over the World Wide Web. Two examples are altpick.com and portfolios.com.

Another way to find photographers and illustrators is to look in newsletters, newspapers, and magazines. A call or E-mail to the art director of the publication will usually yield the artist's name and address. Local artists are sometimes listed in your Yellow Pages.

## Working with an illustrator

As you can imagine, custom illustration is not inexpensive, but it may be less than you think. Charges vary widely; a local illustrator might charge upwards of $2000.

If you haven't used an illustrator before, there are a few tips that will help make your first experience a positive one.

Begin with a phone call to explain your project and expectations. Describe how the illustration will be used and in what type of publication.

You'll get the most from artists by giving them some breathing room. Describing an assignment to "symbolize the global economy" will give the artist much more opportunity to be creative than saying "I want a drawing of a globe on a one dollar bill."

Discuss the medium they use (i.e., pen and ink, digital, watercolors, etc.) and how it reproduces in the process you'll use to print it. Don't forget to point out if you will be printing the finished art in black and white or in color.

These are samples of work by accomplished illustrators, all of whom we contacted after seeing their work in magazines or newspapers. The illustration on the immediate right was produced by a service that specializes in black and white line art.

© Graphics International

© Wayne Vincent. waynevincent.com

Before you talk price, reach an understanding about the rights you are buying. It's important to understand that illustrations and photographs remain the property of the artists. By law, they can reuse the image and charge you a fee if you ever want to reprint a publication using the same illustration. If you need exclusive rights, or rights to reprint the work, arrange them up-front.

Next, negotiate the price. If it's too high, don't hesitate to offer what you can afford. Most artists are willing to work with you in the hope you'll use them again in the future. *The Graphic Artist's Guild Handbook, Pricing and Ethical Guidelines* is a valuable resource for gauging fair prices (available from the ideabook.com store or from the Graphic Artist's Guild, at www.gag.org).

Once they understand the assignment and you have agreed to a price, set a deadline allowing yourself a few days for the possibility of changes or delays.

Now it's time to stand back and let them work their magic. Generally, the illustrator will rough out several different ideas for you to choose from. Select the one that works best and point out anything that is out of place or technically inaccurate. If you make changes after this stage, it will be expensive.

© Peter Hoey. peterhoey.com

© Hal Mayforth. mayforth.com

© Jennifer Hewitson Illustration

## Working with a photographer

Some photographers charge by the day, some by the assignment. Many will accept a variety of assignments, others specialize in either studio or location work.

Studio photography requires that you bring your people or subjects to the studio and set up within reach of the photographer's equipment. A good studio photographer can re-create just about any imaginable scene or mood with a combination of lighting, props, and sets. You might be surprised how many photographs that appear to be shot on location are actually staged in a studio.

A location photographer shoots everything on site. Sometimes it's as simple as traveling to your location to photograph the subject with available light. Other projects might require elaborate preparation, props, and special lighting.

The practice of working with a photographer is much the same as working with an illustrator. You explain the project, set a deadline, and describe how and where the finished photograph will be used to establish the rights and price.

While many photographers prefer the same creative freedom you might afford an illustrator, others prefer a more specific assignment. Photography is typically a bit more literal than illustration and there are often more details to consider.

Once you're under way the photographers will explain their ideas, perhaps sketch them out, or maybe show you photographs of a similar subject or situation they have taken. Most will want you to be present so that you can answer questions that arise as they compose the picture. If you can't be there, be sure to cover as many issues as possible beforehand.

When you see the final photograph or illustration printed on your document, you'll have a new appreciation of just how valuable a custom image can be.

### Scanning and copyright

Scanning is a terrific way to incorporate custom illustrations and photographs in your artwork. But you must own the artwork before you can use it. Illustrators and photographers hold legal rights to their creations from the moment they produce them, and you can't use them without permission—to be on the safe side, written permission.

And just because you change an image doesn't nullify the copyright and confer it to you. In one case, the artist reproduced his version of a copyrighted photograph as a computer drawing. He added elements, changed colors, and used no physical portion of the original, but was still charged with infringement. As Tad Crawford writes in the *Legal Guide for the Visual Artist* (Allworth Press, New York, 1995), "What is the test for copyright infringement? It is whether an ordinary observer, looking at the original work and the work allegedly copied from it, recognizes that a copying has taken place." In other words, you would have to literally transform an image to call it your own.

With the proliferation of computers and scanners, it's a fair bet that the art world will continue to actively search for opportunities to test and reinforce copyright. Don't take it lightly; infringement awards can amount to many thousands of dollars.

## Reproducing the print projects

There are three basic ways to reproduce the *Ideabook* projects. You can output the final project in small quantities directly from your computer's laser or graphics printer, use the computer printer output as master artwork to be reproduced on a high-quality copier, export to the Portable Document Format (PDF), or create files to be output by a commercial or specialty printer on a printing press.

Generally speaking, your laser or graphics printer is ideal for small quantity projects that can be printed on standard 8 1/2 by 11 inch or 8 1/2 by 14 inch papers and labels designed especially for a computer printer.

Once you get above a quantity of 50 to 100 copies of a single page, the laser printer becomes less practical and you're ready to switch to a high-quality copier.

## Working with a commercial printer

If you are doing any serious publishing, a commercial printer is an important resource. Although many of the *Ideabook* projects can be reproduced in small quantities directly from your computer, a commercial printer with a printing press can generally save you time and money when you're printing more than 500 pages.

An outside printer is also essential for printing projects that require the use of papers heavier than your printer can handle or for large projects that require folding and binding.

### FINDING A QUALITY PRINTER

Printing quality varies widely. The best and most obvious way to find out if printers meet your standards is to review their work and have them print a small project for you.

Below is a list of four fundamentals to look for. These are not legal definitions of good printing, but simple indicators of the minimum acceptable quality.

*Reproduction quality*—The printed piece should not be noticeably less sharp and clear than the original.

*Positioning*—The artwork should be positioned on the page within 1/16" of where you laid it out, top and bottom, left and right. It should not slant on the page unless your original did.

*Ink coverage*—The ink color (black is considered a color) should be the same shade and density on all parts of the page and throughout the document. Text that is noticeably heavier or lighter than the original may have been printed using too much or too little ink.

*Dust and debris*—There should not be noticeable dust or debris that didn't appear on the original artwork. An occasional spot on a limited number of copies is unpreventable, but an attentive printer will catch and discard the majority of these pages.

If the printer is using a high-speed copier, they have less control of these fundamentals, so when in doubt, opt for printing on a press versus a copier.

## GETTING A FAIR PRICE

Printing prices vary widely. Some printers estimate jobs based on changing criteria such as how busy they are or how well-suited your job is to the equipment they use. Other printers follow a strict computer formula. In any case, to ensure you're getting a reasonable price, it's best to get price estimates from two or three different printers.

## PREPARING YOUR ARTWORK

Today, printers prefer computer files to artwork on paper. But there are still some situations where you might have to supply a high-quality printout for copying or printing. In that case, the better prepared your artwork is, the more likely your job will return from the printer as you envisioned it. If you are not clear about how to prepare the artwork, ask the printer what they require.

Obviously, if you are simply copying a standard 8 1/2 by 11 inch page, you normally don't need additional preparation. But if your pages are an odd size or they will be folded and bound, you are responsible for giving the printer complete instructions. A few basics:

*Show where to trim and fold*—Use crop marks to show how you want the final pages trimmed. Crop marks are a "Print" option of all desktop publishing programs and some of the more advanced word-processors.

If there isn't room for crop marks, add a thin line around the outside edge and instruct the printer not to print the line but to use it as the trim guide. Use broken (dotted) crop marks outside the print area to show if and where you want pages folded.

*Supply complete instructions*—When it comes to printing, you can't supply too much information. Give the printer complete written instructions, including the ink color(s), what brand, weight, and finish of paper to use, and any special instructions on folding and binding. Be sure to read the printer's contract terms so you clearly understand who is responsible for what.

Before settling on the quantity, ask about the printer's policy on under- and overruns. It is accepted practice for printers to be 10 percent over or under the quantity you request and to charge an equal amount more or less. It is not unusual, however, to agree beforehand that you will not pay extra for quantities beyond what you order.

*Create a mock-up*—Even for something as simple as an 8 1/2" by 11" sheet printed on both sides, you should create a miniature mock-up of how you want the final pages arranged. It doesn't have to be elaborate, just blank paper folded and marked to show what pages print where.

In the case of a brochure, you might want to show the direction of the folds. If you're creating a multipage document, trim out miniature pages, fold and number them to show how the finished pages should be assembled—you can't provide too much information

*Sign off on a proof*—Most printers can provide you with a photographic print of the negative they use to make the printing plates for your job (called a blueline). If your project represents a significant cost or is at all complicated, a blueline is your insurance that everything is positioned correctly. The blueline shows all of the artwork in place, trimmed, folded, and bound. The only thing you can't check on the blueline is color. If the color arrangement is complex, the printer should provide a separate color proof.

Check the blueline to confirm that everything is in place and that pages are in the right order. Point out any missing elements, dust spots, debris, or anything that doesn't look exactly as you expected.

*Double-check the finished job*—When you accept delivery of the completed job, check to see that you're getting roughly the quantity of pieces you ordered. If you have multiple packages or boxes, take samples from each to ensure that the quality is consistent throughout.

### Working with a specialty printer

A specialty printer has the equipment and expertise to print a particular type of project such as decals, pocket folders, or envelopes. Sometimes, a source halfway across the country will beat a local price or provide a higher-quality job simply because they specialize in that service.

Just about all of the basics covered in the previous section on commercial printers also apply here. Printing on coasters or T-shirts is not nearly as easy as printing on paper, so you'll probably have to be a bit more tolerant about production quality and variances in positioning.

Before you use a specialty printer, be sure to contact them for a description of services, pricing, and for samples to ensure they meet your expectations.

If you ask, most printers are more than happy to provide verbal or written details about how you should prepare your artwork for their process. Many publish guidelines on the Web sites.

Complex jobs are often more art than science. There is nothing more key to success than finding a printer who cares about quality and knows how to achieve it.

## Choosing paper

Whether you print directly from your computer or have your project reproduced by a commercial printer, paper obviously plays an important role in print design.

There are many papers specially designed for use with computer printers: super-smooth papers for printing final artwork, fine stationery papers and envelopes, and general-use papers in an amazing variety of colors and textures.

Many office supply stores stock these papers and some direct mail companies specialize in them. Two examples are: paperdirect.com and avery.com.

### STOCK FOR COMMERCIAL PRINTING

Paper is called "stock" in the printing trade. There are literally thousands of different weights, colors, and finishes.

Costs vary widely and can represent a significant portion of your printing bill, especially when you print in large quantities. So be sure to ask your printer to show you the same type of paper in different price ranges and to explain the advantages of each.

Some of the *Ideabook* projects include suggestions for stock selections, including the category, weight, color, and finish.

*Categories and weights*—The *Ideabook* text refers to three different categories of stock: bond, text, and cover. Each is available in a variety of weights.

*Bond* is the stock you probably buy for everyday use with your printer or copier. It ranges from high-quality sheets for stationery to inexpensive sheets for copiers. It is available in a wide choice of colors, but not nearly the variety available in "text" stock. The most common bond weights are 20 lb, 24 lb, 28 lb, and 32 lb.

The *text* category (sometimes called book) includes literally thousands of different sheets used for books, brochures, and other projects that require a light- to medium-weight sheet. The text category includes stock in every imaginable color and finish. The *Ideabook* refers to text weights ranging from 60 lb to 100 lb.

*Cover* stock is used to cover booklets, paperbacks, pocket folders, business cards, and other projects that require a more rigid sheet. The *Ideabook* refers to cover weights between 60 lb and 100 lb.

FINISHES

Besides various weights, you can choose from a seemingly endless selection of surface finishes.

*Uncoated* stock may have a smooth or textured surface. For example, a "laid" finish has a series of tiny ridges that run parallel down the page; a "pebbled" finish matches its description: a haphazard pattern of tiny, random stones. Your printer can show you everything from a conventional smooth finish to a finish that simulates leather.

*Coated* stock is finished with a very thin layer of clay that provides an excellent surface for printing and is often used for 4-color work. Some sheets are high-gloss, others have a dull finish.

To ensure that you get what you expect, ask your printer for samples. They have hundreds of different types and weights of paper available from paper manufacturers and they'll be happy to help you choose a stock appropriate for your project.

If you are creating a multipage brochure or booklet, many printers will make a "dummy" for you using the actual paper to show you how the final piece will look and feel.

Chapter 3

# Using the QuarkXPress Ideabook CD-ROM

To use the PrePage files you must have QuarkXPress (version 4.1 or higher) installed on your computer. It is important to understand that the files in the *Ideabook* CD-ROM are QuarkXPress files; the disk does not include a separate software program. Therefore, you only need the same hardware/software configuration you normally use with the QuarkXPress program itself.

Before diving in, you should be familiar with QuarkXPress program basics. There are no complex special skills needed to use the files. If you have questions about working with QuarkXPress refer to the *QuarkXPress User Guide*—it provides excellent, comprehensive instructions for working with files such as those supplied on the *Ideabook* CD-ROM.

## Getting Started

Place the Ideabook CD-ROM in your CD-ROM drive and...

STEP 1: OPEN A TEMPLATE

1. Start QuarkXPress and choose "File" > "Open"
2. Specify the location of your CD-ROM drive.
3. Select the MAC folder (Macintosh) or the WIN folder (Windows)
4. Select a file and click "Open"

(If you get an error message, try copying the file to your hard drive before you open it. )

STEP 2: SUBSTITUTE FONTS

As the program opens the template, you may be alerted to fonts used in the template that are not found on your system. Substitute fonts with roughly the same design and weight as those you are replacing—for example, choose a serif typeface to replace a serif typeface, bold for bold, and condensed for condensed (see the font list on page 11 for substitution ideas).

Remember, when you substitute one font for another, especially extremely different fonts, the same amount of text will not fit in the same space and the page may look significantly different than it does in this guide.

STEP 3: CHOOSE A PRINTER AND SAVE THE PUBLICATION

1. Once the template is open choose "File" > "Print"
2. Choose the printer you will use to output the final file and click "Capture Settings." Depending on the printer you're using, this may cause some slight changes such as how much text fits in a given paragraph.
3. Choose "File" > "Save As"
4. Select a folder on your hard drive in which to store the saved file.

5. Type the name for the publication and save it.

That's all there is to it! You're ready to edit your new publication as you would any other document.

## UNDERSTANDING THE TEMPLATE LAYOUT

The first time you open a template, try activating the pointer tool and choosing "Edit" > "Select all." This shows you the boundaries of each text box. Depending on the type of document, a page may be made up of a single text box or many. If you're not an experienced user, templates with more than a few text boxes may look a bit confusing, but once you take a close look, you'll find that a great deal of thought goes into how each box is positioned and linked.

## UNDERSTANDING PLACEHOLDERS

The templates use text "placeholders" to demonstrate the font selection, size, and alignment of the text. To help you roughly calculate the number of words used in a particular story, some text includes a word count every 100 words (the count appears in parentheses, i.e., (100), (200), (300).)

To replace the placeholder text:

1. Move the mouse pointer until the text tool I-beam is at the beginning of the text you want to replace.
2. Click and drag the mouse until you reach the end of the text you want to replace and release the mouse button. You can also double-click to select one word, triple-click to select one line, and click four times to choose a paragraph. Choose "Select all" from the "Edit" menu to select the entire story.
3. When you begin typing or paste text from the clipboard, the selected text will be overwritten.

## UNDERSTANDING GRAPHICS PLACEHOLDERS

Graphics "placeholders," such as those shown here, are placed where you would normally position graphics, clip art, and photographs. Replace them with your own artwork then select and delete the placeholders them before printing.

## USING THE STYLE PALETTE

Most of the text used is formatted using the program's powerful styles function. To take full advantage of the templates it is critical that you take a few minutes to learn how to use them.

Styles control the typeface and size, indents, line, and paragraph spacing. When you change the format of the style all of the paragraphs to which the style is applied change automatically—a major time saver. You can easily identify the style applied to any paragraph by clicking the "Text" tool on a line of text and seeing which style is highlighted in the Styles Palette.

The program's guide provides excellent, comprehensive instructions for using and editing styles.

## SUBSTITUTING FONTS

Styles also make it easy to substitute your favorite fonts.

1. To open the Styles Palette

   Choose "View" > "Show Style Sheets"

2. To edit a style

   Choose "Edit" > "Style Sheets"

Remember: when you change the font, size, and spacing of a style, you may not be able to fit the same amount of text as before. So change styles with caution. If a particular change doesn't achieve the desired effect, you can change the style back to the original settings or start again with a new copy of the template.

## VIEWING THE MASTER PAGES

Each template includes one or two master pages that include the elements repeated on all pages of the template. To view or edit those elements access the master pages.

## USING INCHES VERSUS POINTS

Though much of the desktop publishing world uses points and picas as the primary units of measure, most commercial printers and paper companies speak in inches. The descriptions of the *Ideabook* projects include dimensions in inches so you can speak to vendors in their own language. Naturally, you can change the measurement system to points or picas if you like.

## VERY IMPORTANT

Chuck Green (the author) and Logic Arts Corporation (the publisher) have used their best efforts in preparing this book and the document files contained herein. However, the author and publisher make no warranties of any kind, express or implied, with regard to the documentation or files contained in this book or on the accompanying disc, and specifically disclaim, without limitation, any implied warranties of merchantability and fitness for a particular purpose with respect to program listings in the book, the techniques described in the book, and/or the use of the files. In no event shall the author or publisher be responsible or liable for any loss of profit or any other commercial damages, including but not limited to special incidental, consequential, or any other damages in connection with or arising out of furnishing, performance, or use of this book or the program files.

The author and publisher have used their best efforts to proof and confirm the content of the files, but you should proof and confirm information such as dates, measurements, form properties, and any other content for yourself. The author and publisher make no warranties of any kind, express or implied, with regard to that content or its accuracy.

## USING THE TEMPLATE CATALOG

On the pages that follow you'll find detailed descriptions of each template. Use the catalog to locate the document you'd like to create and then use the instructions beginning on page 33 to open the template. Once you have opened it, take a moment to browse through and to read the corresponding catalog description. Experiment with substituting your favorite fonts and print the pages at full size to see how they are put together.

If you have a question about how to prepare the artwork, don't hesitate to ask your local commercial printer to review the artwork before you print the final version.

# Chapter 4
# Advertisements

## 001
## Coupon Ad

Used to create a small space advertisement in the form of a coupon. Check with publication for specific dimensions.

(NOTE: The author and publisher have used their best efforts to proof and confirm the content of the files, but you should proof and confirm information such as dates, measurements, form properties, and any other content for yourself. The author and publisher make no warranties of any kind, express or implied, with regard to that content or its accuracy.)

SIZE 7.5W x 3H
PAGES 1
FOLD —
STOCK —
BINDING —

## 002
## Block Ad

Used to create a small space advertisement. Check with publication for specific dimensions.

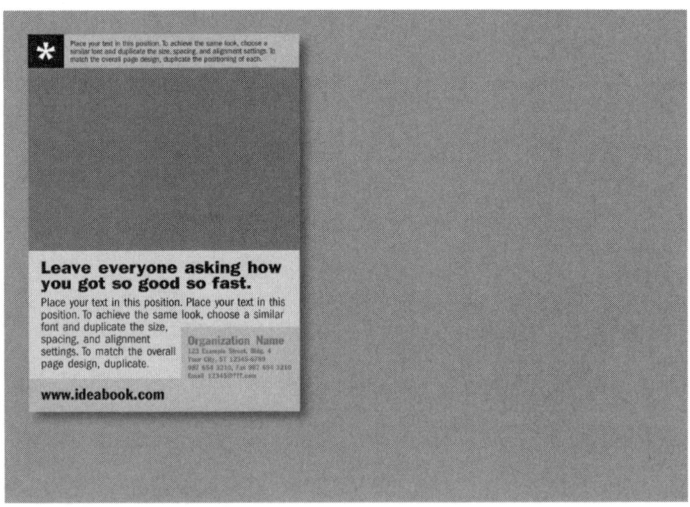


SIZE 4.25W x 6H
PAGES 1
FOLD —
STOCK —
BINDING —

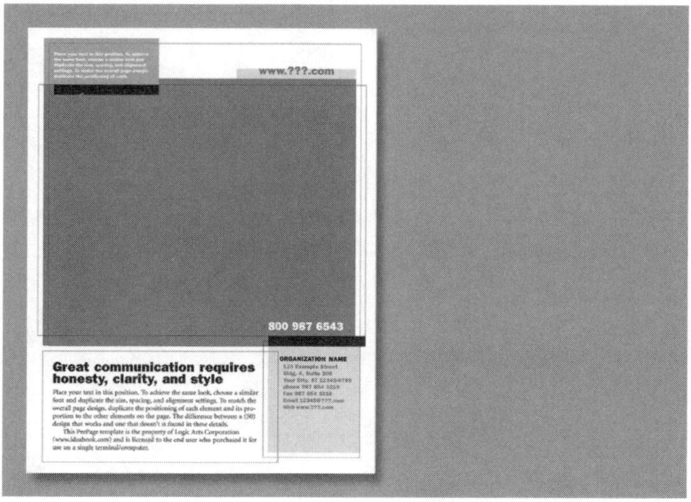


## 003
## Rectangles Ad

Used to create a full page advertisement. Check with publication for specific dimensions.

| | |
|---|---|
| SIZE | 8.5W x 11H |
| PAGES | 1 |
| FOLD | — |
| STOCK | — |
| BINDING | — |

## 004
## Illustrated Ad 1

Used to create a small space advertisement. Check with publication for specific dimensions.

| | |
|---|---|
| SIZE | 2.25W x 9.875H |
| PAGES | 1 |
| FOLD | — |
| STOCK | — |
| BINDING | — |

## 005
## Illustrated Ad 2

Used to create a small space advertisement. Check with publication for specific dimensions.

SIZE 6W x 6H
PAGES 1
FOLD —
STOCK —
BINDING —

## 006
## Illustrated Ad 3

Used to create a small space advertisement. Check with publication for specific dimensions.

SIZE 4.629W x 6.5H
PAGES 1
FOLD —
STOCK —
BINDING —

**007**
**Illustrated Ad 4**

Used to create a small space advertisement. Check with publication for specific dimensions.

| | |
|---|---|
| SIZE | 4.625W x 7.25H |
| PAGES | 1 |
| FOLD | — |
| STOCK | — |
| BINDING | — |

**008**
**Illustrated Ad 5**

Used to create a small space advertisement. Check with publication for specific dimensions.

| | |
|---|---|
| SIZE | 4.625W x 3.625H |
| PAGES | 1 |
| FOLD | — |
| STOCK | — |
| BINDING | — |

## 009
## Illustrated Ad 6

Used to create a small space advertisement. Check with publication for specific dimensions.

| | |
|---|---|
| SIZE | 3.375W x 4.625H |
| PAGES | 1 |
| FOLD | — |
| STOCK | — |
| BINDING | — |

## 010
## Inset Ad

Used to create a small space advertisement. Check with publication for specific dimensions.

| | |
|---|---|
| SIZE | 2.25W x 4.875H |
| PAGES | 1 |
| FOLD | — |
| STOCK | — |
| BINDING | — |

## 011 Object Ad

Used to create a small space advertisement. Check with publication for specific dimensions.

SIZE 2.068W x 9H
PAGES 1
FOLD —
STOCK —
BINDING —

## 012 Phone Book Ad 1

Used to create a small space advertisement for phone book. Check with publication for specific dimensions.

SIZE 4W x 2.375H
PAGES 1
FOLD —
STOCK —
BINDING —

## 013
## Phone Book Ad 2

Used to create a half-page advertisement for phone book. Check with publication for specific dimensions.

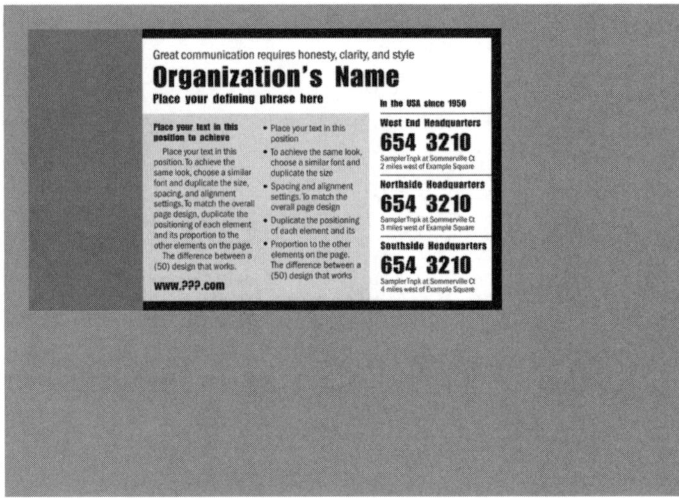


| | |
|---|---|
| SIZE | 8W x 4.875H |
| PAGES | 1 |
| FOLD | — |
| STOCK | — |
| BINDING | — |

## 014
## Tip Ad

Used to create a small space advertisement. Check with publication for specific dimensions.

| | |
|---|---|
| SIZE | 4.25W x 6H |
| PAGES | 1 |
| FOLD | — |
| STOCK | — |
| BINDING | — |

Page 255

Chapter 2

# Books & Booklets

(VARIABLE NUMBER OF PAGES)

## 015
## Block Magazine

Used to create a magazine-like booklet. Page 1: cover; page 2: sample masthead; page 3: contents; page 4-7: sample article.

(NOTE: The author and publisher have used their best efforts to proof and confirm the content of the files, but you should proof and confirm information such as dates, measurements, form properties, and any other content for yourself. The author and publisher make no warranties of any kind, express or implied, with regard to that content or its accuracy.)

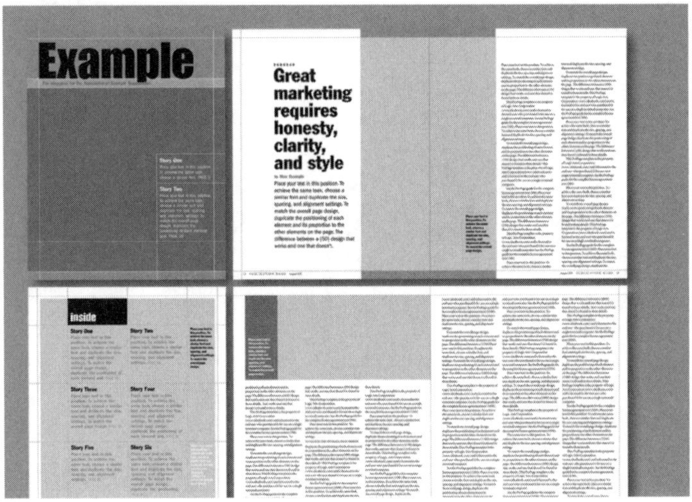


| | |
|---|---|
| SIZE | 8.5W x 11H |
| PAGES | 7 |
| FOLD | — |
| STOCK | cover: 80# gloss cover, text: 50# coated text |
| BINDING | perfect |

## 016
## Chapter Book

Used to create a conventional, non-fiction book. Page 1: title page; page 2 (ii): copyright page; page 3 (iii): acknowledgments; page 4 (iv): blank; page 5 (v) contents; page 6 (vi): blank; page 7 (vi) foreword, page 8 (viii): blank; page 9-12: chapters; page 13: index.

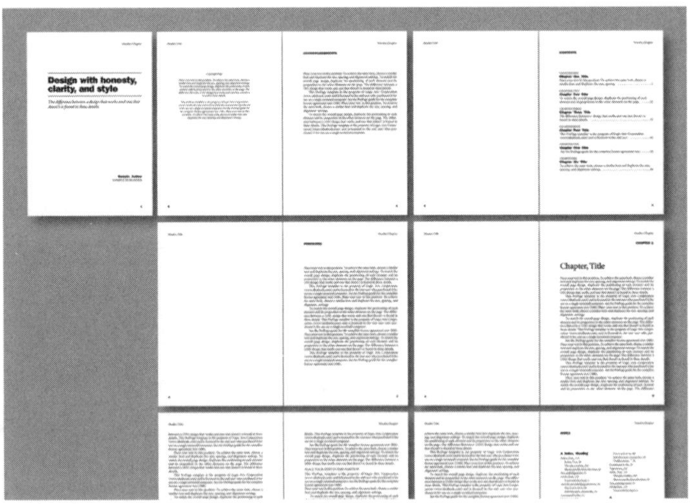


| | |
|---|---|
| SIZE | 6W x 9H |
| PAGES | 13 |
| FOLD | — |
| STOCK | 50# book |
| BINDING | perfect |

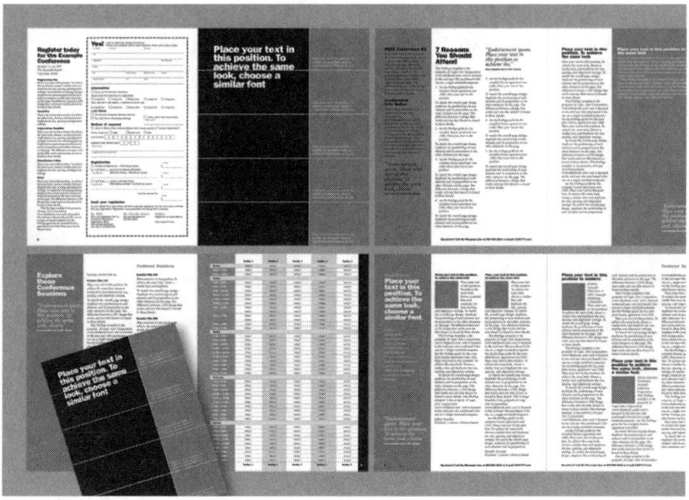

## 017
## Conference Booklet

Used to create a booklet—in this case, for a conference. Page 1: cover; page 2: welcome; page 3: speaker profiles; page 4: seminar descriptions; page 5: calendar; page 6-7: text; page 8: order details and order form.

| | |
|---|---|
| SIZE | 8.5W x 11H |
| PAGES | 8 |
| FOLD | half-fold |
| STOCK | cover: 80# gloss cover, text: 70# coated text |
| BINDING | saddle-stitch |

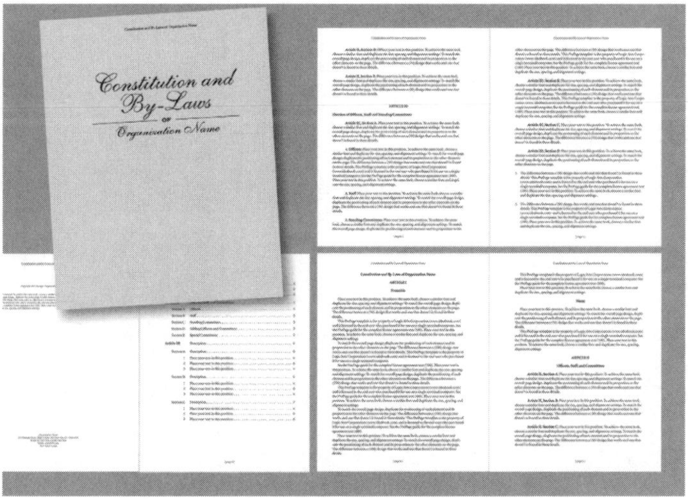


## 018
## Constitution

Used to create a booklet—in this case, for an organizational constitution. Page 1: cover; page 2: copyright; page 3: contents; page 4-7: articles and listings.

| | |
|---|---|
| SIZE | 8.5W x 11H |
| PAGES | 7 |
| FOLD | half-fold |
| STOCK | cover: 65# uncoated cover; 60# uncoated text |
| BINDING | spiral wire binding |

## 019
## Cookbook

Used to create a booklet—in this case, for a fundraiser cookbook. Page 1: cover; page 2–3: recipes; page 4: back cover.

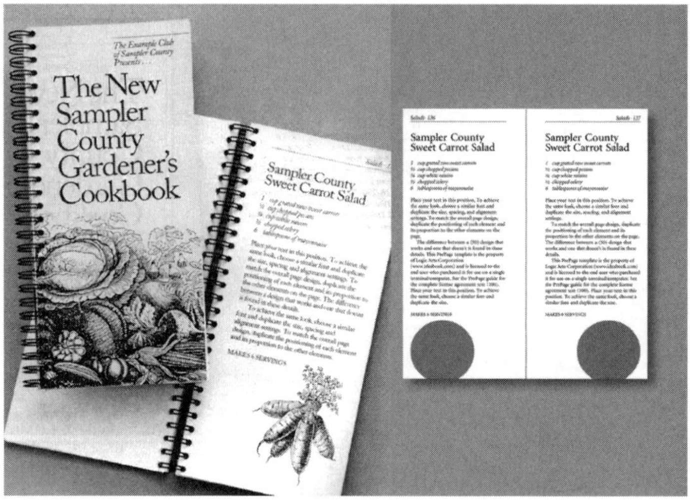


SIZE 4W x 9H
PAGES 4
FOLD half-fold
STOCK cover: 65# uncoated cover; text: 60# uncoated text
BINDING spiral wire binding

## 020
## Directory

Used to create a listing of organizations. Page 1-2: text pages. Divide the directory using the section heads, then list the name of the product, organization or person, add descriptive text, and the appropriate name, address and phone numbers.

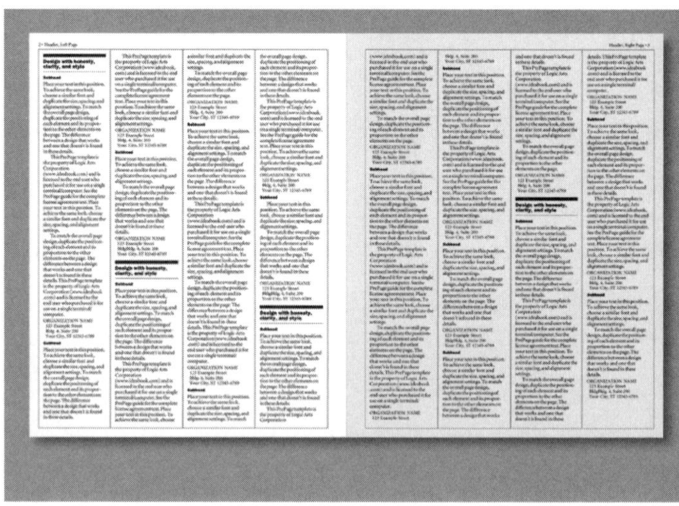

SIZE 8.5W x 11H
PAGES 2
FOLD half-fold
STOCK 60# uncoated text
BINDING saddle-stitch

## 021
## Dust Cover Booklet

Used to create a book cover for the text booklet below (021b). Cover wraps around the front and back pages of the booklet text. Page 1: wrap-around cover. To create a background pattern use a picture font or substitute an illustration.

| | |
|---|---|
| SIZE | 17W x 6.5H (flat); 4.5W x 6.5H (finished) |
| PAGES | 1 |
| FOLD | gate-fold |
| STOCK | 65# uncoated cover |
| BINDING | — |

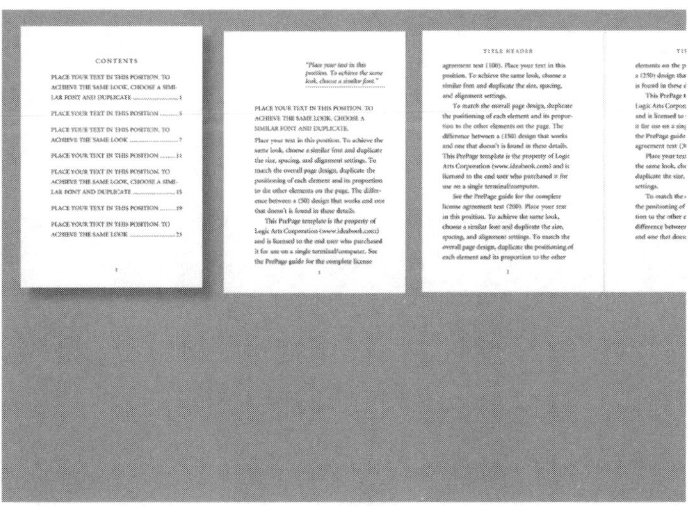


## 021b
## Dust Cover Booklet Text

Used to create the booklet text for dust cover above (021). Cover wraps around the front and back pages of the booklet text. Page 1: cover; page 2: blank; page 3: contents; page 4: blank; page 5-11: text. Assemble the final book by wrapping the cover flaps around the first and last pages of the inside booklet.

| | |
|---|---|
| SIZE | 4.438W x 6.5H (flat) |
| PAGES | 11 |
| FOLD | half-fold |
| STOCK | 60# uncoated text |
| BINDING | saddle-stitch |

## 022
## Event Booklet

Used to create a schedule of events in booklet form. Page 1: cover; page 2: contents; page 3: introduction; pages 4–5: text pages highlight one event per page; page 6: back cover.

SIZE 5.5W x 8.5H
PAGES 6
FOLD half-fold
STOCK cover: 65# uncoated cover, text: 60# uncoated text
BINDING saddle-stitch

## 023
## Event Booklet

Used to create a booklet for charitable auction adaptable for other types of events. Page 1: cover; page 2: contents; page 3: title; page 4: blank; page 5: endorsement; page 6: blank; page 7: overview; page 8: awards; page 9: sponsors; page 10: rules; page 11: program; page 12-13: items; page 14: sponsor advertisements; page 16: back cover.

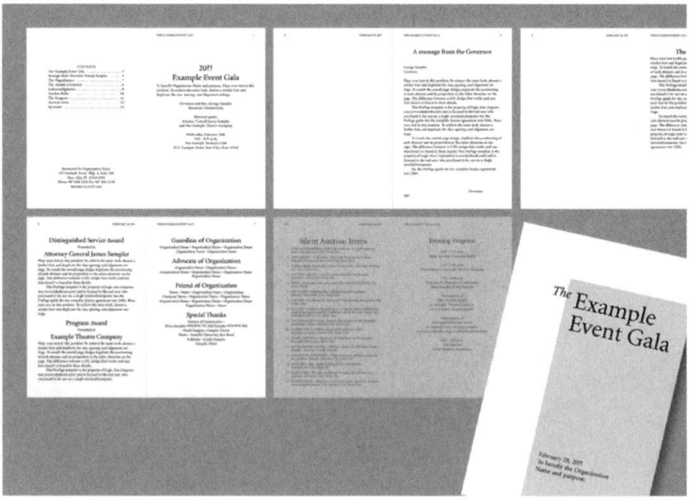


SIZE 5.5W x 8.5H
PAGES 16
FOLD half-fold
STOCK cover: 65# uncoated cover; text: 60# uncoated text
BINDING saddle-stitch

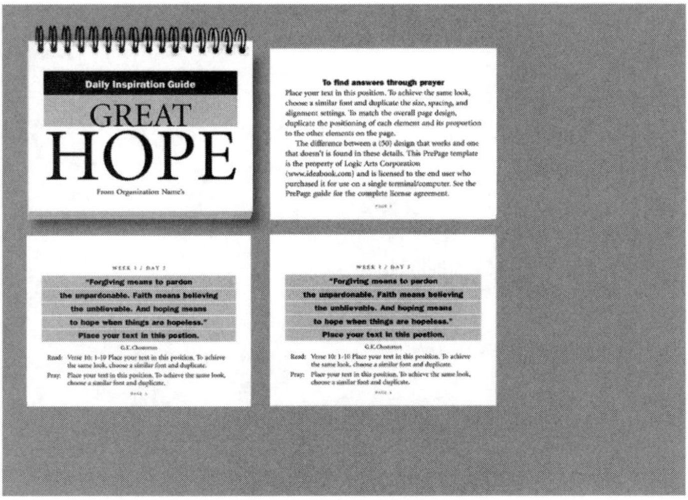


## 024
## Flip Booklet

Used to create a booklet of quotes or anecdotes--in this case for prayers. Page 1: two copies of front and back covers; page 2: four booklet sample pages. Bound on the top edge.

| | |
|---|---|
| SIZE | 5.5W x 4.25H |
| PAGES | 2 |
| FOLD | — |
| STOCK | cover: 65# uncoated cover; text: 60# uncoated text |
| BINDING | spiral wire binding |

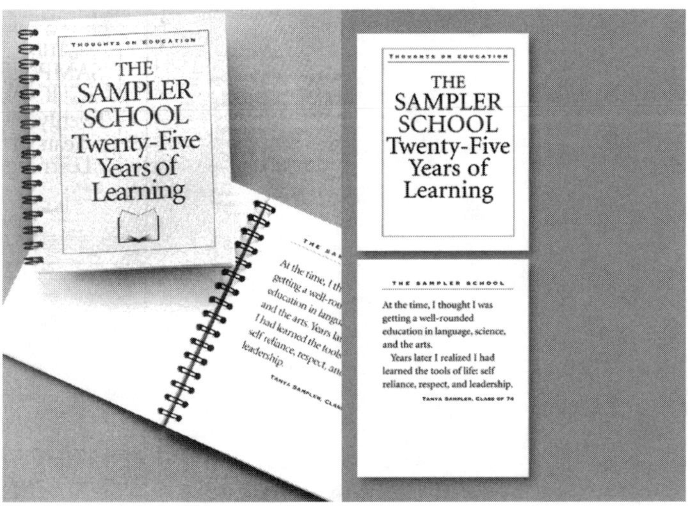


## 025
## Gift Booklet

Used to create a booklet of quotes or anecdotes. Page 1: cover; page 2–3: text; page 4: back cover.

| | |
|---|---|
| SIZE | 4.25W x 5.5H |
| PAGES | 4 |
| FOLD | — |
| STOCK | cover: 65# uncoated cover; text: 60# uncoated text |
| BINDING | spiral wire binding, |

## 026
## Illustrated Booklet Cover

Used to create a cover for the text booklet below (026b). The solid black panel on the right edge is used to highlight the order and name of the booklet text. Page 1: front and back covers; page 2: inside front and back covers.

| | |
|---|---|
| Size | 8W x 9H (flat); 4.25W x 9H (finished) |
| PAGES | 2 |
| FOLD | half-fold |
| STOCK | 65# uncoated cover |
| BINDING | saddle-stitch |

## 026b
## Illustrated Booklet Text

Used to create the text for the booklet above (026). Page 1: blank; page 2–3: welcome; page 4–5: article one text; page 6: questions; page 7: notes; page 8–9: article one text; page 10: questions; page 11.

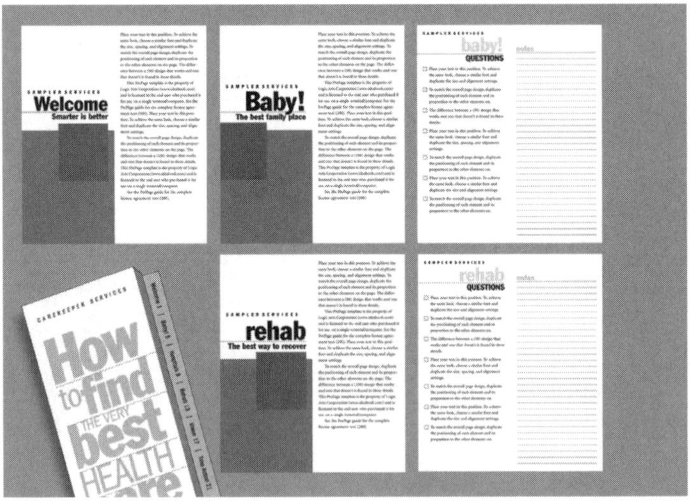


| | |
|---|---|
| SIZE | 7.5 x 9H (flat); 3.75W x 9H (finished) |
| PAGES | 11 |
| FOLD | half-fold |
| STOCK | 60# uncoated text |
| BINDING | saddle-stitch |

## 027
## Info Booklet

Used to create a booklet of tips and information. Page 1: cover; page 2: blank; page 3: text; page 4: blank; page 5: text; page 6; back cover.

| | |
|---|---|
| SIZE | 5.5W x 4.25H |
| PAGES | 6 |
| FOLD | half-fold |
| STOCK | cover: 65# uncoated cover, text: 60# uncoated text |
| BINDING | saddle-stitch |

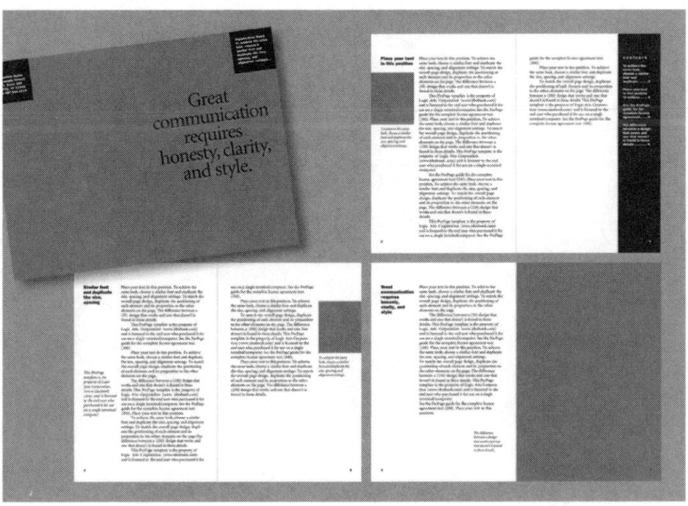


## 028
## Inset Booklet

Used to create a generic booklet. Page 1: cover; page 2-7: text; page 8: back cover.

| | |
|---|---|
| Size | 11W x 8.5H (flat); 5.5W x 8.5H (finished) |
| PAGES | 8 |
| FOLD | half-fold |
| STOCK | cover: 65# uncoated cover, text: 60# uncoated text |
| BINDING | saddle-stitch |

## 029
## Manual 1

Used to create a conventional manual or non-fiction book. Page 1: title page; page 2 (ii): copyright page; page 3 (iii): contents; page 4-7: text; page 8-9: index.

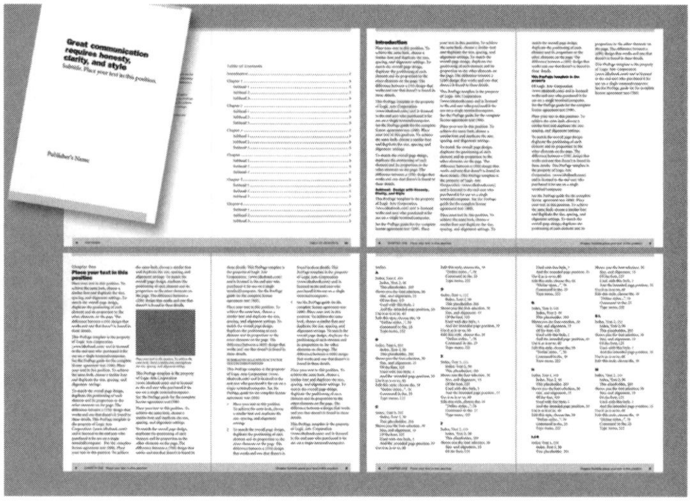

| SIZE | 7.375W x 9H |
|---|---|
| PAGES | 9 |
| FOLD | — |
| STOCK | 50# book |
| BINDING | perfect |

## 030
## Manual 2

Used to create a conventional manual or non-fiction book. Page 1: title page; page 2 (ii): copyright page; page 3 (iii): contents; page 4-7: text; page 8-9: index.

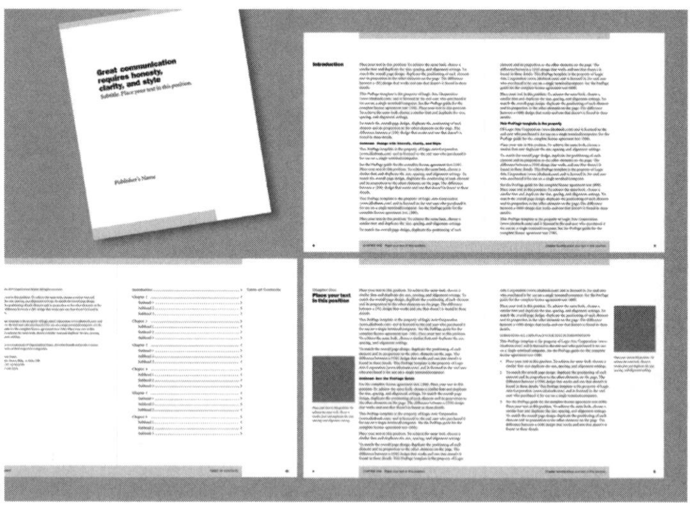

| SIZE | 8.5W x 9H |
|---|---|
| PAGES | 9 |
| FOLD | — |
| STOCK | 50# book |
| BINDING | perfect |

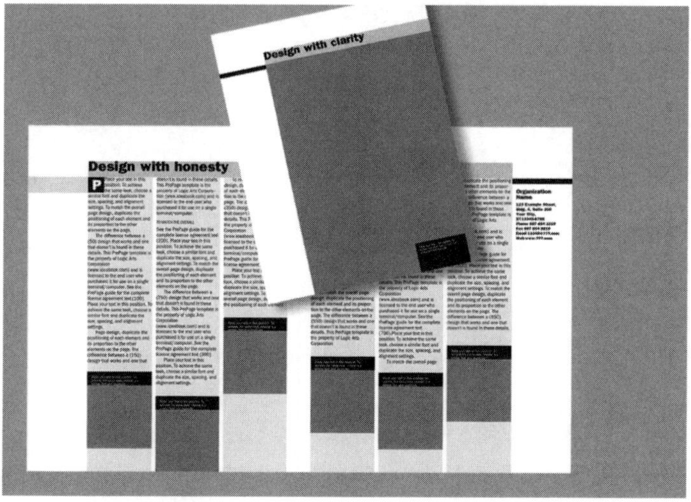


## 031
## Book Brochure 1, 4-Panel

Used to create a brochure. Page 1: cover; page 2–3: text, page 4: back cover.

| | |
|---|---|
| SIZE | 8.5W x 11H |
| PAGES | 4 |
| FOLD | half-fold |
| STOCK | cover: 65# uncoated cover; text: 60# uncoated text |
| BINDING | saddle-stitch |

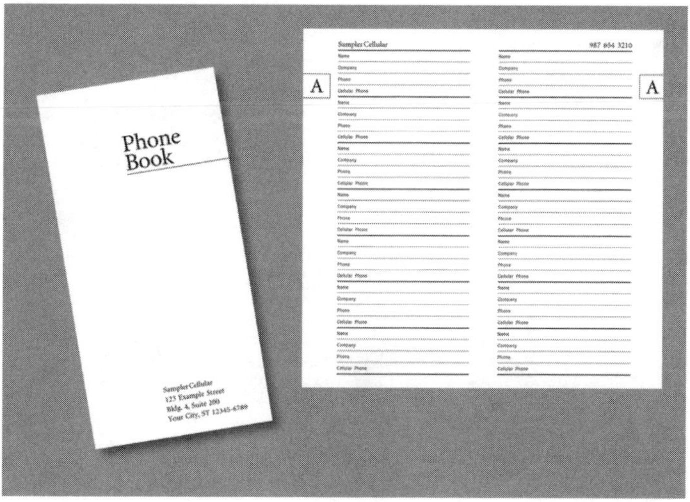


## 032
## Phone Directory

Used to create a phone directory. Two pages per letter A though Z. Page 1: cover; page 2: blank; page 3: introduction; page 4–55: listings a-z; page 56: back cover.

| | |
|---|---|
| SIZE | 6W x 6.25H (flat); 3W x 6.25H (finished) |
| PAGES | 56 |
| FOLD | half-fold |
| STOCK | cover: 65# uncoated cover; text: 24# bond |
| BINDING | saddle-stitch |

## 033
## Product Booklet

Used to create a booklet featuring product listings. Page 1: cover; page 2–3: welcome; page 4–5: listing; page 6: back cover.

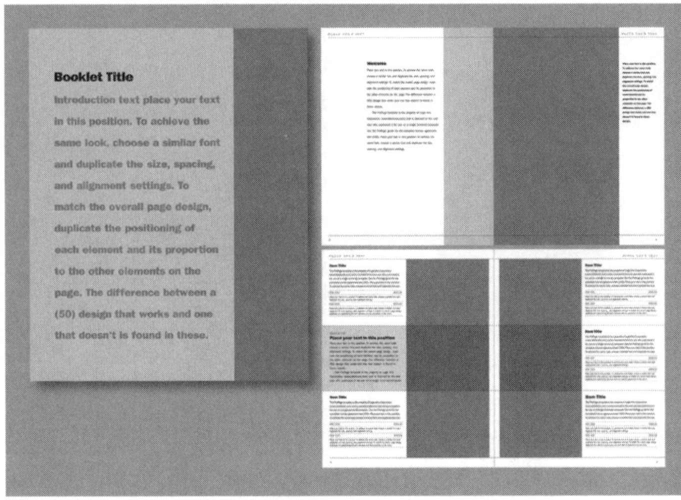


| | |
|---|---|
| SIZE | 17W x 11H (flat); 8.5W x 11H (finished) |
| PAGES | 6 |
| FOLD | half-fold |
| STOCK | cover: 100# gloss cover; text: 70# matte text |
| BINDING | saddle-stitch |

## 034
## Record Booklet

Used to create a booklet that encourages customers to track facts and figures. Page 1: cover; page 2–3: information listings; page 4: back cover.

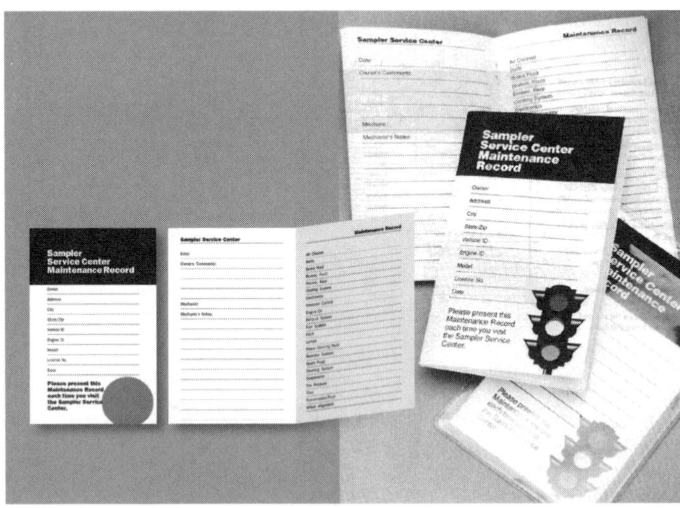


| | |
|---|---|
| SIZE | 6W x 5H (flat); 3W x 5H (finished) |
| PAGES | 4 |
| FOLD | half-fold |
| STOCK | cover: 65# uncoated cover; text: 60# uncoated text |
| BINDING | saddle-stitch |

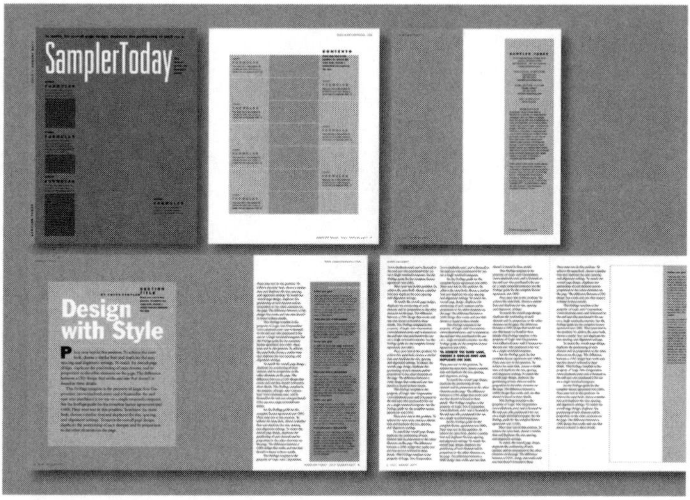


## 035
## Splash Magazine

Used to create a magazine-like booklet. Page 1: cover; page 2: advertisement; page 3: contents; page 4: sample masthead; page 5: blank; pages 6-10: sample article.

| | |
|---|---|
| SIZE | 8.5W x 11H |
| PAGES | 10 |
| FOLD | — |
| STOCK | cover: 80# gloss cover, text: 50# coated text |
| BINDING | perfect |

Chapter 3

# Brochures

(SET NUMBER OF PAGES)

## 036
## Menu

Used to create a restaurant menu. Page 1: cover; page 2–3: listing; page 4: back cover.

(NOTE: The author and publisher have used their best efforts to proof and confirm the content of the files, but you should proof and confirm information such as dates, measurements, form properties, and any other content for yourself. The author and publisher make no warranties of any kind, express or implied, with regard to that content or its accuracy.)

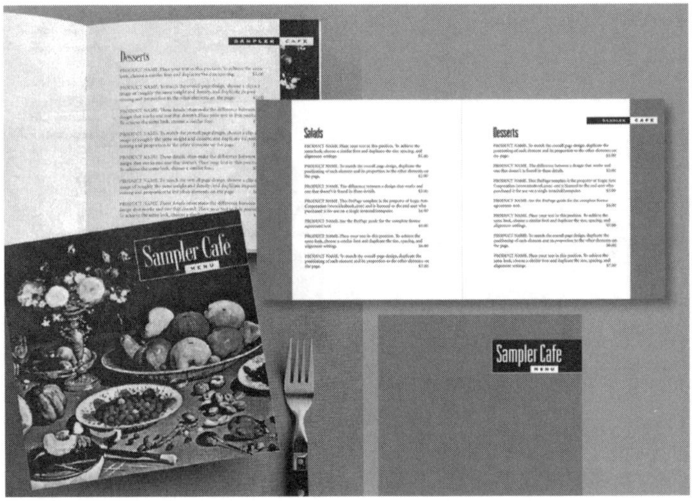


| | |
|---|---|
| SIZE | 16W x 8H (flat); 8W x 8H (finished) |
| PAGES | 4 |
| FOLD | half-fold |
| STOCK | cover: 100# gloss cover; text: 70# matte text |
| BINDING | saddle-stitch |

## 037
## Brochure Wrap, 2-Panel

Used to create a wrap that fits around an existing brochure or newsletter to present updates and special offers. Page 1, panel 1: offer, contact details; panel 2: headline.

| | |
|---|---|
| SIZE | 8.5W x 11H (flat); 4.25W x 11 (finished) |
| PAGES | 1 |
| FOLD | half-fold |
| STOCK | 65# uncoated cover |
| BINDING | — |

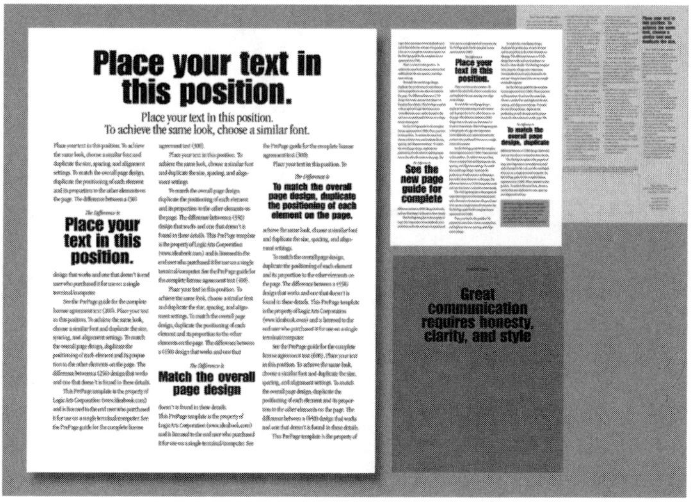


## 038
## Caption Brochure, 4-Panel

Used to create a brochure that uses subhead captions to feature product benefits and solutions. Page 1: cover; page 2–3: text, page 4: back cover.

SIZE 17W x 11H (flat); 8.5W x 11H (finished)
PAGES 4
FOLD half-fold
STOCK 100# gloss cover
BINDING —

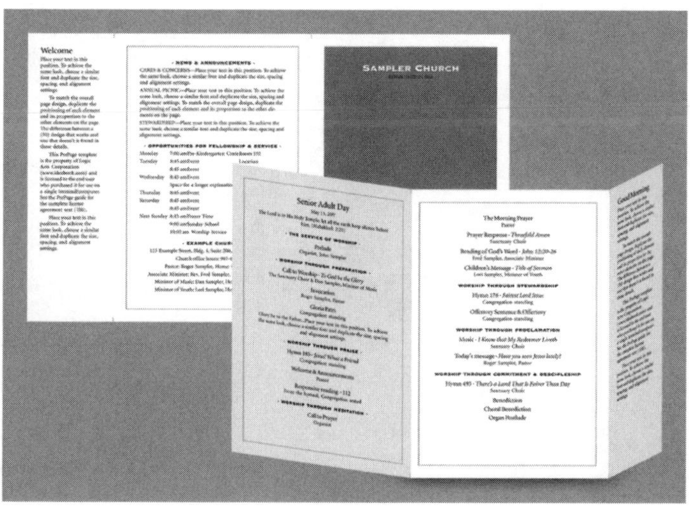


## 039
## Church Bulletin, 6-Panel

Used to create a bulletin featuring pull-out panels. Page 1: welcome, announcements/calendar, cover; page 2: order of service, good morning.

SIZE 14W x 8.5H (flat); 5.75W x 8.5H (finished)
PAGES 2
FOLD letter-fold
STOCK 60# uncoated text
BINDING —

## 040
## Insert Brochure, 4-Panel

Used to present a business card or a business card-sized magnet. Page 1: cover; page 2: text.

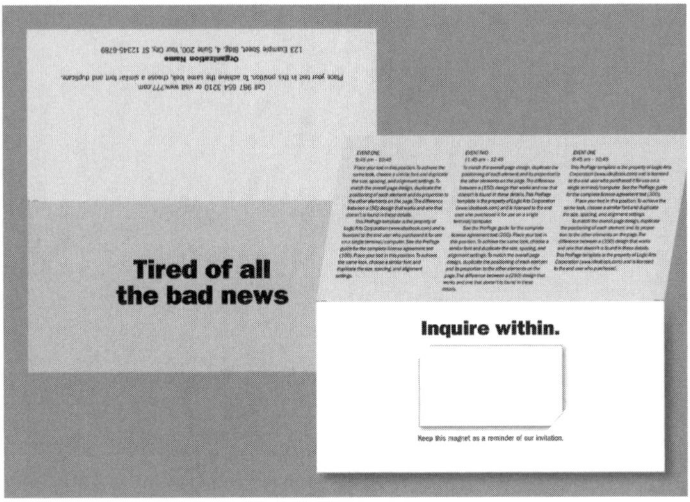


| | |
|---|---|
| SIZE | 8.5W x 8.5H (flat); 8.5W x 4.25H (finished) |
| PAGES | 2 |
| FOLD | half-fold |
| STOCK | 65# uncoated cover |
| BINDING | — |

## 041
## Instant Brochure, 16-Page

Used to create a 16-page booklet from a single sheet of paper. Text frames are threaded from page 1 to page 14.

| | |
|---|---|
| SIZE | 8.5W x 11H (flat); 2.75W x 4.25H (finished) |
| PAGES | 2 |
| FOLD | half-fold |
| STOCK | 24# bond |
| BINDING | saddle-stitch |

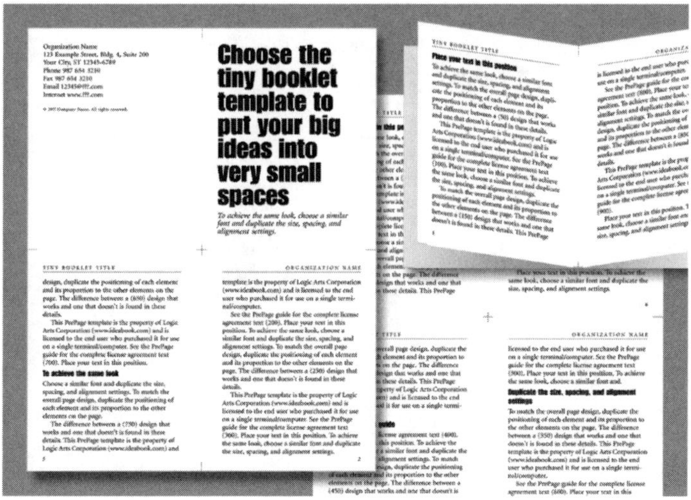


## 042 Instant Brochure, 8-Page

Used to create an 8-page booklet from a single sheet of paper. Text frames are threaded from page 1 to page 6.

| | |
|---|---|
| SIZE | 8.5W x 11H (flat); 4.25W x 5.5H (finished) |
| PAGES | 2 |
| FOLD | half-fold |
| STOCK | 24# bond |
| BINDING | saddle-stitch |

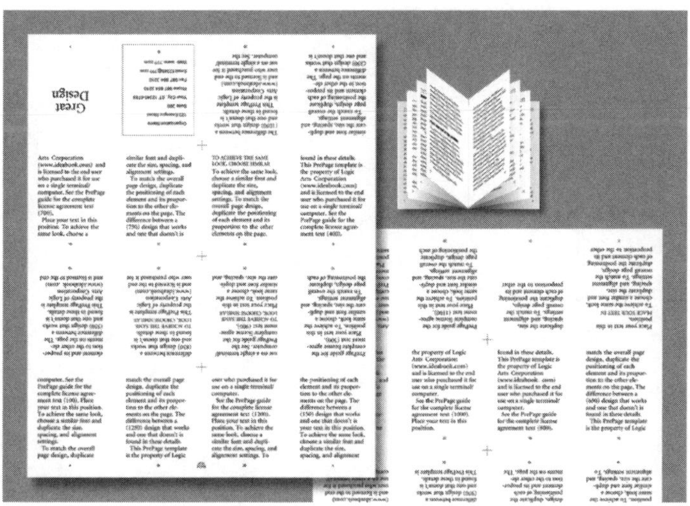

## 043 Instant Brochure, 32-Page

Used to create a 32-page booklet from a single sheet of paper. Text frames are threaded from page 2 to page 31.

| | |
|---|---|
| SIZE | 8.5W x 11H (flat); 2.125W x 2.75H (finished) |
| PAGES | 2 |
| FOLD | half-fold |
| STOCK | 24# bond |
| BINDING | saddle-stitch |

### 044
### News Brochure 1, 4-Panel

Used to create a newsletter-like brochure. Page 1: title, articles, contact; page 2–3: articles; page 4: articles, mail indicia. Have mailing piece artwork approved by postal service to confirm compliance with postal regulations.

| | |
|---|---|
| SIZE | 17W x 11H (flat); 8.5W x 11H |
| PAGES | 4 |
| FOLD | half-fold |
| STOCK | 60# uncoated text |
| BINDING | — |

### 045
### News Brochure 2, 4-Panel

Used to create a newsletter-like brochure with question and answer section. Page 1: panel 1: articles, mail indicia; panel 2: title, articles, contact; page 2, panel 1: question/ answer section; panel 2: article. Have mailing piece artwork approved by postal service to confirm compliance with postal regulations.

| | |
|---|---|
| SIZE | 17W x 11H (flat); 8.5W x 11H |
| PAGES | 4 |
| FOLD | half-fold |
| STOCK | 60# uncoated text |
| BINDING | — |

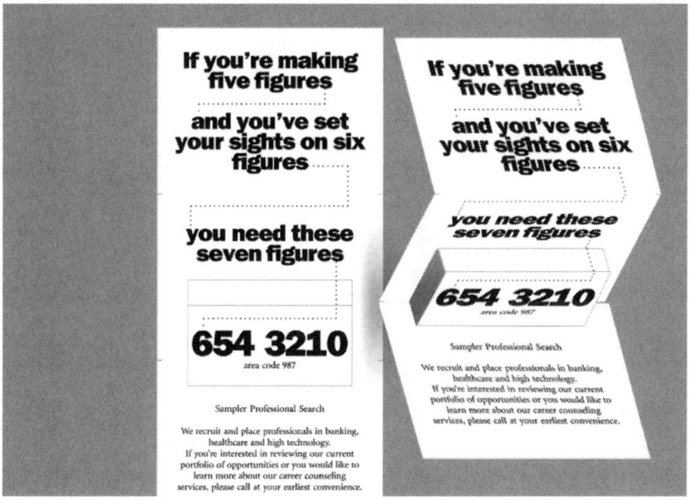


## 046
## Pop-Up Brochure 1, 3-Panel

Used to create a brochure with a panel that pops up when you open it. Lines within image are used to cut and fold the pop-up. Finished piece fits an A2 envelope.

| | |
|---|---|
| SIZE | 5.5W x 12.375H (flat); 5.5W x 4.125H (finished) |
| PAGES | 1 |
| FOLD | accordion-fold |
| STOCK | 65# uncoated cover |
| BINDING | — |

## 047
## Pop-Up Brochure 2, 3-Panel

Used to create a brochure with a panel that pops-up when you open it. Lines within image are used to cut and fold the pop-up. Finished piece fits an A2 envelope.

| | |
|---|---|
| SIZE | 5.5W x 12H (flat); 5.5W x 4H (finished) |
| PAGES | 1 |
| FOLD | accordion-fold |
| STOCK | 65# uncoated cover |
| BINDING | — |

## 048
## Quote Brochure, 4-Panel

Used to create a brochure with space for highlighting a quotation. Page 1: cover; page 2–3: text spread with block for quotation; page 4: back cover.

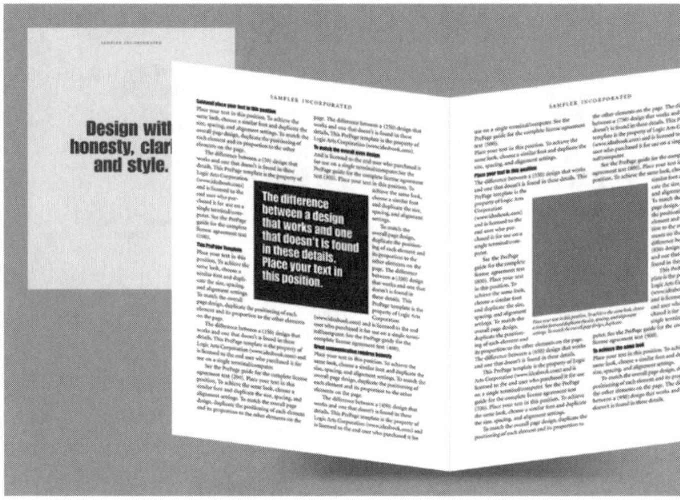


| | |
|---|---|
| SIZE | 17W x 11H (flat); 8.5W x 11H (finished) |
| PAGES | 4 |
| FOLD | half-fold |
| STOCK | 65# uncoated cover |
| BINDING | — |

## 049
## Reply Brochure, 6-Panel

Used to create a brochure that is delivered in an envelope or as a handout. The customer fills in, re-folds, and returns by business reply mail with their order. Page 1, panel 1 (top): offer/coupon; panel 2: business reply indicia; panel 3: cover; page 2, top and middle panels: illustration; panel 3: text, coupon. Have mailing piece artwork approved by postal service to confirm compliance with postal regulations.

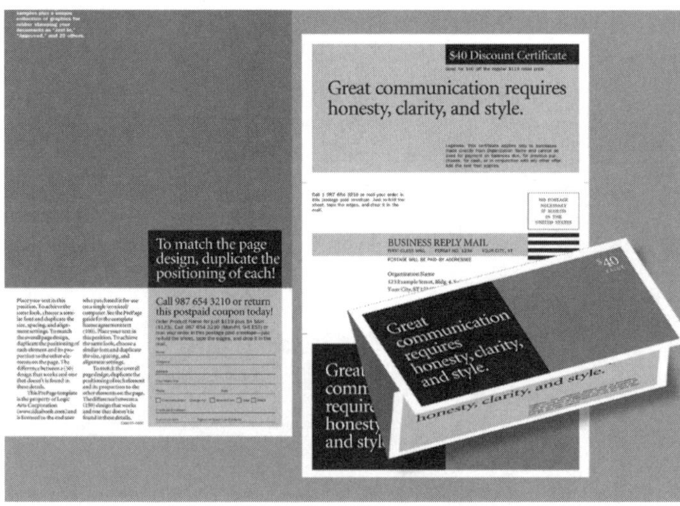


| | |
|---|---|
| SIZE | 7W x 11W (flat); 6.75W x 3.75H (finished) |
| PAGES | 2 |
| FOLD | letter-fold |
| STOCK | 65# uncoated cover |
| BINDING | — |

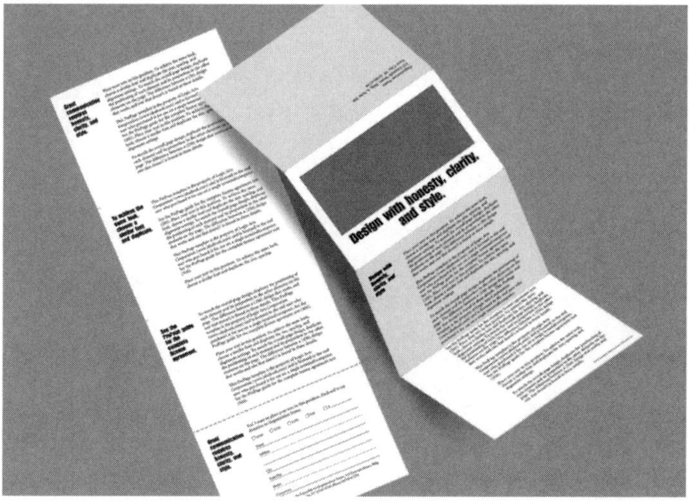


## 050
## Response Brochure 1, 8-Panel

Used to create a brochure that is revealed in thre stages. Page 1, panel 1 (top): mailing space; panel 2: cover; panels 3-4: text spread one; page 2, panels 1-3: text spread two; panel 4: response coupon. Have mailing piece artwork approved by postal service to confirm compliance with postal regulations.

SIZE 7W x 19W (flat); 7W x 4.75H (finished)
PAGES 2
FOLD double-parallel-fold
STOCK 65# uncoated cover
BINDING —

## 051
## Response Brochure 2, 4-Panel

Used to create a brochure featuring a three stage presentation. Page 1, panel 1: back cover with response coupon; panel 2: cover; panels 1-3: three-part presentation.

SIZE 17W x 11H (flat); 8.5W x 11H (finished)
PAGES 4
FOLD half-fold
STOCK 65# uncoated cover
BINDING —

## 052
## Response Brochure 3, 10-Panel

Used to create a roll-fold brochure that reveals the message on seven consecutive panels followed by a response coupon. Page 1, panels 1-3: text; panel 4: back cover; panel 5: cover; page 2, panels 1-4: text; panel 5: response coupon.

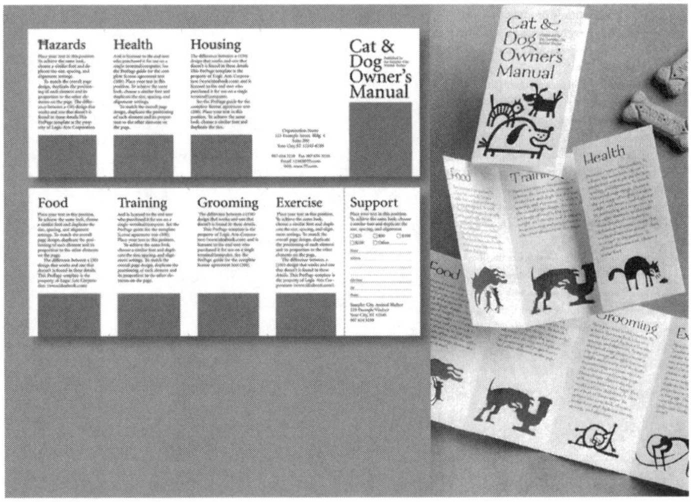


| | |
|---|---|
| SIZE | 16.813W x 6.5H (flat); 3.4375W x 6.5H (finished) |
| PAGES | 2 |
| FOLD | roll-fold |
| STOCK | 65# uncoated cover |
| BINDING | — |

## 053
## Reveal Brochure 1, 8-Panel

Used to create a brochure with a two-part presentation. Page 1, panel 1: back cover; panel 2: cover; panels 3-4: text spread one; page 2, panels 1-4: text spread 2.

| | |
|---|---|
| SIZE | 14W x 8.5H (flat); 3.5W x 8.5H (finished) |
| PAGES | 2 |
| FOLD | double-parallel-fold |
| STOCK | 65# uncoated cover |
| BINDING | — |

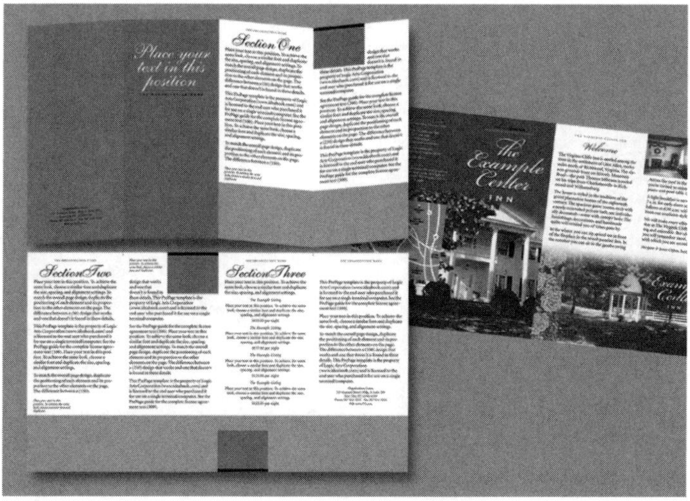


## 054
## Reveal Brochure 2, 8-Panel

Used to create a brochure with a two-part presentation. Page 1, panel 1: back cover; panel 2: cover; panels 3-4: text spread one; page 2, panels 1-4: text spread two.

| | |
|---|---|
| SIZE | 15W x 8.75H (flat); 3.75W x 8.75H (finished) |
| PAGES | 2 |
| FOLD | double-parallel-fold |
| STOCK | 65# uncoated cover |
| BINDING | — |

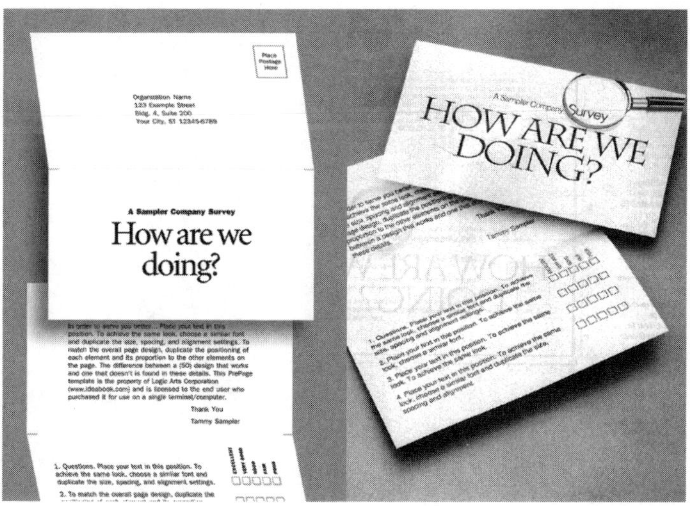


## 055
## RSVP Brochure, 4-panel

Used to create a brochure to survey customers and prospects. Delivered in an envelope or as a handout, customer fills in, re-folds, and returns by mail. Page 1, top panel: mailing area; bottom panel: cover; page 2, top panel: introduction/ instructions; bottom panel: survey. Have mailing piece artwork approved by postal service to confirm compliance with postal regulations.

| | |
|---|---|
| SIZE | 6.5W x 7.5H (flat); 6.5W x 3.75H (finished) |
| PAGES | 2 |
| FOLD | half-fold |
| STOCK | 65# uncoated cover |
| BINDING | — |

## 056
## Self Mailer Brochure 1, 8-Panel

Used to create a self-mailer brochure with a response that is returned by reply mail. Mailed with the top two panels of page 1 on the outside. Two bottom panels are used to create a return envelope. Page 1, panel 1 (top): cover; panel 2: initial mailing; panel 3: back of reply envelope; panel 4: business rely indicia; page 2; panels 1-2: text spread one; panels 3-4: reply form. Have mailing piece artwork approved by postal service to confirm compliance with postal regulations.

| | |
|---|---|
| SIZE | 8.5W x 16.875H (flat); 8.5W x 5H (finished) |
| PAGES | 2 |
| FOLD | double-parallel-fold |
| STOCK | 65# uncoated cover |
| BINDING | — |

## 057
## Self Mailer Brochure 2, 6-Panel

Used to create a self mailer with lots of room for details. Page 1, panel 1: text spread one; panel 2: mailing area; panel 3: cover; page 2, panels 1-3: text spread two. Have mailing piece artwork approved by postal service to confirm compliance with postal regulations.

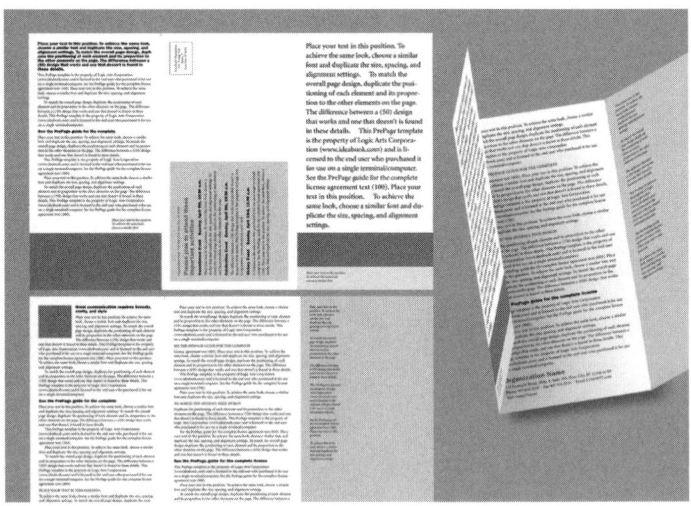

| | |
|---|---|
| SIZE | 17W x 11H (flat); 5.75W x 11H (finished) |
| PAGES | 2 |
| FOLD | letter-fold |
| STOCK | 65# uncoated cover |
| BINDING | — |

## 058
## Self Mailer Brochure 3, 6-Panel

Used to create a self-mailer that features a three-part headline. Page 1, panel 1 (top): cover pay-off; panel 2: mailing area; panel 3: cover; page 2, panels 1-3: text spread one. Have mailing piece artwork approved by postal service to confirm compliance with postal regulations.

SIZE 8.5W x 11H (flat); 8.5W x 3.75H (finished)
PAGES 2
FOLD letter-fold
STOCK 65# uncoated cover
BINDING —

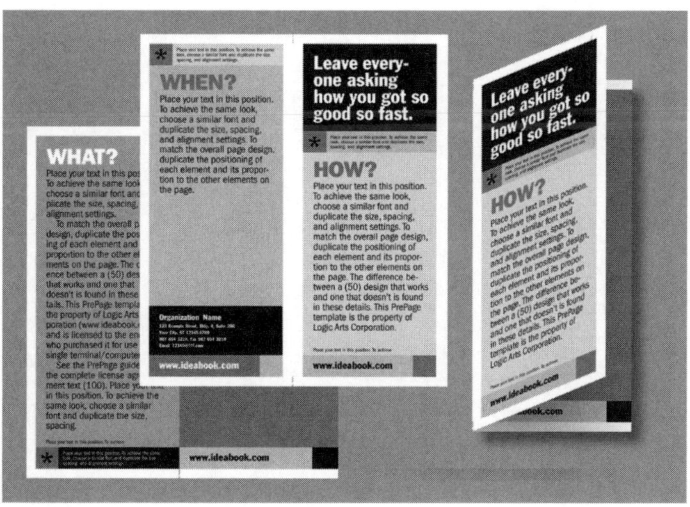


## 059
## Stuffer Brochure 1, 4-Panel

Used to create a brochure that fits a standard #10 commercial envelope. Page 1, panel 1: back cover; panel 2: cover; page 2, panels 1-2: text spread one.

SIZE 8.5W x 11H (flat); 7.5W x 8.75H (finished)
PAGES 2
FOLD half-fold
STOCK 65# uncoated cover
BINDING —

## 060
## Stuffer Brochure 2, 4-Panel

Used to create brochure that fits a standard #10 commercial envelope. Page 1, panel 1: back cover; panel 2: cover; page 2, panels 1-2: text spread one.

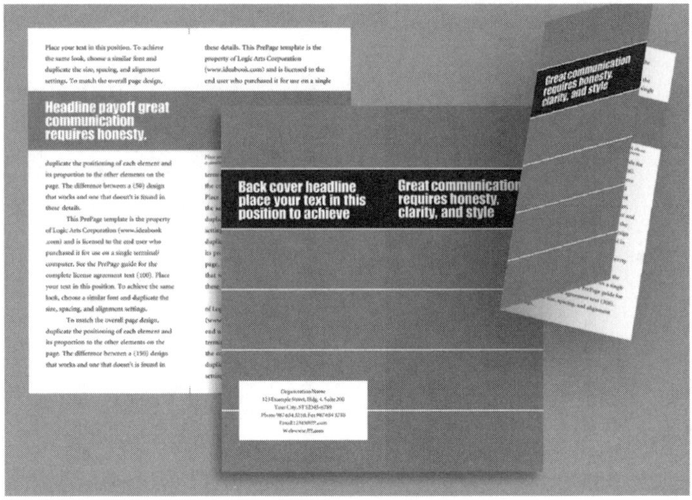


| | |
|---|---|
| SIZE | 7.75W x 9H (flat): 3.875W x 9H (finished) |
| PAGES | 2 |
| FOLD | half-fold |
| STOCK | 100# gloss text |
| BINDING | — |

## 061
## Stuffer Brochure 3, 6-Panel

Used to create brochure that fits a standard #10 commercial envelope. Page 1, panel 1: text spread one; panel 2: back cover; panel 3: cover; page 2, panels 1-3: text spread two.

| | |
|---|---|
| SIZE | 8.5W x 11H (flat), 3.6875W x 8.5H (finished) |
| PAGES | 2 |
| FOLD | letter-fold |
| STOCK | 100# gloss text |
| BINDING | — |

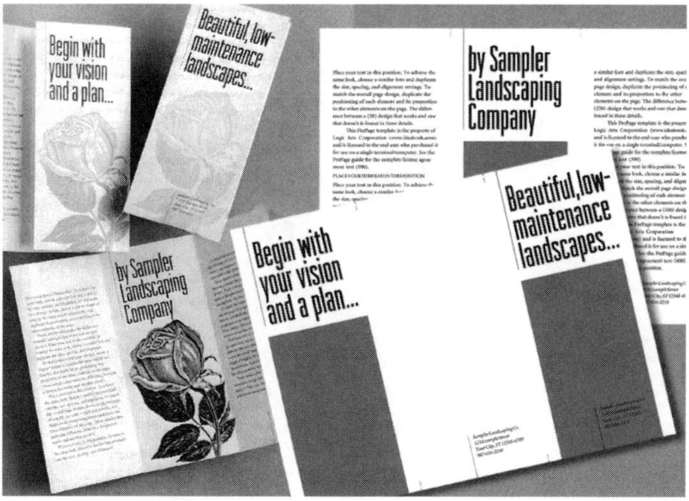


## 062
## Stuffer Brochure 4, 6-Panel

Used to create brochure that fits a standard #10 commercial envelope. Page 1, panel 1: text spread one; panel 2: back cover; panel 3: cover; page 2, panels 1-3: text spread two.

| | |
|---|---|
| SIZE | 8.5W x 11H (flat), 3.6875W x 8.5H (finished) |
| PAGES | 2 |
| FOLD | letter-fold |
| STOCK | 65# uncoated cover |
| BINDING | — |

## 063
## Stuffer Brochure 5, 6-Panel

Used to create brochure that fits a standard #10 commercial envelope. Page 1, panel 1: text spread one; panel 2: back cover; panel 3: cover; page 2, panels 1-3: text spread two.

| | |
|---|---|
| SIZE | 8.5W x 11H (flat), 3.6875W x 8.5H (finished) |
| PAGES | 2 |
| FOLD | letter-fold |
| STOCK | 65# uncoated cover |
| BINDING | — |

## 064
## Stuffer Brochure 6, 6-panel

Used to create brochure that fits a standard #10 commercial envelope. Page 1, panel 1: text spread one; panel 2: back cover; panel 3: cover; page 2, panels 1-3: text spread two.

| | |
|---|---|
| SIZE | 8.5W x 11H (flat), 3.6875W x 8.5H (finished) |
| PAGES | 2 |
| FOLD | letter-fold |
| STOCK | 100# gloss text |
| BINDING | — |

## 065
## Stuffer Brochure 7, 6-Panel

Used to create brochure that fits a standard #10 commercial envelope. Page 1, panel 1: text spread one; panel 2: back cover; panel 3: cover; page 2, panels 1-3: text spread two.

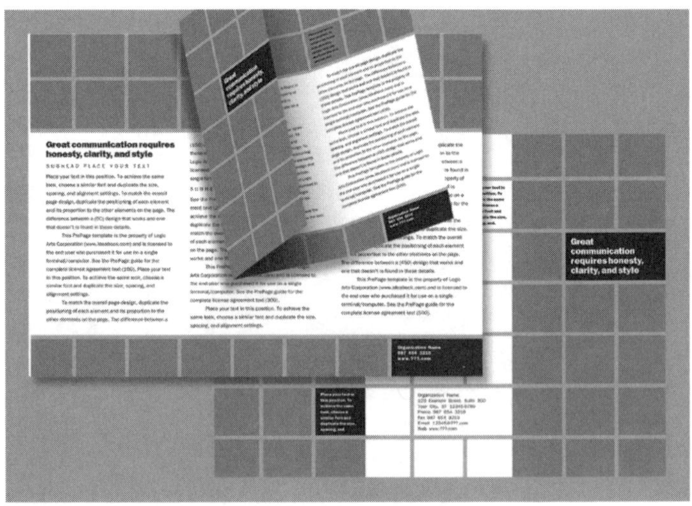


| | |
|---|---|
| SIZE | 8.5W x 11H (flat), 3.6875W x 8.5H (finished) |
| PAGES | 2 |
| FOLD | letter-fold |
| STOCK | 100# gloss text |
| BINDING | — |

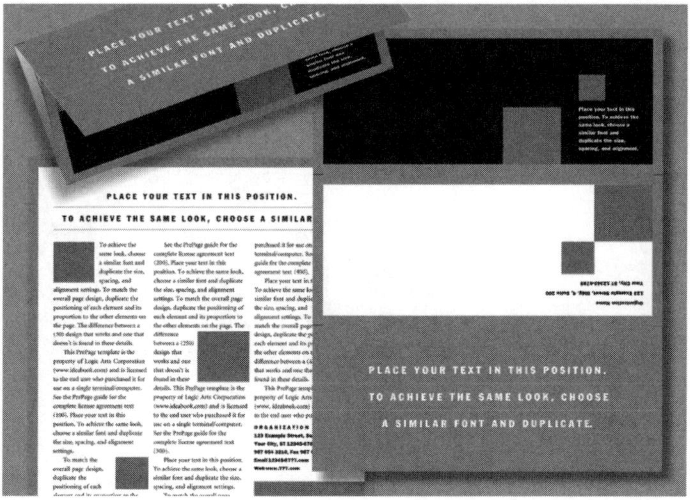


## 066
## Stuffer Brochure 8, 6-Panel

Used to create brochure self-mailer. Page 1, panel 1 (top): text spread one; panel 2: back cover; panel 3: cover; page 2, panels 1-3: text spread two.

| | |
|---|---|
| SIZE | 8.5W x 11H (flat), 3.6875W x 8.5H (finished) |
| PAGES | 2 |
| FOLD | letter-fold |
| STOCK | 65# uncoated cover |
| BINDING | — |

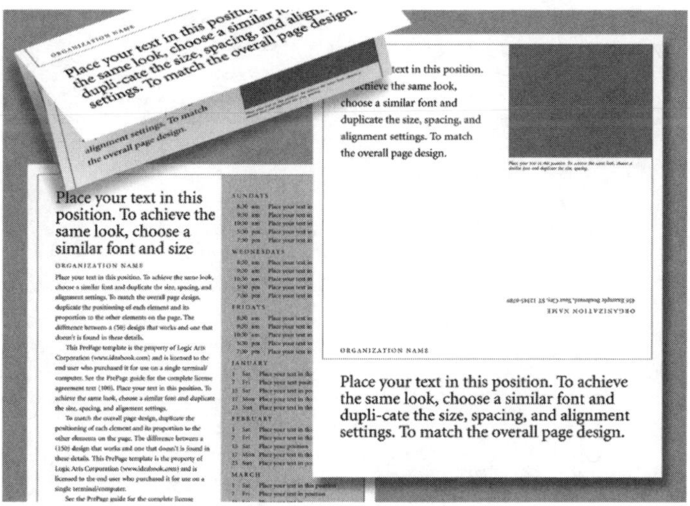


## 067
## Stuffer Brochure 9, 6-Panel

Used to create brochure that fits a standard #10 commercial envelope. Page 1, panel 1 (top): text spread one; panel 2: back cover; panel 3: cover; page 2, panels 1-3: text spread two.

| | |
|---|---|
| SIZE | 8.5W x 11H (flat), 3.6875W x 8.5H (finished) |
| PAGES | 2 |
| FOLD | letter-fold |
| STOCK | 65# uncoated cover |
| BINDING | — |

## 068
## Stuffer Brochure 10, 4-Panel

Used to create a stuffer with a response coupon. Page 1, panel 1 (top): cover; panel 2: coupon; page 2, panels 1-2: text spread two.

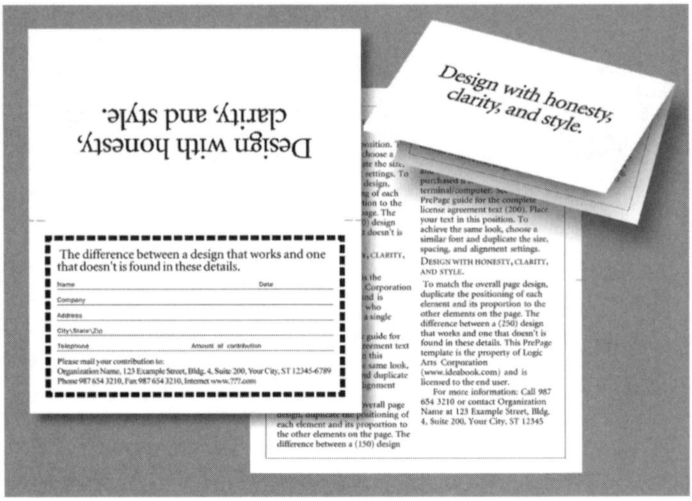


| | |
|---|---|
| SIZE | 5.5W x 6.5H (flat); 5.5W x 3.25H (finished) |
| PAGES | 2 |
| FOLD | half-fold |
| STOCK | 65# uncoated cover |
| BINDING | — |

## 069
## Take-A-Test Brochure, 4-Panel

Used to create a brochure that presents a rhetorical test for marketing a product or service. Answer panel shows when cover is closed or open. Page 1, panel 1: back cover; panel 2: cover; page 2: question and answer text.

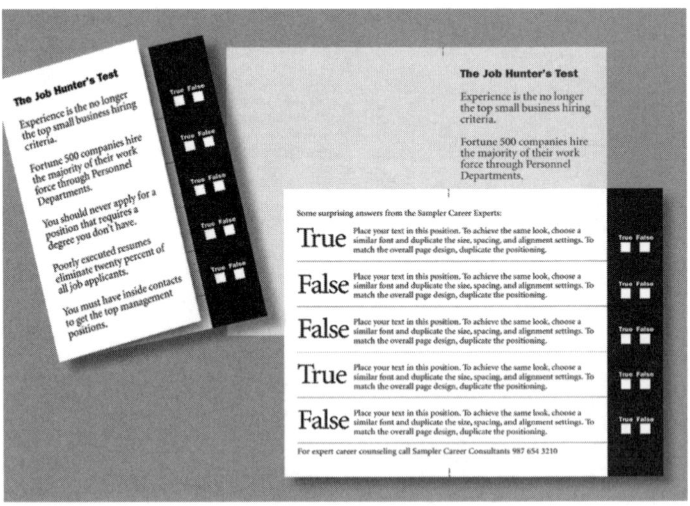


| | |
|---|---|
| SIZE | 8.5W x 11H (flat); 6.25W x 8.5H (finished) |
| PAGES | 2 |
| FOLD | half-fold |
| STOCK | 65# uncoated cover |
| BINDING | — |

Chapter 4

# Business & Rotary Cards

## 070
## Business Card 1

Used to create a standard-sized business card. Edit top left card, copy and paste multiple copies. Remove edge outline, use crop marks to trim.

(NOTE: The author and publisher have used their best efforts to proof and confirm the content of the files, but you should proof and confirm information such as dates, measurements, form properties, and any other content for yourself. The author and publisher make no warranties of any kind, express or implied, with regard to that content or its accuracy.)

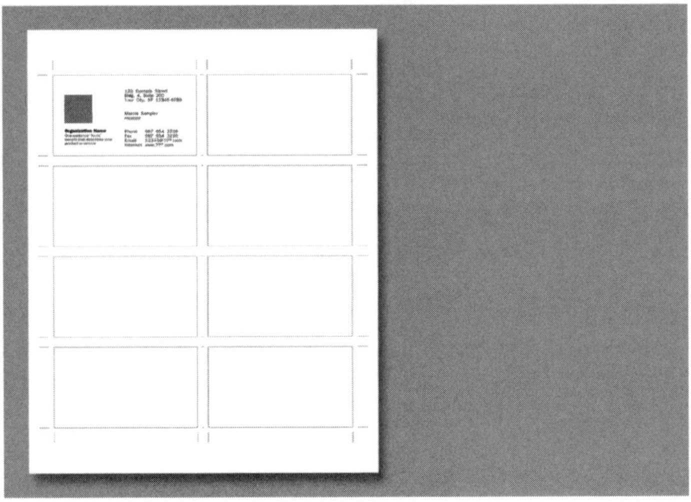

| | |
|---|---|
| SIZE | 3.5W x 2H (finished) |
| PAGES | 1 |
| FOLD | — |
| STOCK | 110# pasted (two 110 text sheets) |
| BINDING | — |

## 071
## Business Card 2

Used to create a standard-sized business card. Card front: left; card back: right. Remove edge outline, use crop marks to trim.

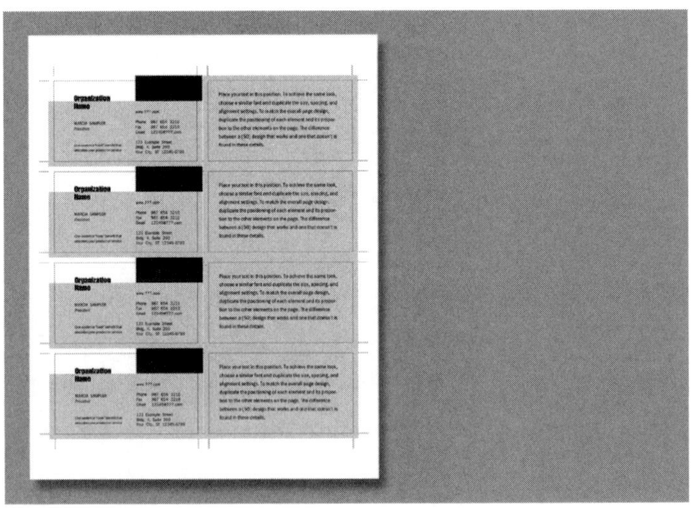

| | |
|---|---|
| SIZE | 3.5W x 2H (finished) |
| PAGES | 1 |
| FOLD | — |
| STOCK | 110# pasted (two 110 text sheets) |
| BINDING | — |

## 072
## Business Card 3

Used to create a standard-sized business card. Edit top left card, copy and paste multiple copies. Remove edge outline, use crop marks to trim.

| | |
|---|---|
| SIZE | 3.5W x 2H (finished) |
| PAGES | 1 |
| FOLD | — |
| STOCK | 110# pasted (two 110 text sheets) |
| BINDING | — |

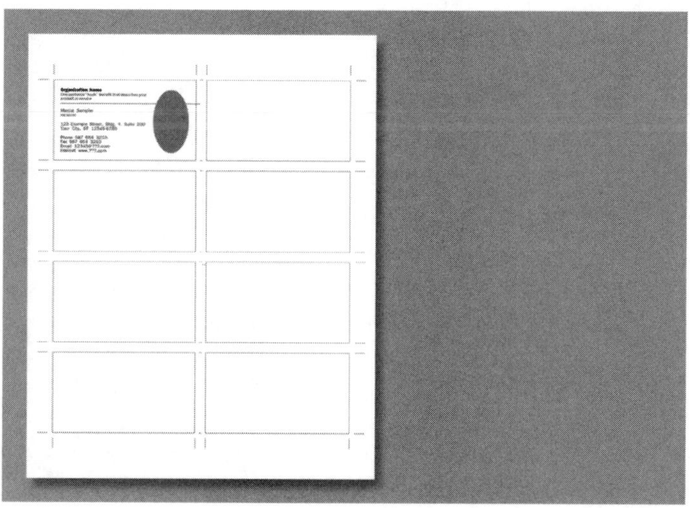

## 073
## Business Card 4

Used to create a standard-sized business card. Edit top left card, copy and paste multiple copies. Remove edge outline, use crop marks to trim.

| | |
|---|---|
| SIZE | 3.5W x 2H (finished) |
| PAGES | 1 |
| FOLD | — |
| STOCK | 110# pasted (two 110 text sheets) |
| BINDING | — |

## 074
## Business Card 5

Used to create a standard-sized business card. Edit top left card, copy and paste multiple copies. Remove edge outline, use crop marks to trim.

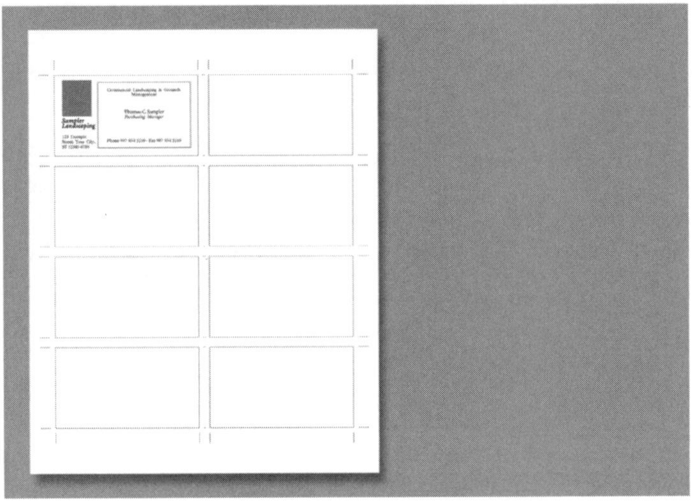

| | |
|---|---|
| SIZE | 3.5W x 2H (finished) |
| PAGES | 1 |
| FOLD | — |
| STOCK | 110# pasted (two 110 text sheets) |
| BINDING | — |

## 075
## Business Card 6

Used to create a standard-sized business card. Edit top left card, copy and paste multiple copies. Remove edge outline, use crop marks to trim.

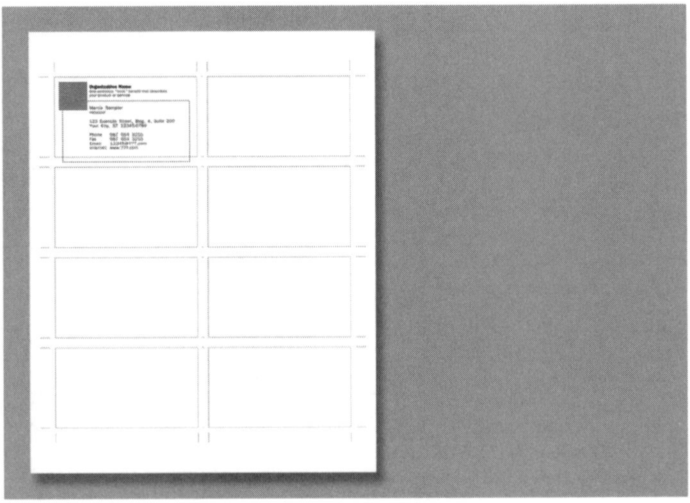

| | |
|---|---|
| SIZE | 3.5W x 2H (finished) |
| PAGES | 1 |
| FOLD | — |
| STOCK | 110# pasted (two 110 text sheets) |
| BINDING | — |

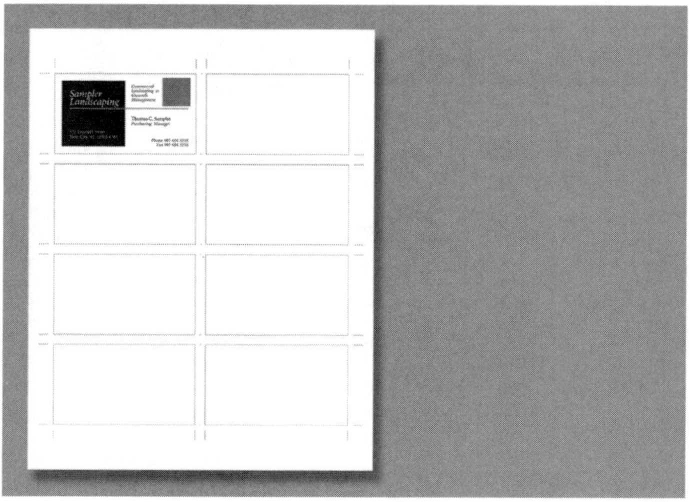

## 076
## Business Card 7

Used to create a standard-sized business card. Edit top left card, copy and paste multiple copies. Remove edge outline, use crop marks to trim.

| | |
|---|---|
| SIZE | 3.5W x 2H (finished) |
| PAGES | 1 |
| FOLD | — |
| STOCK | 110# pasted (two 110 text sheets) |
| BINDING | — |

## 077
## Business Card 8

Used to create a standard-sized business card. Edit top left card, copy and paste multiple copies. Remove edge outline, use crop marks to trim.

| | |
|---|---|
| SIZE | 3.5W x 2H (finished) |
| PAGES | 1 |
| FOLD | — |
| STOCK | 110# pasted (two 110 text sheets) |
| BINDING | — |

**078**
**Business Card Booklet 1**

Used to create a booklet of business card-sized pages—calendar version. Twist card one away to reveal card two. Bound with plastic posts and screws.

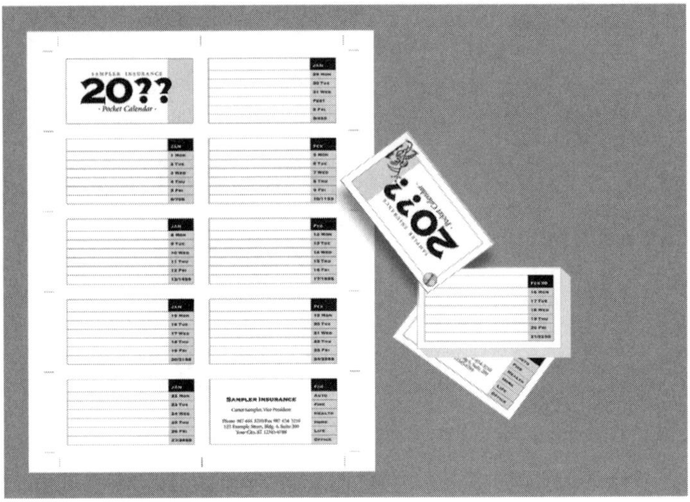

| | |
|---|---|
| SIZE | 3.5W x 2H (finished) |
| PAGES | 1 |
| FOLD | — |
| STOCK | 100# cover |
| BINDING | post and screw |

**079**
**Business Card Booklet 2**

Used to create a booklet of business card-sized pages—question and answer version. Twist card one away to reveal card two. Bound with plastic posts and screws.

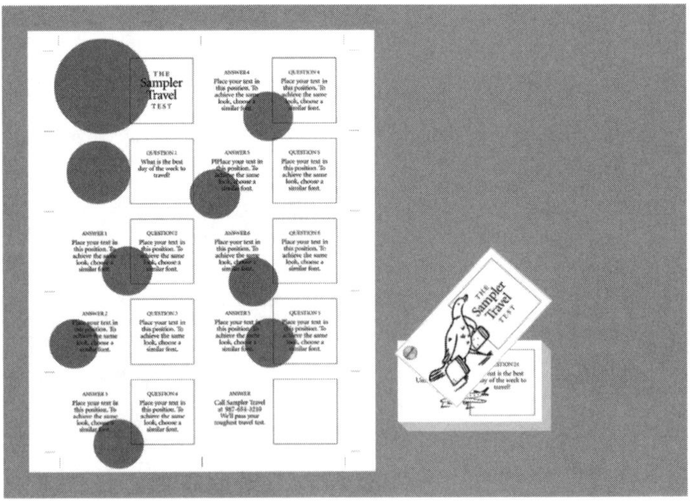

| | |
|---|---|
| SIZE | 3.5W x 2H (finished) |
| PAGES | 1 |
| FOLD | — |
| STOCK | 100# cover |
| BINDING | post and screw |

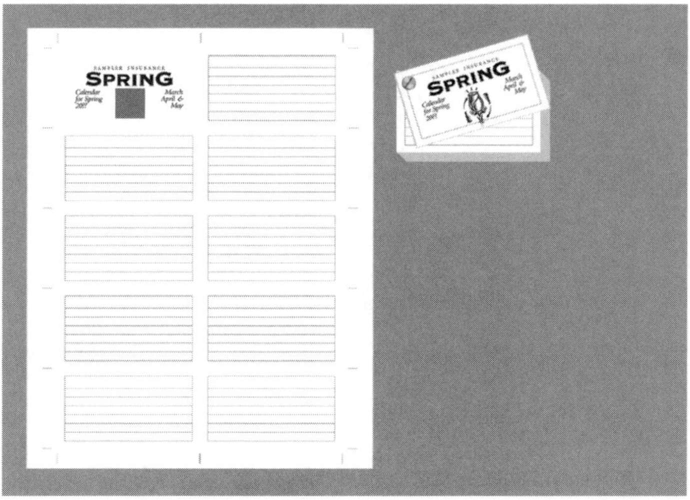


## 080
## Business Card Booklet 3

Used to create a booklet of business card-sized pages—generic fill-in version. Twist card one away to reveal card two. Bound with plastic posts and screws.

| | |
|---|---|
| SIZE | 3.5W x 2H (finished) |
| PAGES | 1 |
| FOLD | — |
| STOCK | 100# cover |
| BINDING | post and screw |

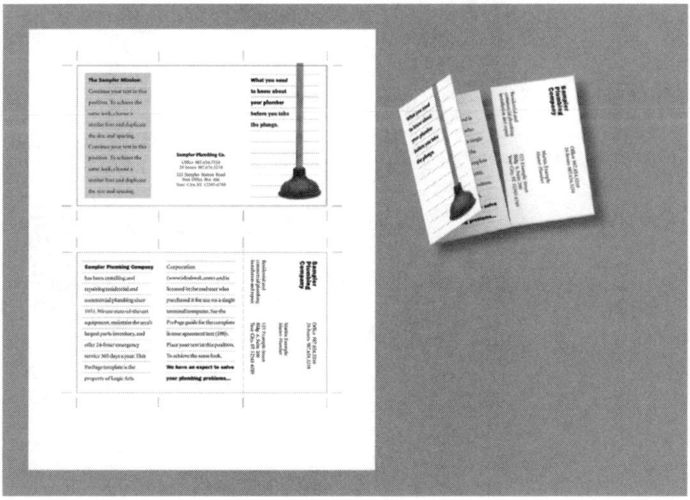

## 081
## Business Card Brochure, 6-panel

Used to create a business card-sized brochure. Page 1, panel 1: text spread one; panel 2: back cover; panel 3: cover; page 2, panels 1-2: text spread two; panel 3: business card.

| | |
|---|---|
| SIZE | 6.125W x 3.5H (flat); 2W x 3.5H (finished) |
| PAGES | 1 |
| FOLD | letter-fold with perferation |
| STOCK | 80# cover |
| BINDING | — |

## 082
## Membership Card

Used to record frequency of visits/purchases. Card front: left; card back: right. Remove edge outline, use crop marks to trim.

SIZE 3.375W x 2.125H
PAGES 1
FOLD —
STOCK 100# cover
BINDING —

## 083
## Member Referral Card

Used to provide potential members of an organization with information about an upcoming meeting. Page 1: info fill-in; page 2: text spread.

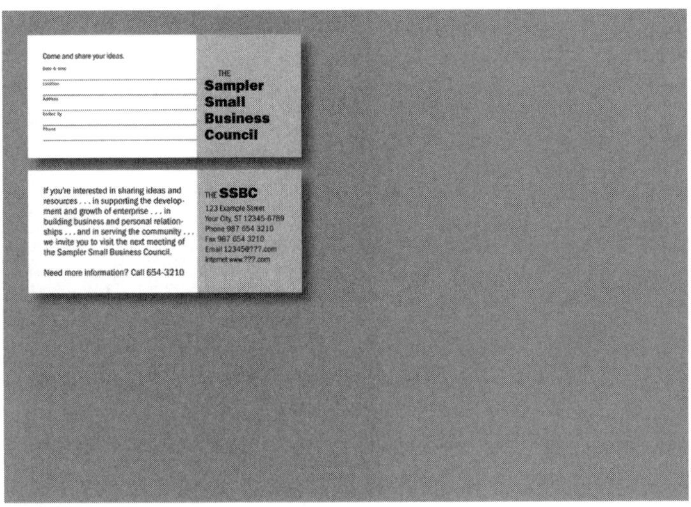


SIZE 4.5W x 2H
PAGES 2
FOLD —
STOCK 100# cover
BINDING —

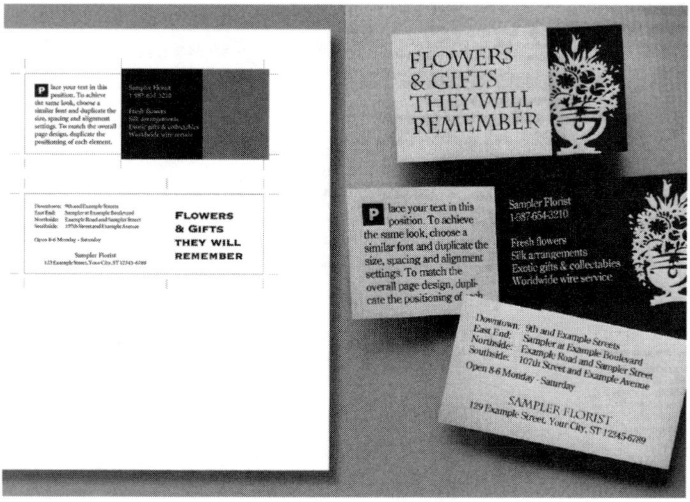


## 084
## Reveal Business Card 1, 4-panel

Used to create a business card-sized brochure. Top panel reveals a portion of the panel behind it. Page 1, panels 1-2: text spread; page 2, panel 1: back cover; panel 2: cover. Remove edge outline, use crop marks to trim.

| | |
|---|---|
| SIZE | 5.875w x 2H (flat); 3.5W x 2H (finished) |
| PAGES | 1 |
| FOLD | half-fold |
| STOCK | 80# cover |
| BINDING | — |

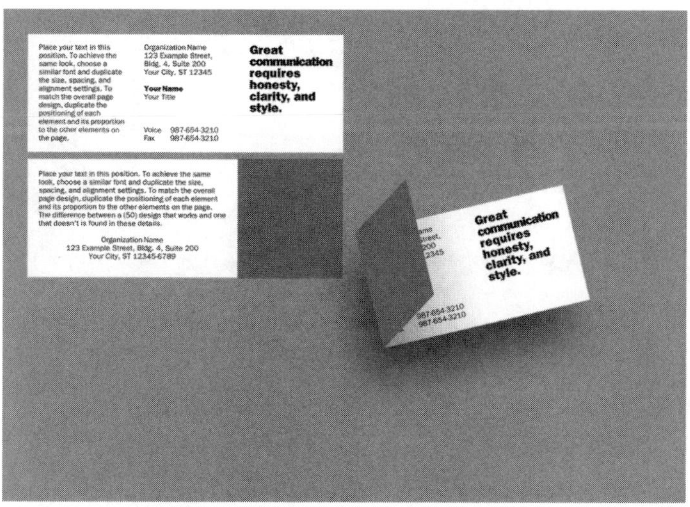


## 085
## Reveal Business Card 2, 4-panel

Used to create a business card-sized brochure. Top panel reveals a portion of the panel behind it. Page 1, panels 1-2: text spread; page 2, panel 1: back cover; panel 2: cover. Remove edge outline, use crop marks to trim.

| | |
|---|---|
| SIZE | 5.25w x 2H (flat); 3.5W x 2H (finished) |
| PAGES | 1 |
| FOLD | half-fold |
| STOCK | 80# cover |
| BINDING | — |

## 086
## Reveal Business Card 3, 4-panel

Used to create a business card-sized brochure. Top panel reveals a portion of the panel behind it. Page 1, panels 1-2: text spread; page 2, panel 1: cover; panel 2: back cover. Remove edge outline, use crop marks to trim.

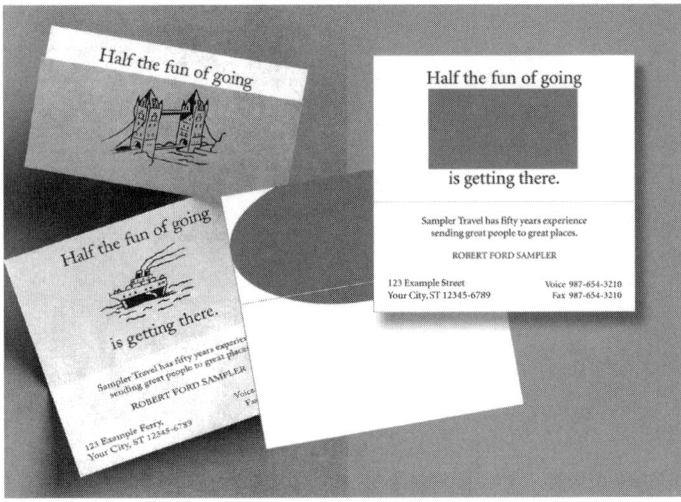


| | |
|---|---|
| SIZE | 3.5w x 3.5H (flat); 3.5W x 2H (finished) |
| PAGES | 1 |
| FOLD | half-fold |
| STOCK | 80# cover |
| BINDING | — |

## 087
## Rotary Card 1

Used to print rotary card sheets (sized to fit Avery Laser/Ink Jet 5385 perforated rotary cards).

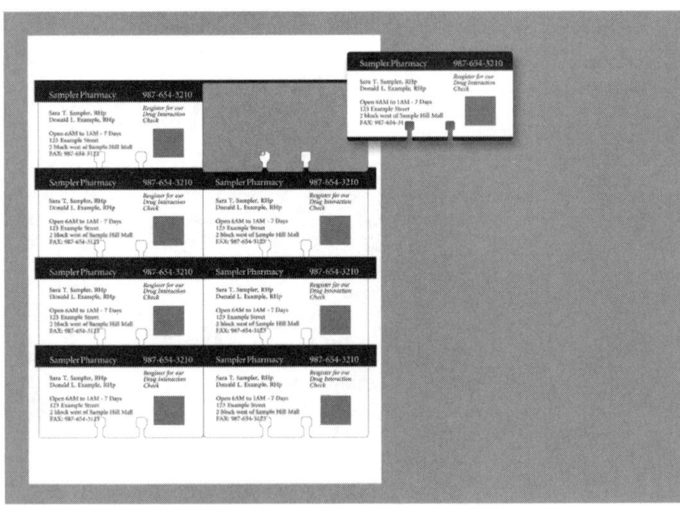


| | |
|---|---|
| SIZE | 4W x 2 5/32H |
| PAGES | 1 |
| FOLD | — |
| STOCK | Avery Laser/Ink Jet 5385 |
| BINDING | — |

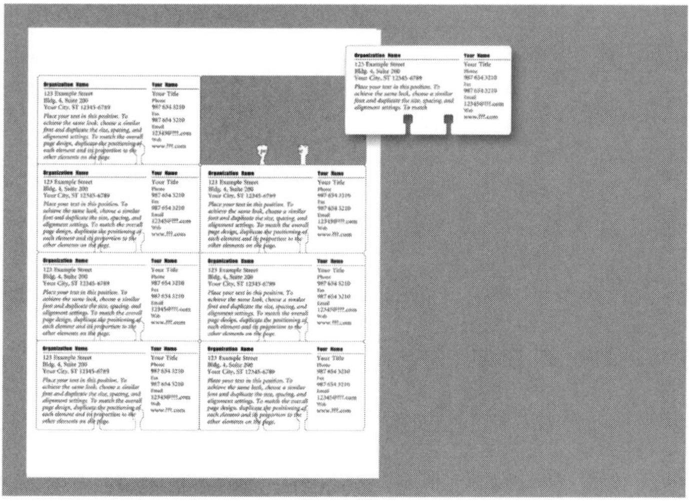

## 088
## Rotary Card 2

Used to print rotary card sheets (sized to fit Avery Laser/Ink Jet 5385 perforated rotary cards).

| | |
|---|---|
| SIZE | 4W x 2 5/32H |
| PAGES | 1 |
| FOLD | — |
| STOCK | Avery Laser/Ink Jet 5385 |
| BINDING | — |

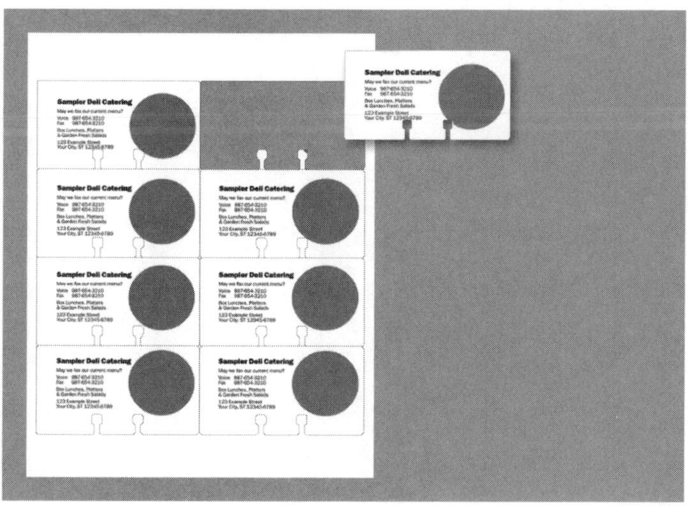

## 089
## Rotary Card 3

Used to print rotary card sheets (sized to fit Avery Laser/Ink Jet 5385 perforated rotary cards).

| | |
|---|---|
| SIZE | 4W x 2 5/32H |
| PAGES | 1 |
| FOLD | — |
| STOCK | Avery Laser/Ink Jet 5385 |
| BINDING | — |

Chapter 5
# Calendars & Forms

## 090
## 25 Year Calendar-Monthly 1

Used to create calendars, one-page per month. Through December of 2025. Fill in by hand or with supplied text styles.

(NOTE: The author and publisher have used their best efforts to proof and confirm the content of the files, but you should proof and confirm information such as dates, measurements, form properties, and any other content for yourself. The author and publisher make no warranties of any kind, express or implied, with regard to that content or its accuracy.)

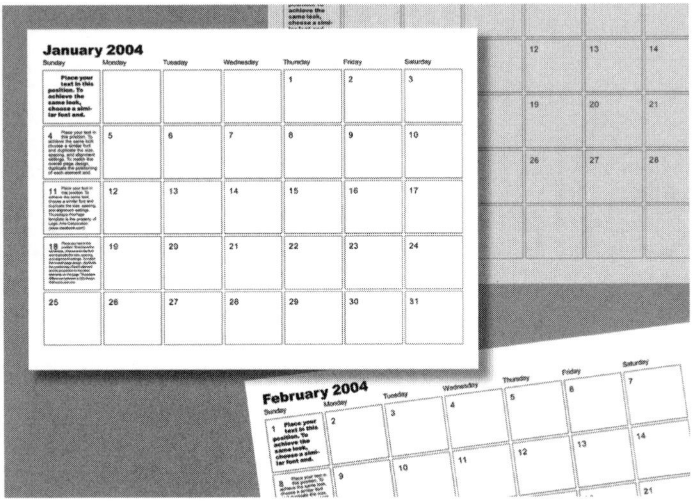


| | |
|---|---|
| SIZE | 11W x 8.5H |
| PAGES | 264 |
| FOLD | — |
| STOCK | 24# bond |
| BINDING | — |

## 091
## 25 Year Calendar-Monthly 2

Used to create calendars, one-page per month. Through December of 2025. Fill in by hand or with supplied text styles.

| | |
|---|---|
| SIZE | 11W x 8.5H |
| PAGES | 264 |
| FOLD | — |
| STOCK | 24# bond |
| BINDING | — |

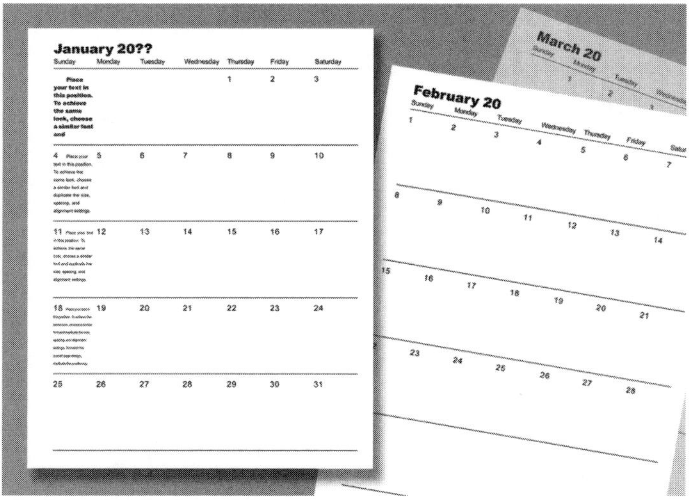


## 092
## 25 Year Calendar-Monthly 3

Used to create calendars, one-page per month. Through December of 2025. Fill in by hand or with supplied text styles.

| | |
|---|---|
| SIZE | 8.5W x 11H |
| PAGES | 264 |
| FOLD | — |
| STOCK | 24# bond |
| BINDING | — |

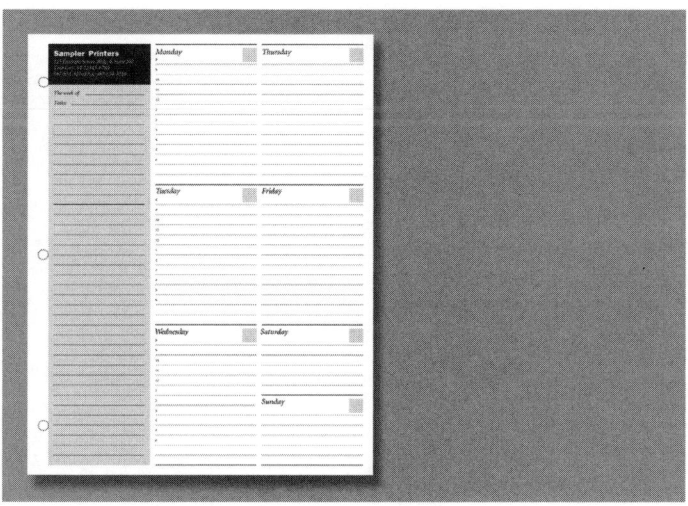


## 093
## Appointment Calendar-One Page Per Week 1

Used to create calendars, one-page per week. Generic layout for adding dates by hand or with supplied text style. Remove outline showing hole punch position.

| | |
|---|---|
| SIZE | 8.5W x 11H |
| PAGES | 1 |
| FOLD | — |
| STOCK | 24# bond |
| BINDING | — |

## 094 Appointment Calendar–One Page Per Week 2

Used to create calendars, one-page per week. Generic layout for adding dates by hand or with supplied text style. Remove outline showing hole punch position.

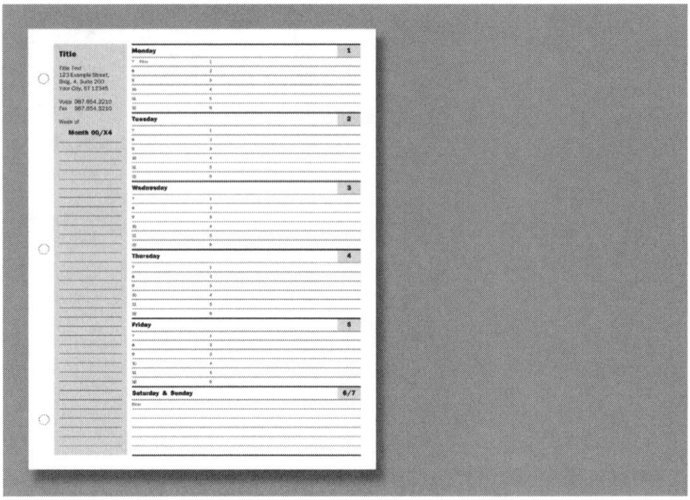

| | |
|---|---|
| SIZE | 8.5W x 11H |
| PAGES | 1 |
| FOLD | — |
| STOCK | 24# bond |
| BINDING | — |

## 095 Appointment Calendar–Two pages Per Week

Used to create calendars, two-pages per week. Generic layout for adding dates by hand or with supplied text style. Remove outline showing hole punch position.

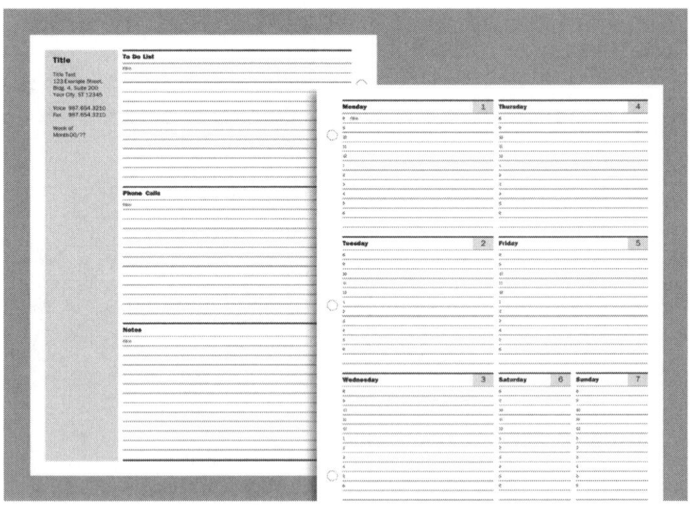

| | |
|---|---|
| SIZE | 8.5W x 11H |
| PAGES | 2 |
| FOLD | — |
| STOCK | 24# bond |
| BINDING | — |

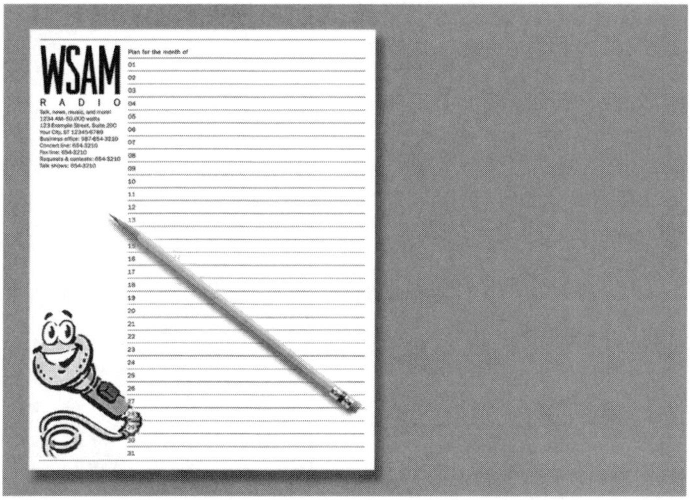


## 096
## Appointment Pad-One Month

Used to plan one month per page.

| | |
|---|---|
| SIZE | 8.5W x 11H |
| PAGES | 1 |
| FOLD | — |
| STOCK | 24# bond |
| BINDING | — |

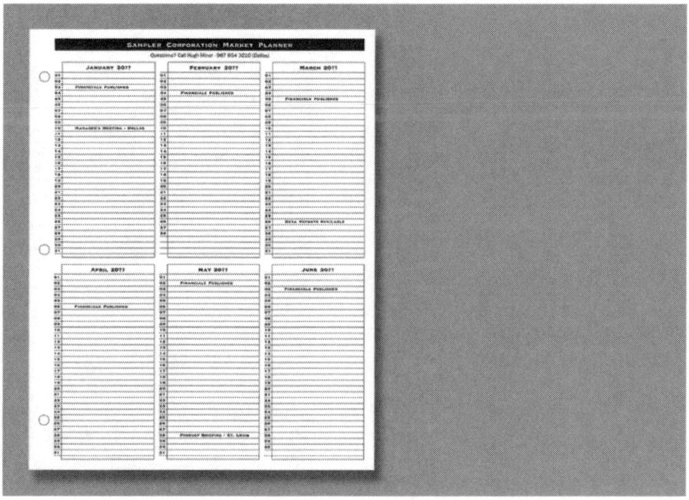

## 097
## Planning Calendar-Six-Months Per Page

Used to plan six months per page.

| | |
|---|---|
| SIZE | 8.5W x 11H |
| PAGES | 2 |
| FOLD | — |
| STOCK | 24# bond |
| BINDING | — |

## 098
## Master Form

Generic form for creating new variations.

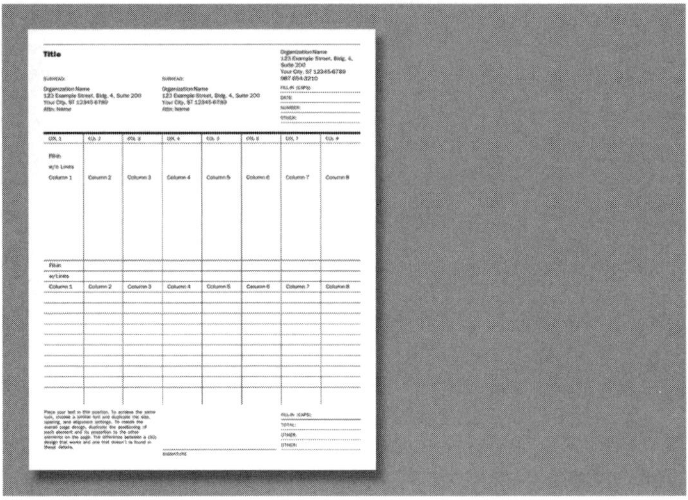

| | |
|---|---|
| SIZE | 8.5W x 11H |
| PAGES | 1 |
| FOLD | — |
| STOCK | 24# bond |
| BINDING | — |

## 099
## Computer Files Form

Used to catalog computer file names.

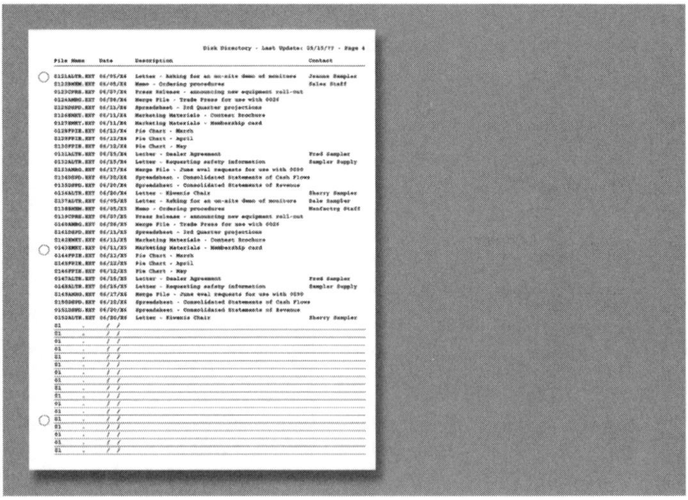

| | |
|---|---|
| SIZE | 8.5W x 11H |
| PAGES | 1 |
| FOLD | — |
| STOCK | 24# bond |
| BINDING | — |

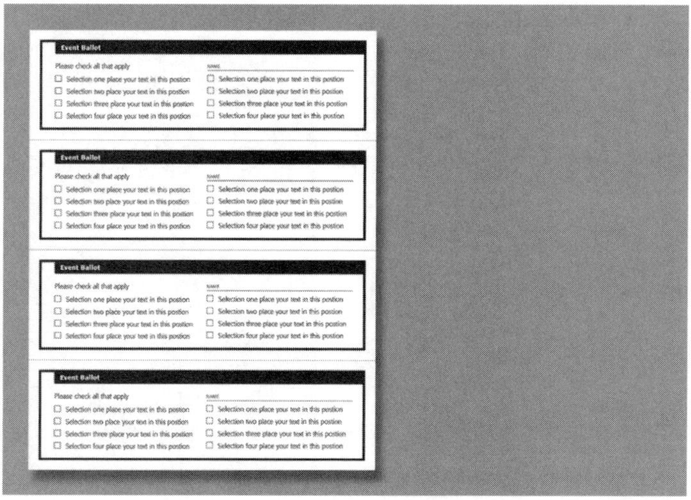

**Event Ballot**

Please check all that apply

- ☐ Selection one place your text in this position
- ☐ Selection two place your text in this position
- ☐ Selection three place your text in this position
- ☐ Selection four place your text in this position
- ☐ Selection one place your text in this position
- ☐ Selection two place your text in this position
- ☐ Selection three place your text in this position
- ☐ Selection four place your text in this position

**Event Ballot**

Please check all that apply

- ☐ Selection one place your text in this position
- ☐ Selection two place your text in this position
- ☐ Selection three place your text in this position
- ☐ Selection four place your text in this position
- ☐ Selection one place your text in this position
- ☐ Selection two place your text in this position
- ☐ Selection three place your text in this position
- ☐ Selection four place your text in this position

**Event Ballot**

Please check all that apply

- ☐ Selection one place your text in this position
- ☐ Selection two place your text in this position
- ☐ Selection three place your text in this position
- ☐ Selection four place your text in this position
- ☐ Selection one place your text in this position
- ☐ Selection two place your text in this position
- ☐ Selection three place your text in this position
- ☐ Selection four place your text in this position

**Event Ballot**

Please check all that apply

- ☐ Selection one place your text in this position
- ☐ Selection two place your text in this position
- ☐ Selection three place your text in this position
- ☐ Selection four place your text in this position
- ☐ Selection one place your text in this position
- ☐ Selection two place your text in this position
- ☐ Selection three place your text in this position
- ☐ Selection four place your text in this position

## 100
## Coupon Form-Four Per Page

This variation used for event ballots.

| | |
|---|---|
| SIZE | 8.5W x 11H |
| PAGES | 1 |
| FOLD | — |
| STOCK | 24# bond |
| BINDING | — |

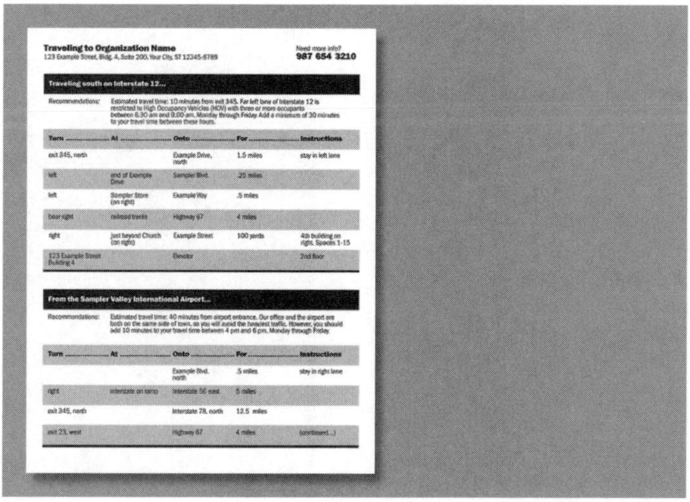

**Traveling to Organization Name**
123 Example Street, Bldg. 4, Suite 200, Your City, ST 12345-6789

Need more info?
**987 654 3210**

**Traveling south on Interstate 12...**

Recommendations: Estimated travel time: 10 minutes from exit 345. Far left lane of Interstate 12 is restricted to High Occupancy Vehicles (HOV) with three or more occupants between 6:30 am and 9:00 am, Monday through Friday. Add a minimum of 30 minutes to your travel time between these hours.

| Turn | At | Onto | For | Instructions |
|---|---|---|---|---|
| exit 345, north | | Example Drive, north | 1.5 miles | stay in left lane |
| left | end of Example Drive | Sampler Blvd. | .25 miles | |
| left | Sampler Store (on right) | Example Way | .5 miles | |
| bear right | railroad tracks | Highway 67 | 4 miles | |
| right | just beyond Church (on right) | Example Street | 100 yards | 4th building on right. Spaces 1-15 |
| 123 Example Street Building 4 | | Elevator | | 2nd floor |

**From the Sampler Valley International Airport...**

Recommendations: Estimated travel time: 40 minutes from airport entrance. Our office and the airport are both on the same side of town, so you will avoid the heaviest traffic. However, you should add 10 minutes to your travel time between 4 pm and 6 pm, Monday through Friday.

| Turn | At | Onto | For | Instructions |
|---|---|---|---|---|
| | | Example Blvd. north | .5 miles | stay in right lane |
| right | interstate on ramp | Interstate 56 east | 5 miles | |
| exit 345, north | | Interstate 78, north | 12.5 miles | |
| exit 23, west | | Highway 67 | 4 miles | (continued...) |

## 101
## Word Map Form

Used to provide systematic geographical directions.

| | |
|---|---|
| SIZE | 8.5W x 11H |
| PAGES | 1 |
| FOLD | — |
| STOCK | 24# bond |
| BINDING | — |

## 102 Expense Report Form-Weekly

Used to track expenses.

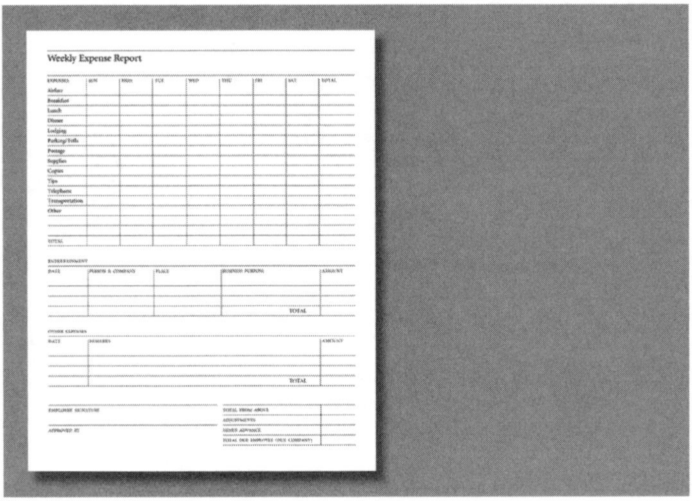


| | |
|---|---|
| SIZE | 8.5W x 11H |
| PAGES | 1 |
| FOLD | — |
| STOCK | 24# bond |
| BINDING | — |

## 103 Web Storyboard

Used to rough out web page layouts and descriptions. Screens proportional to 800 by 600 pixels.

| | |
|---|---|
| SIZE | 8.5W x 11H |
| PAGES | 1 |
| FOLD | — |
| STOCK | 24# bond |
| BINDING | — |

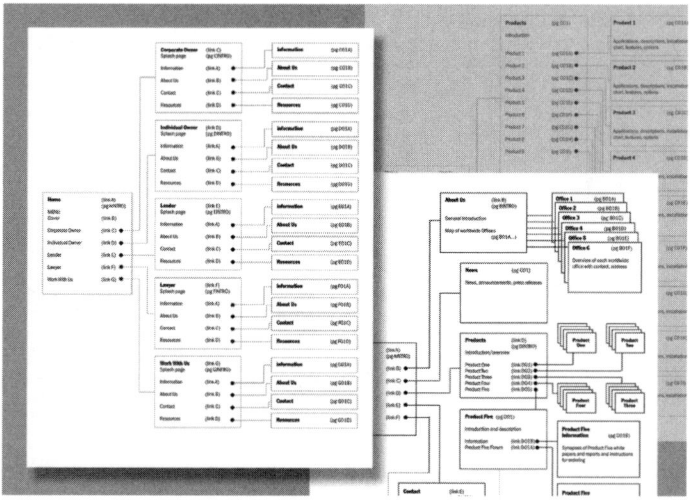

## 104
## Web Flow Chart 1

Used to diagram web site pages. Three variations.

SIZE 8.5W x 11H
PAGES 3
FOLD —
STOCK 24# bond
BINDING —

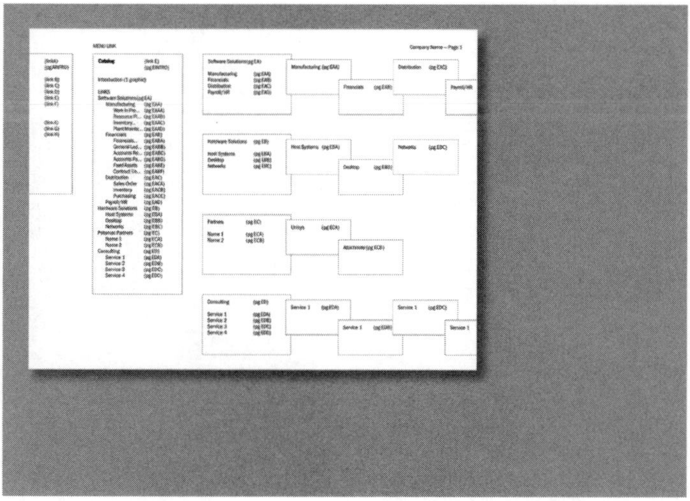

## 105
## Web Flow Chart 2

Used to diagram web site pages.

SIZE 11W x 8.5H
PAGES 1
FOLD —
STOCK 24# bond
BINDING —

## 106
## Font Map Form

Used to show all standard and special characters included with a font. Change the style labeled "02 Font" to font you want to map and the page will show special characters.

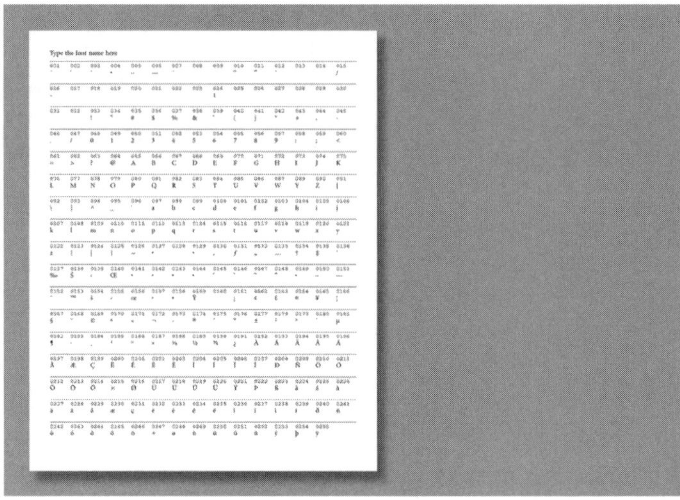

| | |
|---|---|
| SIZE | 8.5W x 11H |
| PAGES | 1 |
| FOLD | — |
| STOCK | 24# bond |
| BINDING | — |

## 107
## Invoice Form

Used to invoice clients.

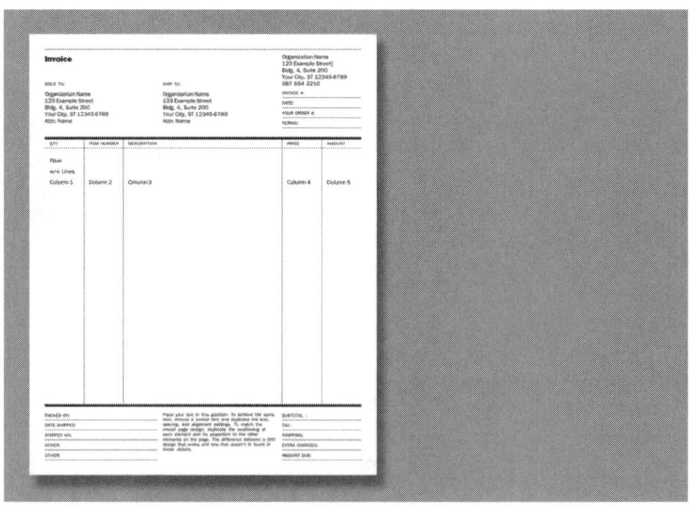

| | |
|---|---|
| SIZE | 8.5W x 11H |
| PAGES | 1 |
| FOLD | — |
| STOCK | 24# bond |
| BINDING | — |

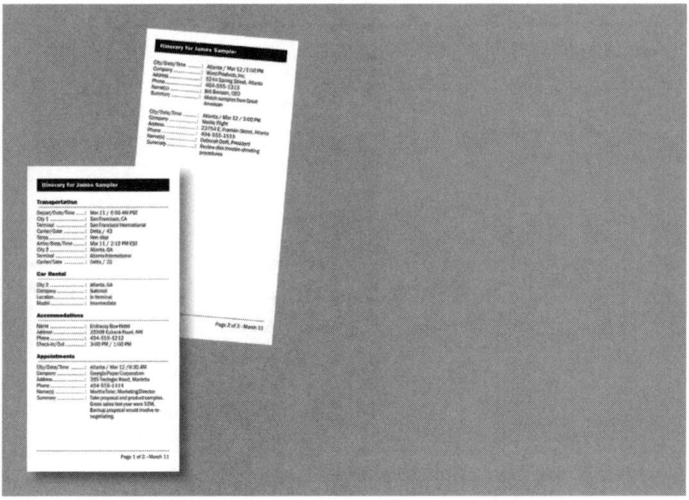


## 108
## Itinerary Form

Used to summarize travel itinerary.

SIZE 3.75W x 7.5H
PAGES 2
FOLD —
STOCK 24# bond
BINDING —

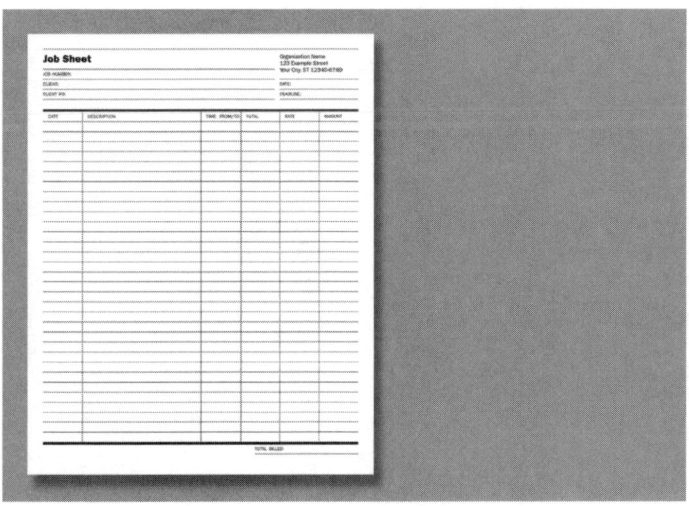


## 109
## Job Sheet Form

Used to record dates, times, rates, and totals of job tasks.

SIZE 8.5W x 11H
PAGES 1
FOLD —
STOCK 24# bond
BINDING —

## 110
## Purchase Order Form

Used for making purchases.

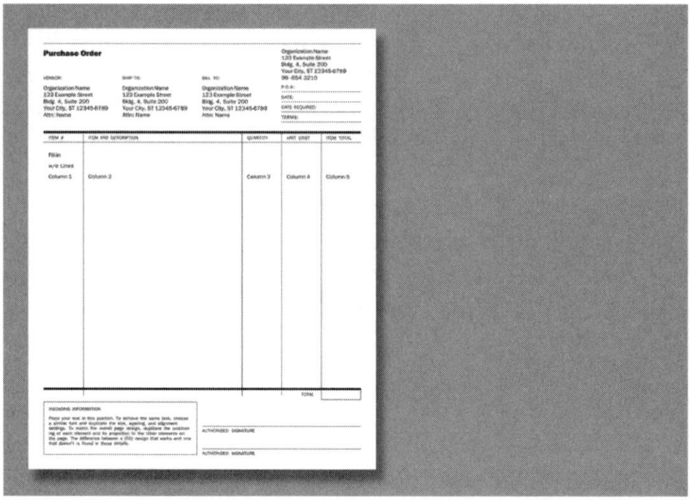

SIZE 8.5W x 11H
PAGES 1
FOLD —
STOCK 24# bond
BINDING —

## 111
## Registration Form

Used to register multiple attendees for an event.

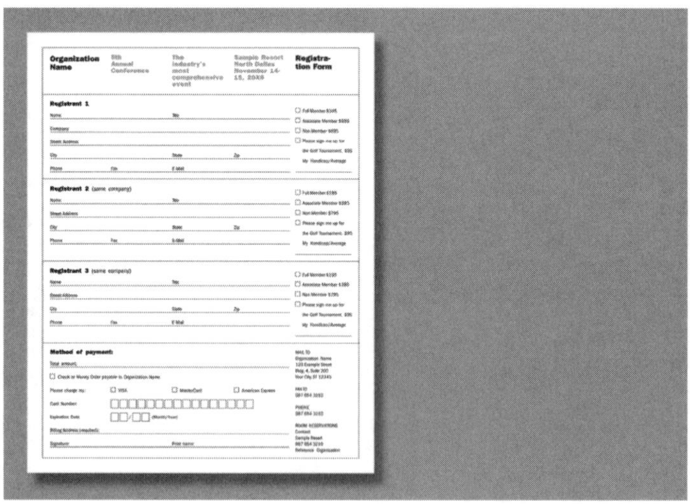

SIZE 8.5W x 11H
PAGES 1
FOLD —
STOCK 24# bond
BINDING —

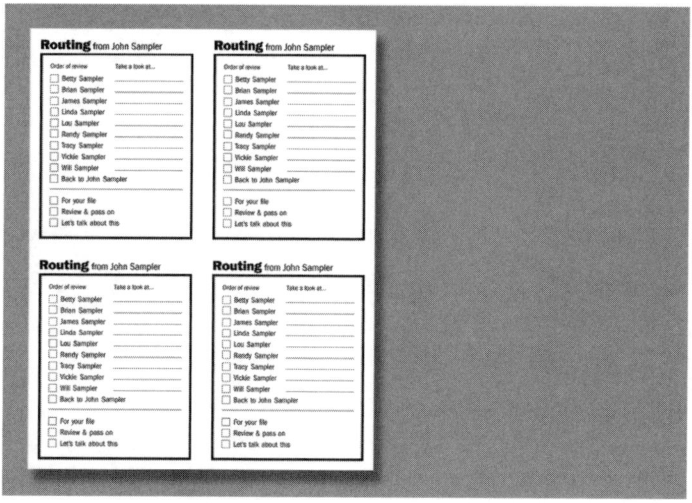


## 112
## Routing Record Form

Attached to files, mail, and publications to facilitate routing.

SIZE 4.25W x 5.5H
PAGES 1
FOLD —
STOCK 24# bond
BINDING —

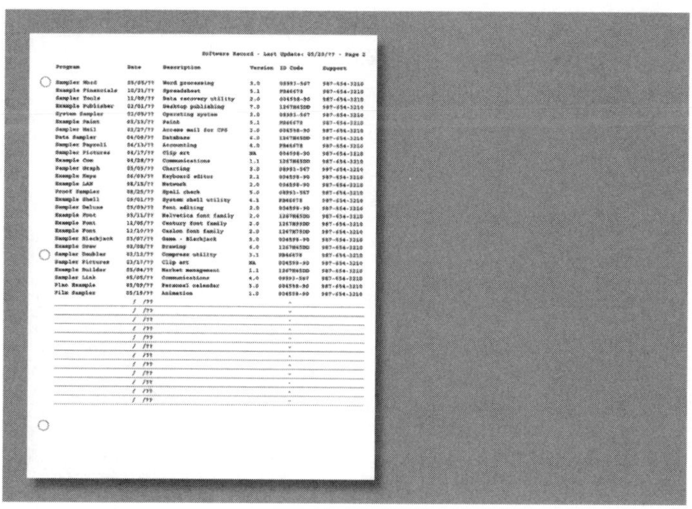


## 113
## Software Record Form

Used to track software programs, versions, and support numbers.

SIZE 8.5W x 11H
PAGES 1
FOLD —
STOCK 24# bond
BINDING —

## 114
## Order Form

Used to take catalog or mail orders.

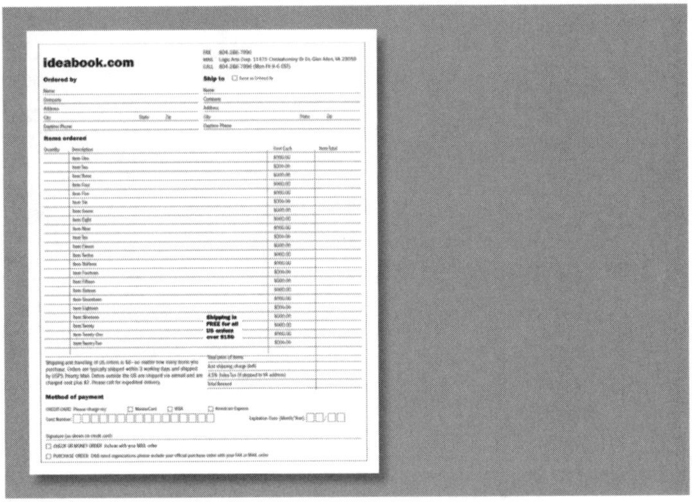


| SIZE | 8.5W x 11H |
|---|---|
| PAGES | 1 |
| FOLD | — |
| STOCK | 24# bond |
| BINDING | — |

## 115
## Time Sheet Form 1

Used to track estimated and actual time spent on a project.

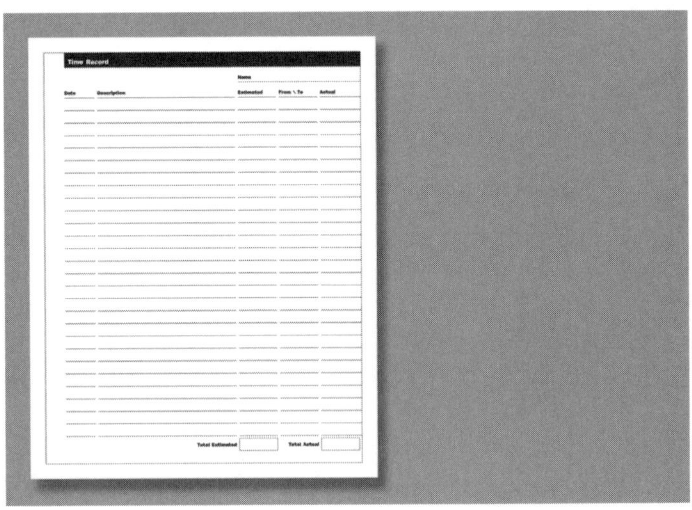


| SIZE | 8.5W x 11H |
|---|---|
| PAGES | 1 |
| FOLD | — |
| STOCK | 24# bond |
| BINDING | — |

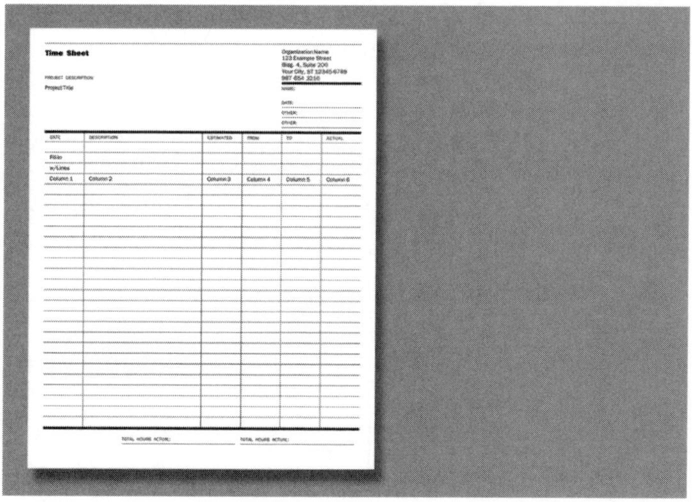


## 116
## Time Sheet Form 2

Used to track estimated and actual time spent on a project.

| | |
|---|---|
| SIZE | 8.5W x 11H |
| PAGES | 1 |
| FOLD | — |
| STOCK | 24# bond |
| BINDING | — |

Chapter 6

# Cards, Invitations, & Notes

## 117 Event Invitation

Used to invite the reader to an event and to communicate the necessary details. Page 1, panel 1 (top): back cover; panel 2: cover; page 2, panel 1: cover illustration caption; panel 2: text spread one. Fits standard A7 announcement envelope.

(NOTE: The author and publisher have used their best efforts to proof and confirm the content of the files, but you should proof and confirm information such as dates, measurements, form properties, and any other content for yourself. The author and publisher make no warranties of any kind, express or implied, with regard to that content or its accuracy.)

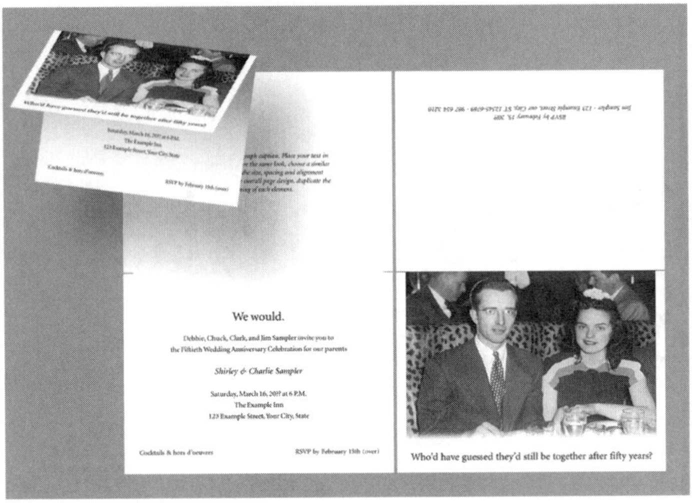


| | |
|---|---|
| SIZE | 6.625W x 10H (flat); 6.625W x 5H (finished) |
| PAGES | 2 |
| FOLD | half-fold |
| STOCK | 65# uncoated cover |
| BINDING | — |

## 118 Announcement

Used to announce an event, ceremony, or action. Page 1, panel 1 (top): back cover; panel 2: cover; page 2, panel 1: blank; panel 2: text spread one. Fits standard A6 announcement envelope.

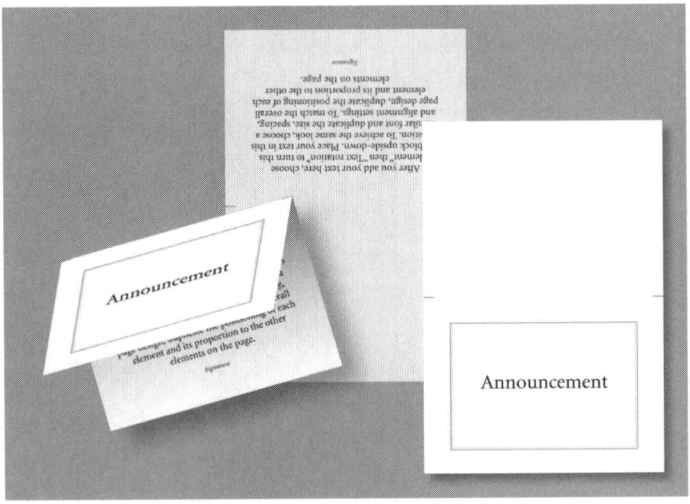


| | |
|---|---|
| SIZE | 5.875W x 8.875H (flat); 5.875W x 4.4375H (finished) |
| PAGES | 2 |
| FOLD | half-fold |
| STOCK | 65# uncoated cover |
| BINDING | — |

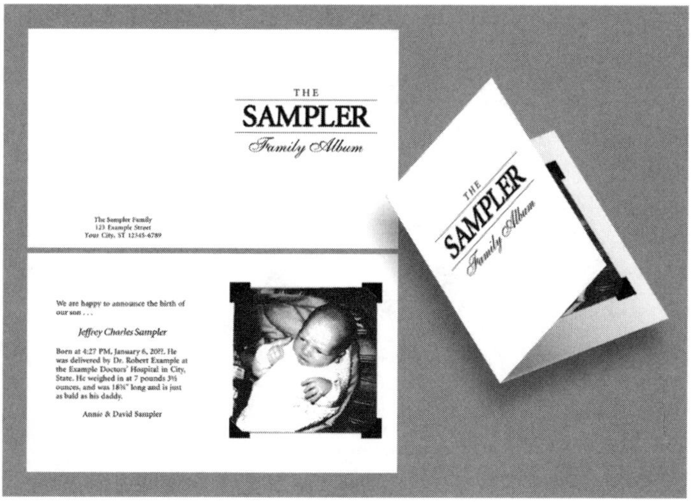


## 119
## Birth Announcement

Used to announce a birth and to provide the customery details. Page 1, panel 1 (top): back cover; panel 2: cover; page 2, panel 1: text spread one; panel 2: space squares to fit photograph, cut slots through center of black squares and insert photo corners. Fits standard A6 announcement envelope.

| | |
|---|---|
| SIZE | 9W x 6H (flat); 4.5W x 6H (finished) |
| PAGES | 2 |
| FOLD | half-fold |
| STOCK | 65# uncoated cover |
| BINDING | — |

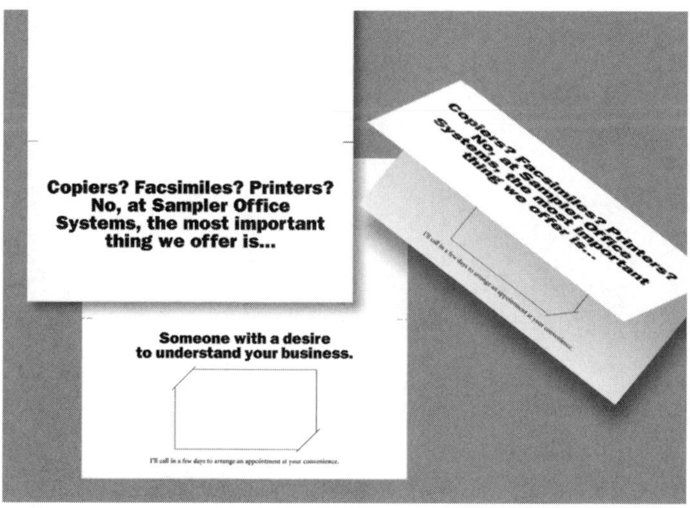


## 120
## Business Greeting Card

Used to present a business card. Page 1, panel 1: back cover; panel 2: cover; page 2, panel 1: blank; panel 2: cut slots and insert card corners.

| | |
|---|---|
| SIZE | 8W x 8H (flat); 8W x 4H (finished) |
| PAGES | 2 |
| FOLD | half-fold |
| STOCK | 65# uncoated cover |
| BINDING | — |

## 121
## Die-Cut Invitation

Used to invite the reader to an event and to communicate the necessary details. Die cut and folded as shown in illustration. Page 1: outside headline panels; page 2: background illustrations.

SIZE 8.5W x 11H (flat); 5.5W x 4.25H (finished)
PAGES 2
FOLD french-fold
STOCK 65# uncoated cover
BINDING —

## 122
## Gift Card Bookmark

Used to present a book as a gift. Page 1 (left): front; (right): back.

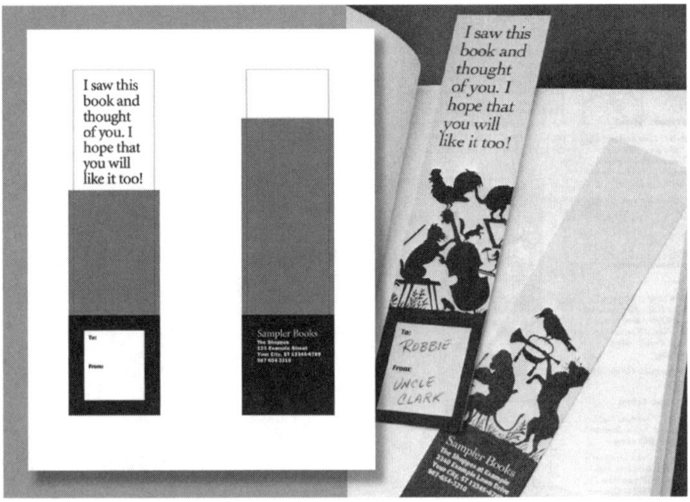


SIZE 6W x 4.5H
PAGES 1
FOLD —
STOCK 100# uncoated cover
BINDING —

## 123
## Greeting Card

Used to create a single-sheet greeting card. Page 1, panel 1 (top left): text spread one; panel 2: illustration; panel 3: back cover; panel 4: cover.

| | |
|---|---|
| SIZE | 8.5W x 11H (flat); 4.25W x 5.5H (finished) |
| PAGES | 1 |
| FOLD | french-fold |
| STOCK | 60# uncoated text |
| BINDING | — |

## 124
## Illustrated Invitation

Used to invite the reader to an event and to communicate the necessary details. Page 1, panel 1 (top): back cover; panel 2: cover; page 2, panels 1-2: illustration; panel 2: text spread one. Fits standard A6 announcement envelope.

| | |
|---|---|
| SIZE | 6W x 9H (flat); 6W x 4.5H (finished) |
| PAGES | 2 |
| FOLD | half-fold |
| STOCK | 65# uncoated cover |
| BINDING | — |

## 125
## Origami Invitation

Used to create an origami invitation in the form of a bird. Invites the reader to an event and to communicate the necessary details. Page 1: invitation; page 2: folding instructions.

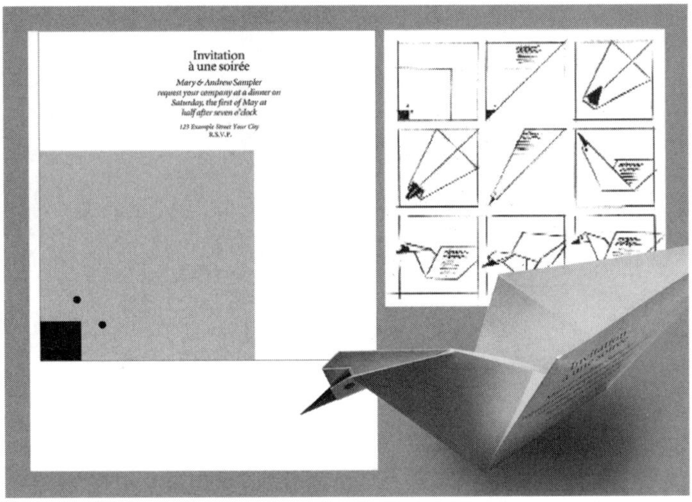


| | |
|---|---|
| SIZE | 8.25W x 8.25H (flat) |
| PAGES | 2 |
| FOLD | custom fold |
| STOCK | 60# uncoated text |
| BINDING | — |

## 126
## Picture Invitation

Used to invite the reader to an event and to communicate the necessary details. Page 1, panel 1 (top left): cover; panel 2: blank; panel 3: back cover; panel 4: text spread one.

| | |
|---|---|
| SIZE | 8.5W x 11H (flat); 4.25W x 5.5H (finished) |
| PAGES | 1 |
| FOLD | french-fold |
| STOCK | 60# uncoated text |
| BINDING | — |

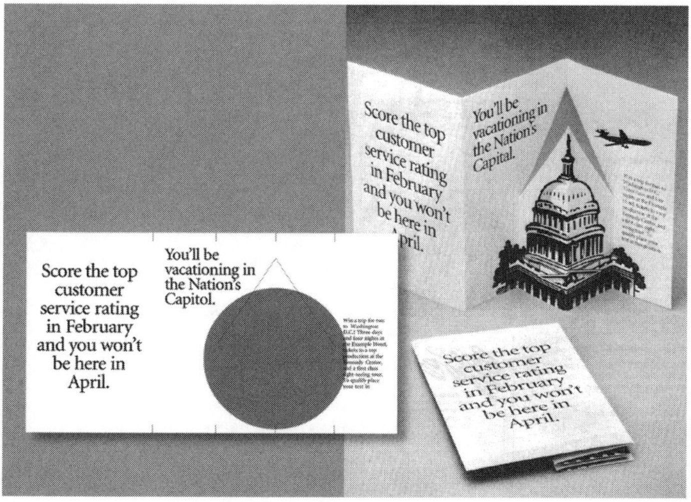


## 127
## Pop-Up Card

Used to create a die-cut, pop-up card. Illustration pushes forward as card is opened. Page 1, panel 1: cover; panel 2–3: text spread.

| | |
|---|---|
| SIZE | 11W x 6H (flat); 3.75W x 6H (finished) |
| PAGES | 1 |
| FOLD | double-parallel-fold |
| STOCK | 65# uncoated cover |
| BINDING | — |

## 128
## Signature Card

Used to attach business card to proposals, reports, brochures, and so on. Cut slots and insert card corners. Page 1, top panel: back; bottom panel: front.

| | |
|---|---|
| SIZE | 7.25W x 5.25H (flat); 7.25W x 3.5H (finished) |
| PAGES | 2 |
| FOLD | half-fold |
| STOCK | 65# uncoated cover |
| BINDING | — |

## 129
## Signature Card-Two per page

Used to attach business card to proposals, reports, brochures, and so on. Cut slots and insert card corners. Page 1, panel 1 (top): back; panel 2 (bottom): front.

SIZE 10W x 8.5H (flat); 5W x 5.125H (finished)
PAGES 1
FOLD half-fold
STOCK 65# uncoated cover
BINDING —

## 130
## Step Invitation

Used to invite the reader to an event and to reveal the necessary details in three steps. Page 1, panel 1 (top): cover; panel 2: text spread one; panel 3: text spread three. Accordion-fold.

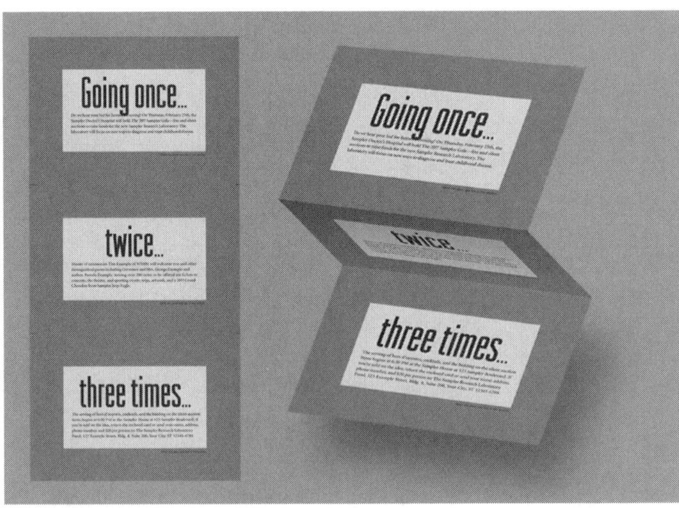


SIZE 6.25W x 4.5H
PAGES 1
FOLD accordion-fold
STOCK 65# uncoated cover
BINDING —

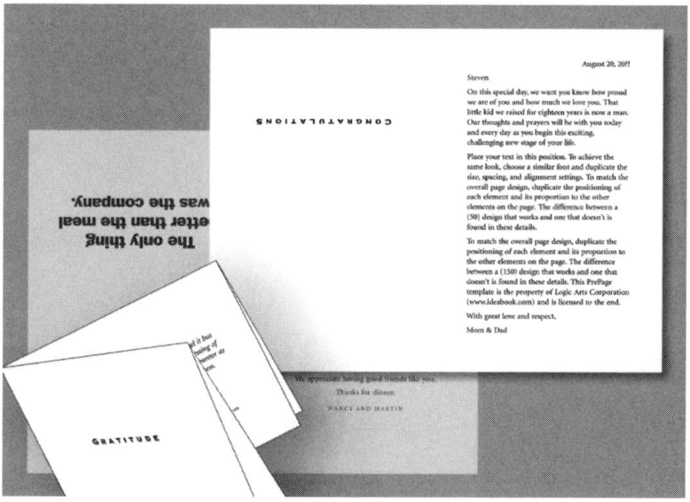

## 131
## Text Note

Used to create a single-sheet note card. Page 1, panel 1 (top left): cover; panel 2 and 4: text; panel 3: back cover, blank.

| | |
|---|---|
| SIZE | 11W x 8.5H (flat); 5.5W x 4.25H (finished) |
| PAGES | 3 |
| FOLD | french-fold |
| STOCK | 24# bond |
| BINDING | — |

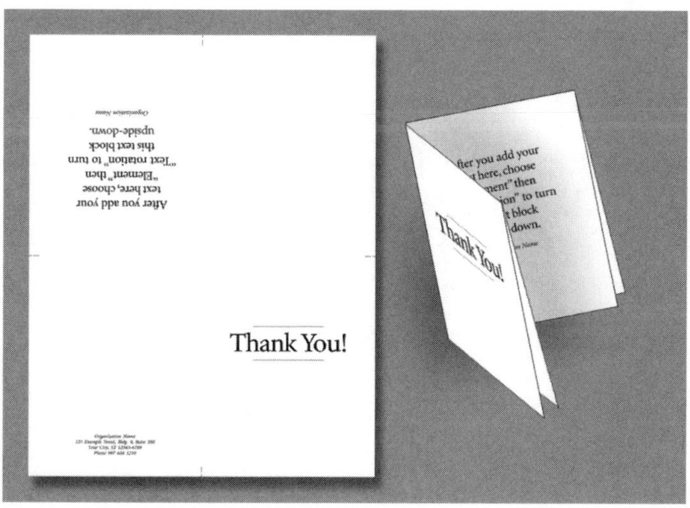

## 132
## Thank You Card

Used to create a single-sheet greeting card. Page 1, panel 1 (top left): cover; panel 2: blank; panel 3: back cover; panel 4: text spread one.

| | |
|---|---|
| SIZE | 8.5W x 11H (flat); 4.25W x 5.5H (finished) |
| PAGES | 1 |
| FOLD | french-fold |
| STOCK | 24# bond |
| BINDING | — |

Chapter 7

# Catalogs & Product Sheets

## 133
## Three Item Catalog

Used to create a catalog featuring three items per page. Page 1: cover; page 2–3: text spread; page 4: back cover.

(NOTE: The author and publisher have used their best efforts to proof and confirm the content of the files, but you should proof and confirm information such as dates, measurements, form properties, and any other content for yourself. The author and publisher make no warranties of any kind, express or implied, with regard to that content or its accuracy.)

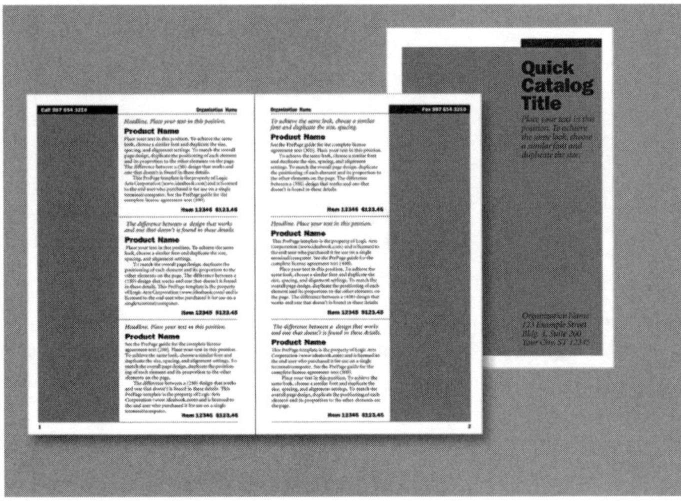


| | |
|---|---|
| SIZE | 8.5W x 11H (flat); 5.5W x 8.5H (finished) |
| PAGES | 4 |
| FOLD | half-fold |
| STOCK | 60# uncoated text |
| BINDING | saddle-stitch |

## 134
## Four Item Catalog

Used to create a catalog featuring four items per page. Page 1: cover; page 2–3: text spread; pages 4: back cover.

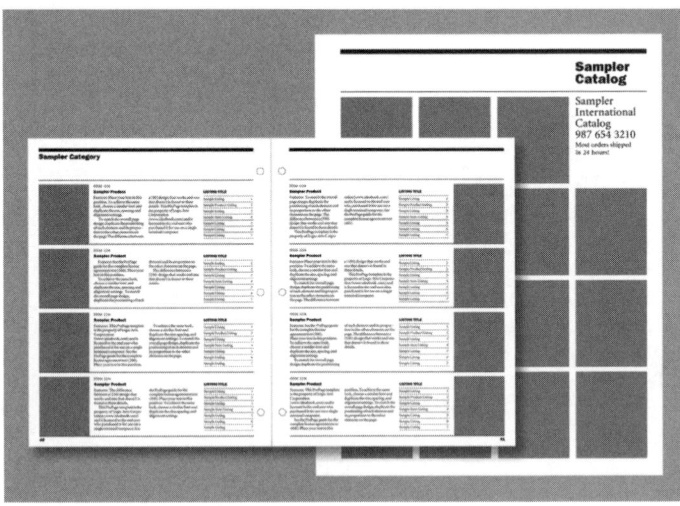


| | |
|---|---|
| SIZE | 8.5W x 11H |
| PAGES | 3 |
| FOLD | — |
| STOCK | 60# uncoated text |
| BINDING | — |

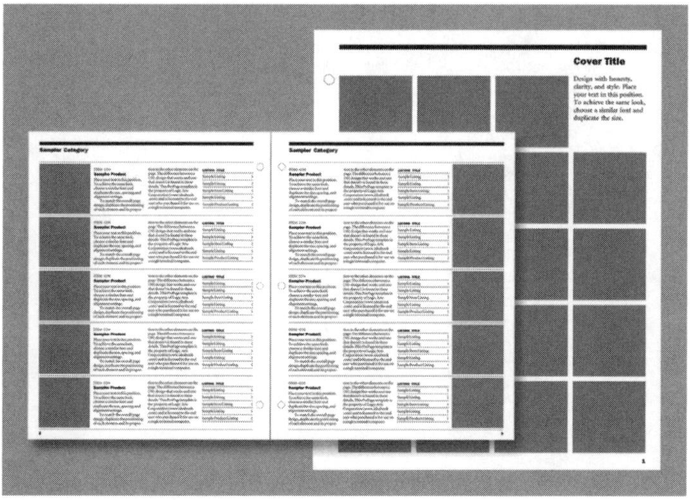


## 135
## Five Item Catalog

Used to create a catalog featuring five items per page. Page 1: cover; page 2-3: text spread; page 4: back cover.

| | |
|---|---|
| SIZE | 8.5W x 11H |
| PAGES | 3 |
| FOLD | — |
| STOCK | 60# uncoated text |
| BINDING | — |

## 136
## Plug-In Catalog

Used to create a catalog built from plug-in text, illustration, and photographic modules. Page 1: cover; page 2: welcome, contents; page 3: order form; pages 4-7: catalog text; page 8: back cover.

| | |
|---|---|
| SIZE | 8.5W x 11H |
| PAGES | 8 |
| FOLD | — |
| STOCK | 60# uncoated text |
| BINDING | — |

## 137
## Table Catalog

Used to create a catalog structured on item tables. Page 1: cover; page 2: welcome; page 3: contents; pages 4–5: catalog text; page 6: back cover.

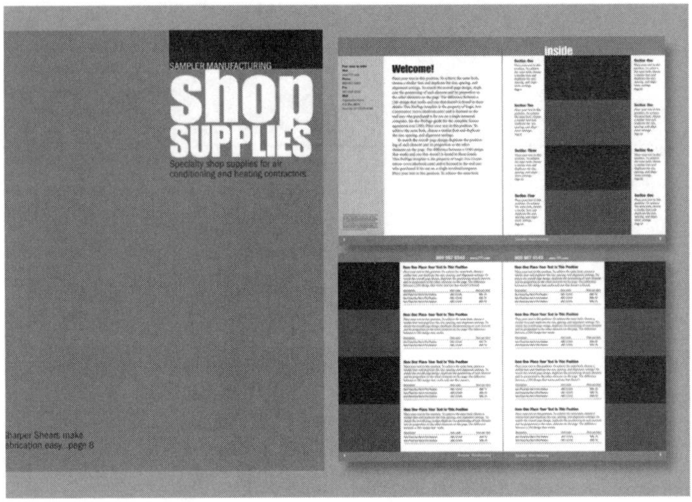


| | |
|---|---|
| SIZE | 8.5W x 11H |
| PAGES | 6 |
| FOLD | — |
| STOCK | 60# uncoated text |
| BINDING | — |

## 138
## Product Sheet-Single Product

Used to create a product sheet featuring a description, facts and figures, and an illustration.

| | |
|---|---|
| SIZE | 8.5W x 11H |
| PAGES | 1 |
| FOLD | — |
| STOCK | 60# uncoated text |
| BINDING | — |

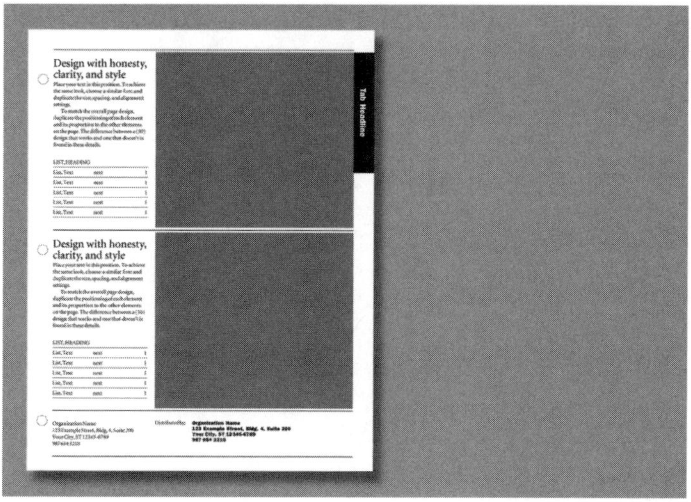


## 139
## Product Sheet-Two Products

Used to create a product sheet featuring two sets of descriptions, facts and figures, and illustrations.

| | |
|---|---|
| SIZE | 8.5W x 11H |
| PAGES | 1 |
| FOLD | — |
| STOCK | 60# uncoated text |
| BINDING | — |

Chapter 8
# Certificates

## 140
## Bar Certificate

Used to create an award certificate featuring an inspirational quotation.

(NOTE: The author and publisher have used their best efforts to proof and confirm the content of the files, but you should proof and confirm information such as dates, measurements, form properties, and any other content for yourself. The author and publisher make no warranties of any kind, express or implied, with regard to that content or its accuracy.)

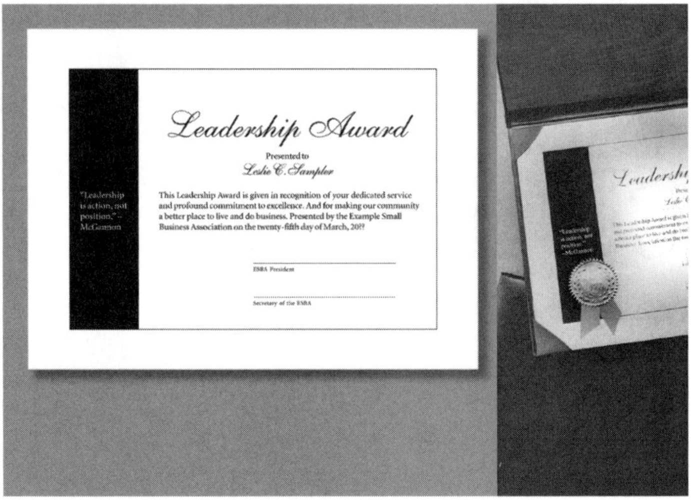


| SIZE | 11W x 8.5H |
|---|---|
| PAGES | 1 |
| FOLD | — |
| STOCK | 60# uncoated text |
| BINDING | — |

## 141
## Classic Certificate

Used to create an award certificate featuring a decorative seal.

| SIZE | 11W x 8.5H |
|---|---|
| PAGES | 1 |
| FOLD | — |
| STOCK | 60# uncoated text |
| BINDING | — |

## 142
## Elegant Certificate

Used to create an award certificate featuring an illustration.

SIZE 11W x 8.5H
PAGES 1
FOLD —
STOCK 60# uncoated text
BINDING —

## 143
## Illustrated Certificate

Used to create an award certificate featuring an illustration.

SIZE 11W x 8.5H
PAGES 1
FOLD —
STOCK 60# uncoated text
BINDING —

**144**
**Left/Right Certificate**

Used to create an award certificate that highlights the award title.

SIZE 11W x 8.5H
PAGES 1
FOLD —
STOCK 60# uncoated text
BINDING —

**145**
**Quote Certificate**

Used to create an award certificate featuring an inspirational quotation.

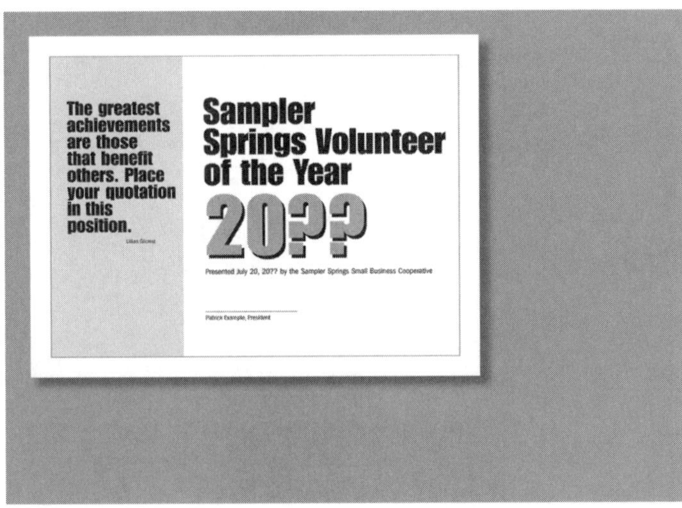


SIZE 11W x 8.5H
PAGES 1
FOLD —
STOCK 60# uncoated text
BINDING —

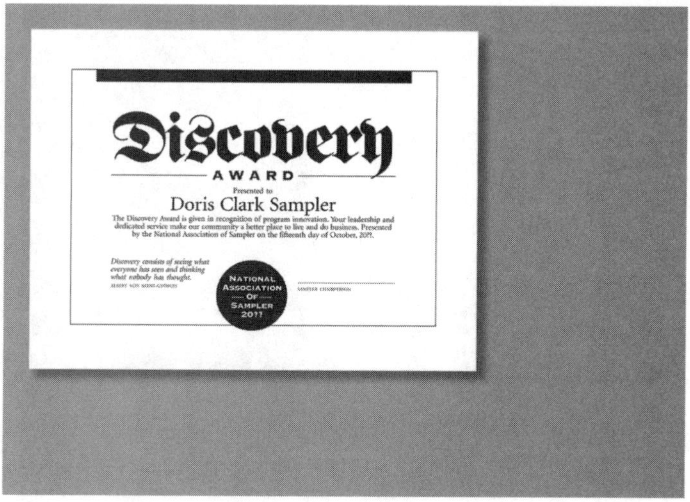


## 146
## Seal Certificate

Used to create an award certificate featuring a decorative seal.

| | |
|---|---|
| SIZE | 11W x 8.5H |
| PAGES | 1 |
| FOLD | — |
| STOCK | 60# uncoated text |
| BINDING | — |

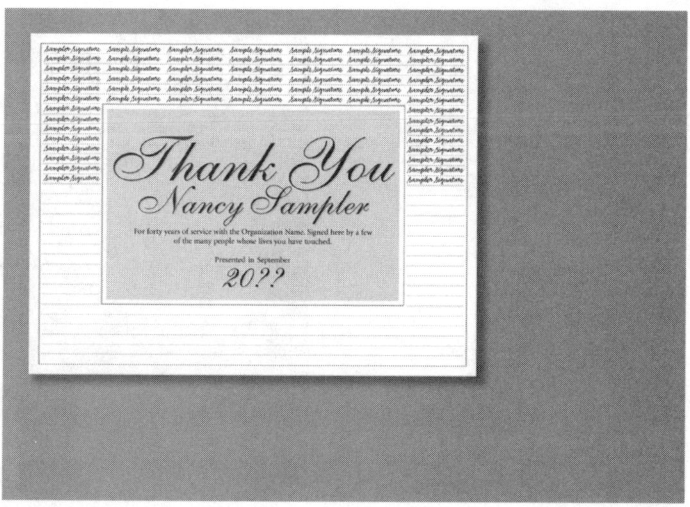


## 147
## Signature Certificate

Used to create an award certificate that is signed by the group members who present it.

| | |
|---|---|
| SIZE | 11W x 8.5H |
| PAGES | 1 |
| FOLD | — |
| STOCK | 60# uncoated text |
| BINDING | — |

## 148
## Square Certificate

Used to create an award certificate with a distinctive wallpaper background. To recreate the pattern use a picture font or substitute your own illustrations.

| SIZE | 8.5W x 8.5H |
|---|---|
| PAGES | 1 |
| FOLD | — |
| STOCK | 60# uncoated text |
| BINDING | — |

## 149
## Stack Certificate 1

Used to create an award certificate featuring an illustration.

| SIZE | 8.5W x 11H |
|---|---|
| PAGES | 1 |
| FOLD | — |
| STOCK | 60# uncoated text |
| BINDING | — |

## 150
## Stack Certificate 2

Used to create an award certificate featuring an illustration.

| | |
|---|---|
| SIZE | 8.5W x 11H |
| PAGES | 1 |
| FOLD | — |
| STOCK | 60# uncoated text |
| BINDING | — |

## 151
## Team Certificate

Used to create an award certificate featuring a group photograph (the photo caption at the right names those in the photograph).

| | |
|---|---|
| SIZE | 11W x 8.5H |
| PAGES | 1 |
| FOLD | — |
| STOCK | 60# uncoated text |
| BINDING | — |

## 152 Vintage Certificate

Used to create an award certificate featuring a decorative seal.

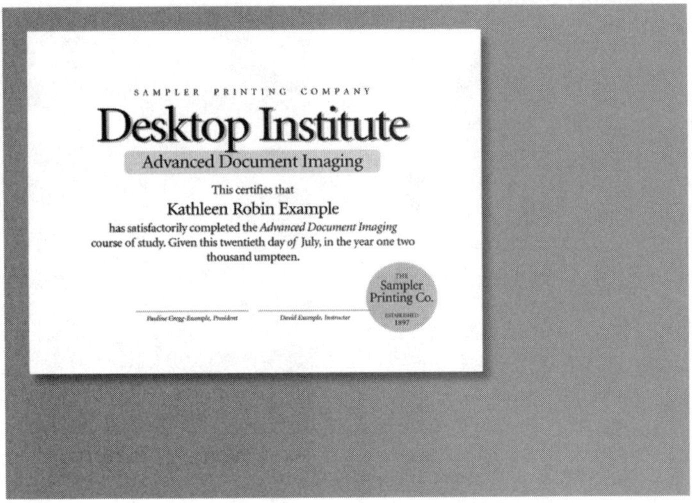


| SIZE | 11W x 8.5H |
|---|---|
| PAGES | 1 |
| FOLD | — |
| STOCK | 60# uncoated text |
| BINDING | — |

Chapter 9

# Correspondence & Messages

## 153 Envelope, Executive-Size

Used to create a monarch-sized envelope. Used with executive- and personal-sized letterhead (files 162 and 163).

(NOTE: The author and publisher have used their best efforts to proof and confirm the content of the files, but you should proof and confirm information such as dates, measurements, form properties, and any other content for yourself. The author and publisher make no warranties of any kind, express or implied, with regard to that content or its accuracy.)

| | |
|---|---|
| SIZE | 7W x 3.875H |
| PAGES | 1 |
| FOLD | — |
| STOCK | — |
| BINDING | — |

## 154 Envelope, Business-Size

Used to create a business-sized (#10) envelope.

| | |
|---|---|
| SIZE | 9.5W x 4.125H |
| PAGES | 1 |
| FOLD | — |
| STOCK | — |
| BINDING | — |

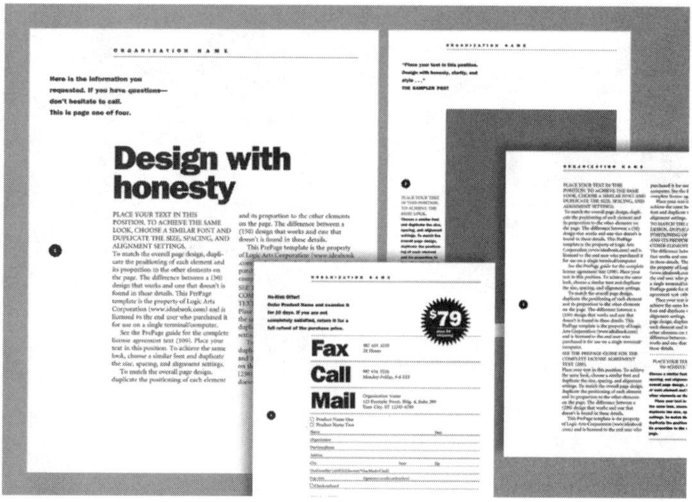


## 155
## Fax Presentation 1

Used to create multi-page, illustrated fax presentation of products or services. Page 1-3: text; page 4: reply form.

| SIZE | 8.5W x 11H |
|---|---|
| PAGES | 4 |
| FOLD | — |
| STOCK | 24# bond |
| BINDING | — |

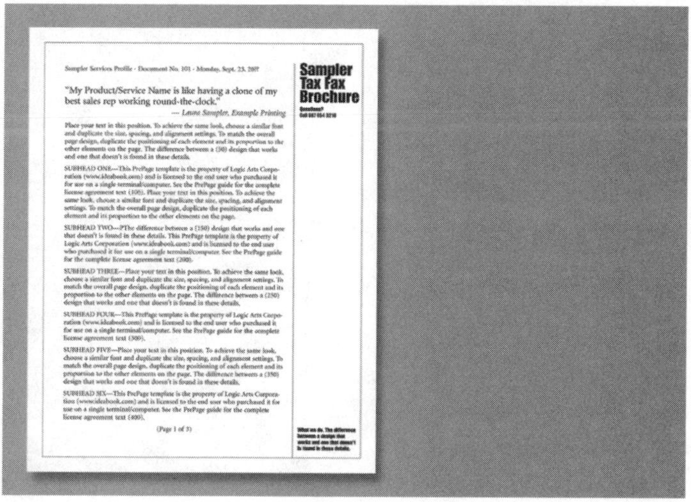


## 156
## Fax Presentation 2

Used to create a fax presentation of products or services.

| SIZE | 8.5W x 11H |
|---|---|
| PAGES | 1 |
| FOLD | — |
| STOCK | 24# bond |
| BINDING | — |

## 157
## Fax Message Cover

Used to create cover sheets for faxed messages. Three versions.

| | |
|---|---|
| SIZE | 8.5W x 11H |
| PAGES | 3 |
| FOLD | — |
| STOCK | 24# bond |
| BINDING | — |

## 158
## Fax Message— Two Per Page

Used to create cover sheets for faxed messages.

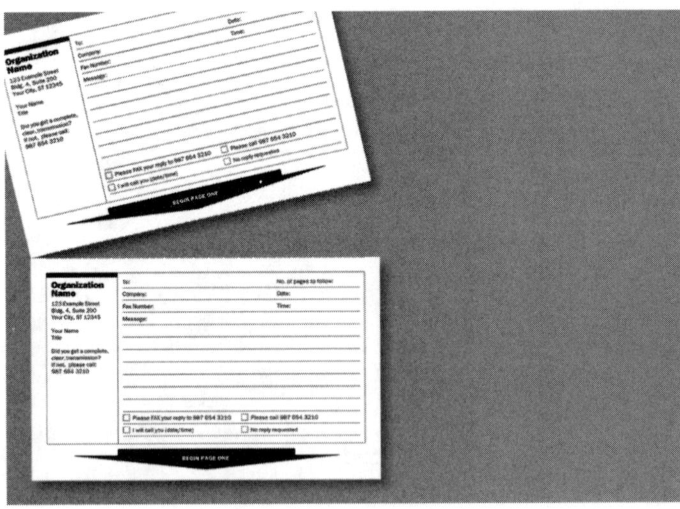


| | |
|---|---|
| SIZE | 8.5W x 11H (flat); 8.5W x 5.5H (trimmed) |
| PAGES | 1 |
| FOLD | — |
| STOCK | 24# bond |
| BINDING | — |

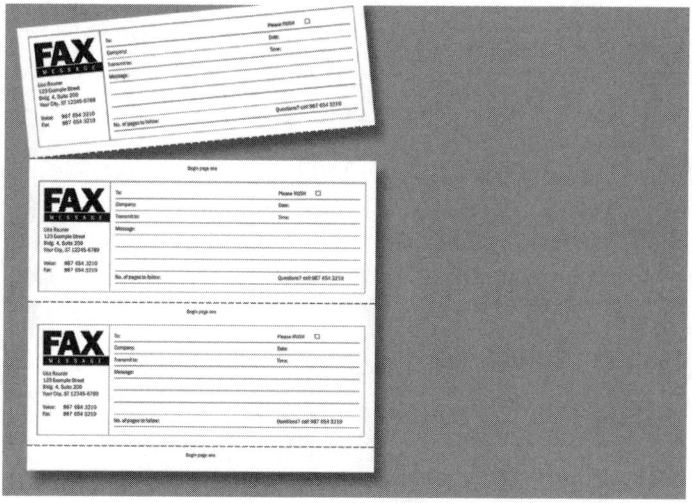


### 159
### Fax Message—Three Per Page

Used to create cover sheets for faxed messages.

| | |
|---|---|
| SIZE | 8.5W x 11H (flat); 8.5W x 3.5625H (trimmed) |
| PAGES | 1 |
| FOLD | — |
| STOCK | 24# bond |
| BINDING | — |

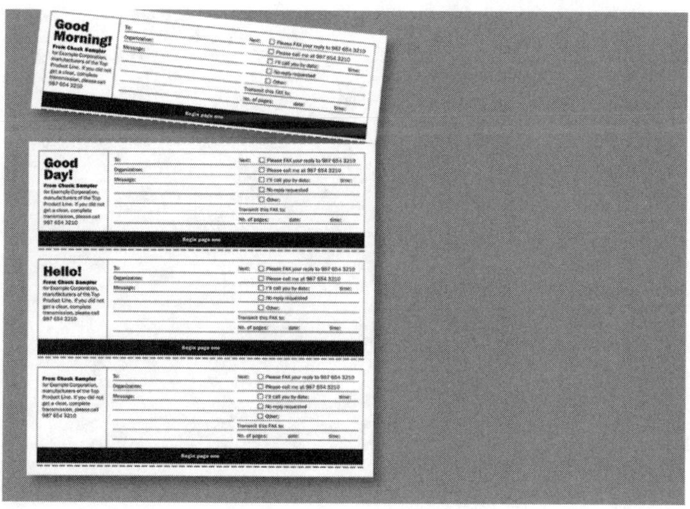


### 160
### Fax Message—Four Per Page

Used to create cover sheets for faxed messages.

| | |
|---|---|
| SIZE | 8.5W x 11H (flat); 8.5W x 2.6875H (trimmed) |
| PAGES | 1 |
| FOLD | — |
| STOCK | 24# bond |
| BINDING | — |

## 161
## All-In-One Mailer

Used to create a self-mailer from a single sheet. Have mailing piece artwork approved by the postal service to confirm compliance with postal regulations. Page 1, panel 1 (top): back; panel 2 (bottom): cover; panel 2–3: for handwriting text message.

| | |
|---|---|
| SIZE | 8.5W x 11H (flat); 8.5W x 5.5H (finished) |
| PAGES | 2 |
| FOLD | half-fold |
| STOCK | 65# uncoated cover |
| BINDING | — |

## 162
## Letterhead, Executive

Used to create an executive-sized letterhead. Used with executive-sized envelope (file 153).

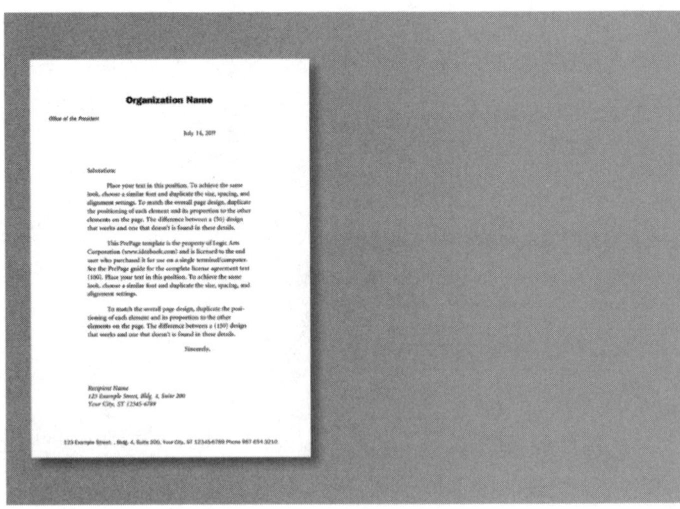


| | |
|---|---|
| SIZE | 7.25W x 10.5H |
| PAGES | 1 |
| FOLD | letter-fold |
| STOCK | 24# bond |
| BINDING | — |

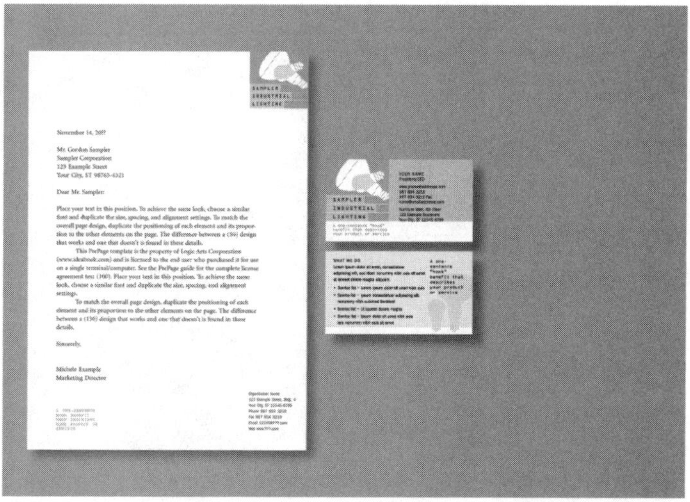

## 163
## Letterhead, Personal

Used to create a personal-sized letterhead and matching card. Used with executive-sized envelope (file 153). Page 1: letterhead; page 2, (top): business card front; (bottom): business card front.

| | |
|---|---|
| SIZE | 7.25W x 10.5H |
| PAGES | 1 |
| FOLD | letter-fold |
| STOCK | Letterhead: 24# bond;<br>business card: 110# pasted (two 110 text sheets) |

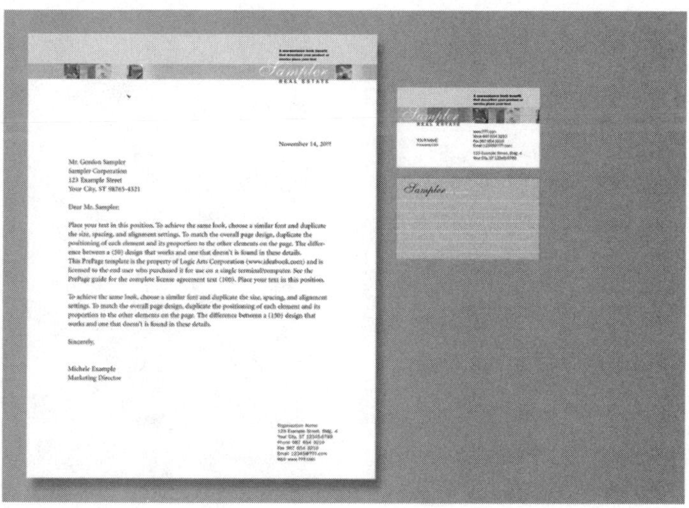

## 164
## Business Letterhead/ Business Card 1

Used to create a business letterhead and matching card. Page 1: letterhead; page 2, (top): business card front; (bottom): business card front.

| | |
|---|---|
| SIZE | letterhead: 8.5W x 11H; business card: 3.5W x 2H |
| PAGES | 2 |
| FOLD | letter-fold |
| STOCK | Letterhead: 24# bond;<br>business card: 110# pasted (two 110 text sheets) |

## 165
## Business Letterhead/ Business Card 2

Used to create a business letterhead and matching card. Page 1: letterhead; page 2, (top): business card front; (bottom): business card front.

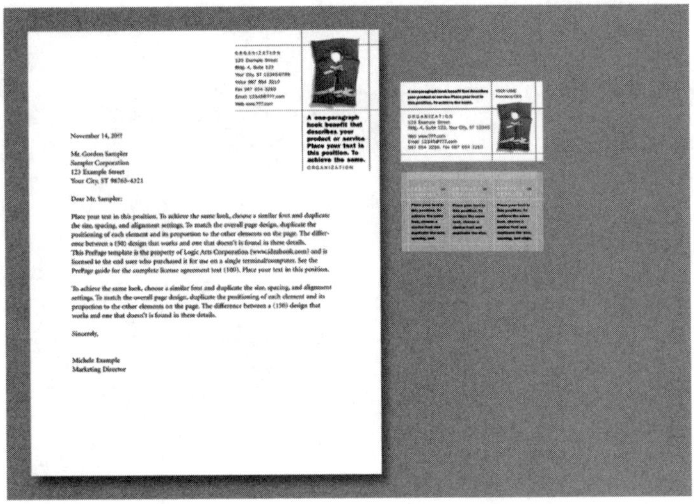

| | |
|---|---|
| SIZE | letterhead: 8.5W x 11H; business card: 3.5W x 2H |
| PAGES | 2 |
| FOLD | letter-fold |
| STOCK | Letterhead: 24# bond;<br>business card: 110# pasted (two 110 text sheets) |

## 166
## Business Letterhead/ Business Card 3

Used to create a business letterhead and matching card. Page 1: letterhead; page 2, (top): business card front.

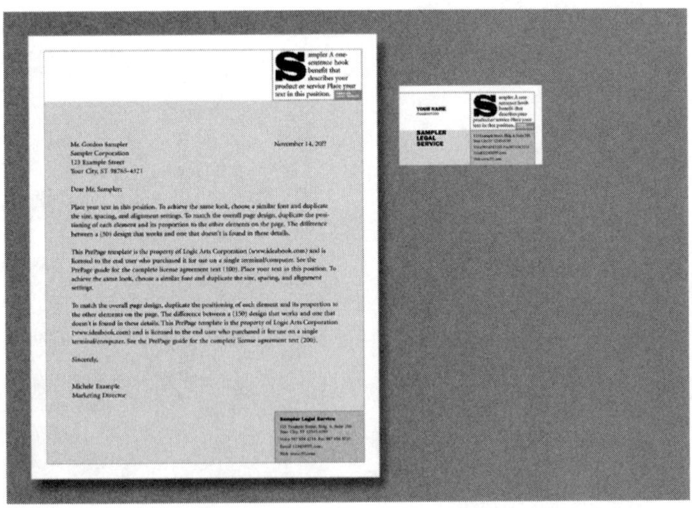

| | |
|---|---|
| SIZE | letterhead: 8.5W x 11H; business card: 3.5W x 2H |
| PAGES | 2 |
| FOLD | letter-fold |
| STOCK | Letterhead: 24# bond;<br>business card: 110# pasted (two 110 text sheets) |

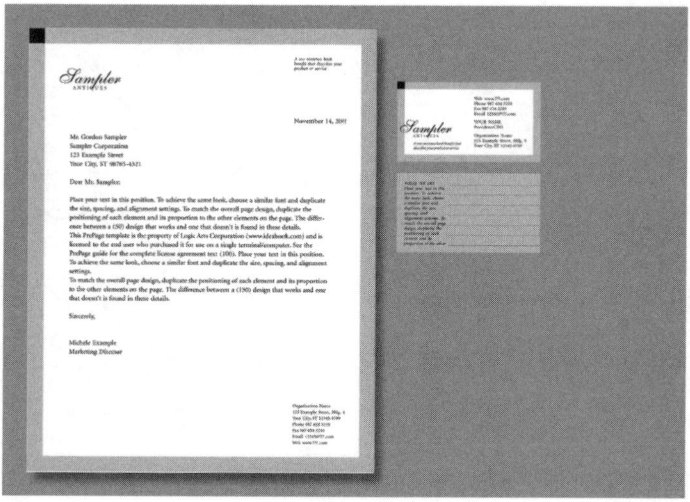


## 167
## Business Letterhead/ Business Card 4

Used to create a business letterhead and matching card. Page 1: letterhead; page 2, (top): business card front; (bottom): business card front.

| | |
|---|---|
| SIZE | letterhead: 8.5W x 11H; business card: 3.5W x 2H |
| PAGES | 2 |
| FOLD | letter-fold |
| STOCK | Letterhead: 24# bond;<br>business card: 110# pasted (two 110 text sheets) |

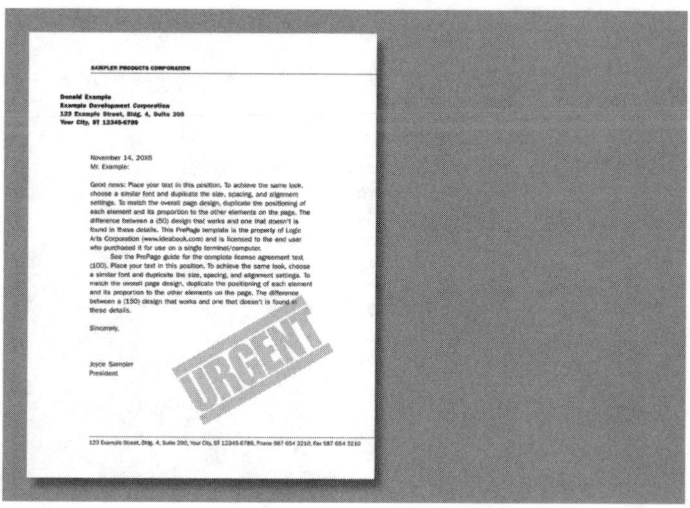


## 168
## Business Letterhead 5

Used to create a business letterhead with a changeable page stamp (URGENT).

| | |
|---|---|
| SIZE | 8.5W x 11H |
| PAGES | 1 |
| FOLD | letter-fold |
| STOCK | 24# bond |
| BINDING | — |

## 169
## Business Letterhead/ Business Card 6

Used to create a business letterhead and matching card. Page 1: letterhead; page 2, (top): business card front.

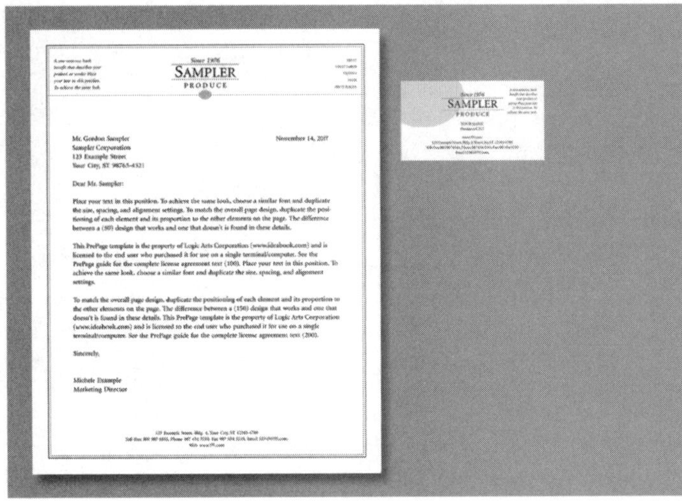


| | |
|---|---|
| SIZE | letterhead: 8.5W x 11H; business card: 3.5W x 2H |
| PAGES | 2 |
| FOLD | letter-fold |
| STOCK | Letterhead: 24# bond;<br>business card: 110# pasted (two 110 text sheets) |

## 170
## Memo

Used to create a memorandum with an illustration.

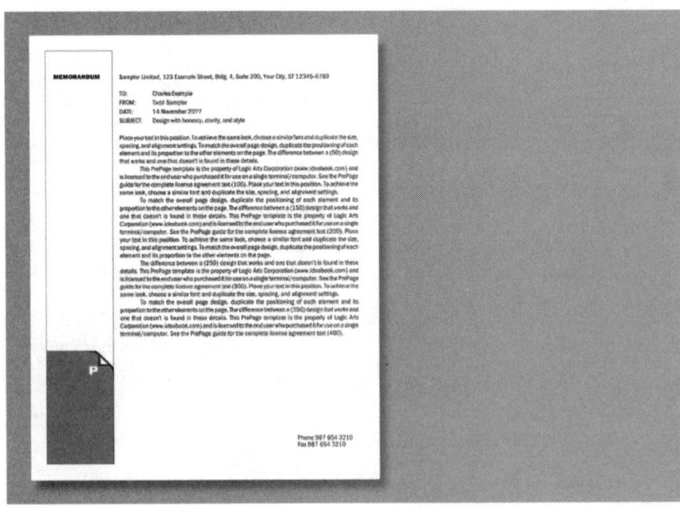


| | |
|---|---|
| SIZE | 8.5W x 11H |
| PAGES | 1 |
| FOLD | letter-fold |
| STOCK | 24# bond |
| BINDING | — |

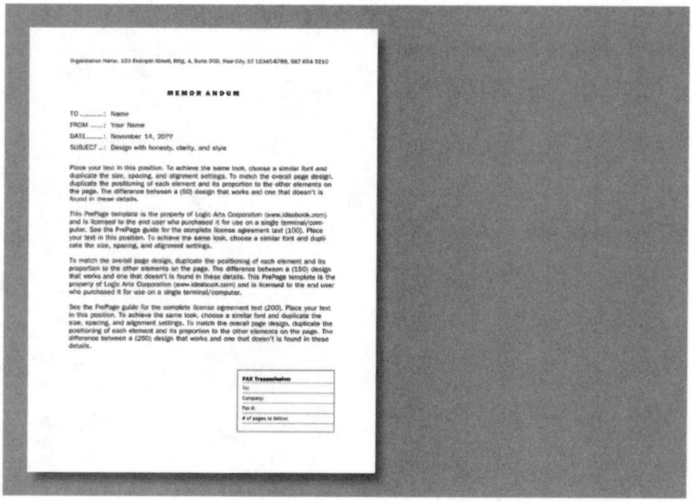


## 171 Memo Fax

Used to create a memorandum with a memo box.

| | |
|---|---|
| SIZE | 8.5W x 11H |
| PAGES | 1 |
| FOLD | letter-fold |
| STOCK | 24# bond |
| BINDING | — |

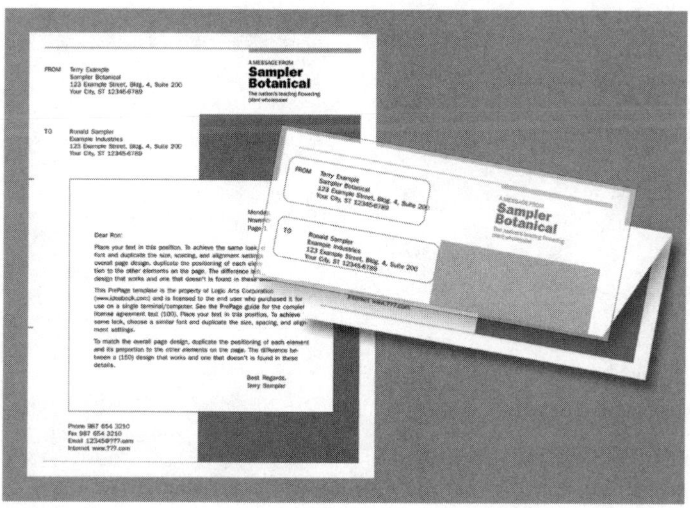


## 172 Memo Mailer

Used to create a memorandum with an illustrated background. Z-folded, the return and recipient's addresses show through the windows of a standard #9 double-window envelope.

| | |
|---|---|
| SIZE | 8.5W x 11H |
| PAGES | 1 |
| FOLD | accordion-fold |
| STOCK | 24# bond |
| BINDING | — |

## 173
## Message Pad

Used to create a detailed message pad.

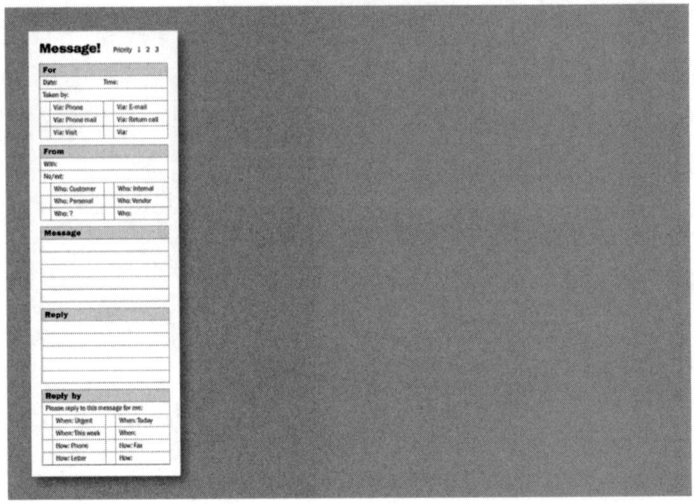


SIZE 2.75W x 8.5H
PAGES 1
FOLD —
STOCK 24# bond
BINDING Pad

## 174
## Personal Note 1

Used to create personal-sized notepaper to fit an A-6 envelope.

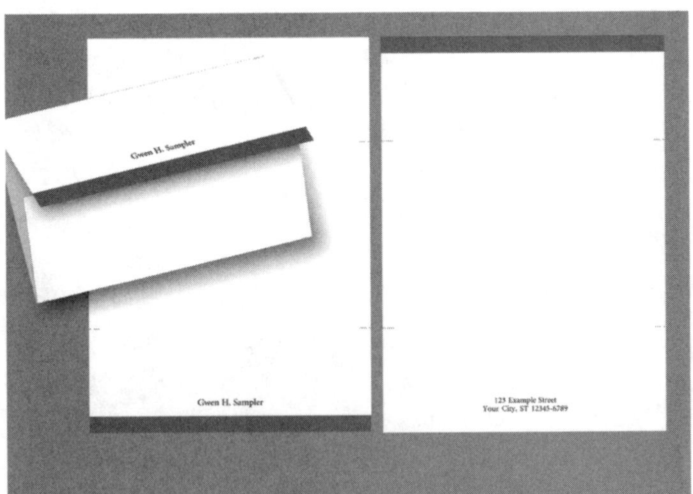


SIZE 6W x 8.5H
PAGES 2
FOLD letter-fold
STOCK 24# bond
BINDING —

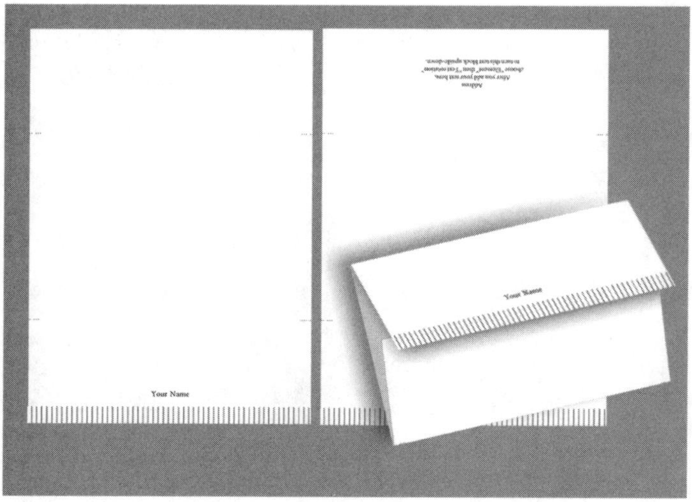


## 175
## Personal Note 2

Used to create personal-sized notepaper to fit an A-6 envelope.

| | |
|---|---|
| SIZE | 6W x 8.5H |
| PAGES | 2 |
| FOLD | letter-fold |
| STOCK | 24# bond |
| BINDING | — |

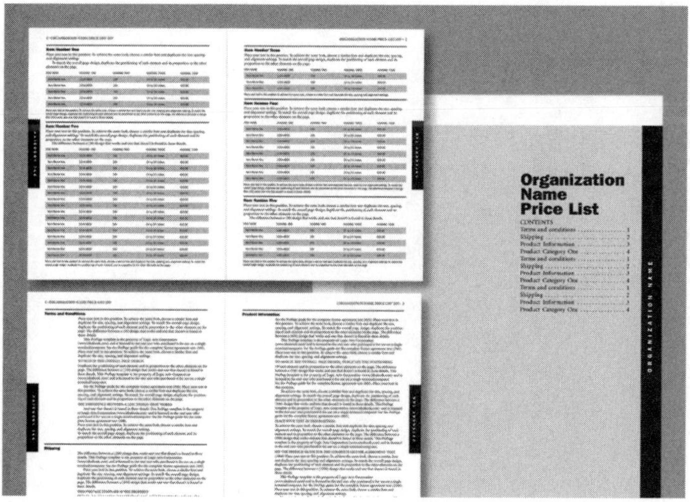


## 176
## Price List

Used to create a detailed listing of purchasing and pricing information. Page 1: cover; pages 2–3: text; pages 3–5: price listings; page 6: back cover.

| | |
|---|---|
| SIZE | 8.5W x 11H |
| PAGES | 6 |
| FOLD | — |
| STOCK | 60# uncoated text |
| BINDING | — |

## 177
## Product Sheet

Used to create a product sheet.

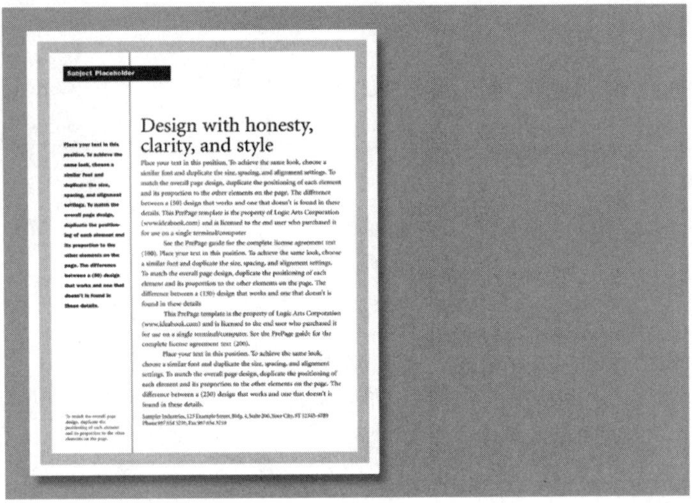


| | |
|---|---|
| SIZE | 8.5W x 11H |
| PAGES | 1 |
| FOLD | — |
| STOCK | 60# uncoated text |
| BINDING | — |

Chapter 10
# Direct Mail & Postcards

## 178
## Billboard Envelopes

Used to create artwork for a business envelope layouts (five versions).

(NOTE: The author and publisher have used their best efforts to proof and confirm the content of the files, but you should proof and confirm information such as dates, measurements, form properties, and any other content for yourself. The author and publisher make no warranties of any kind, express or implied, with regard to that content or its accuracy.)

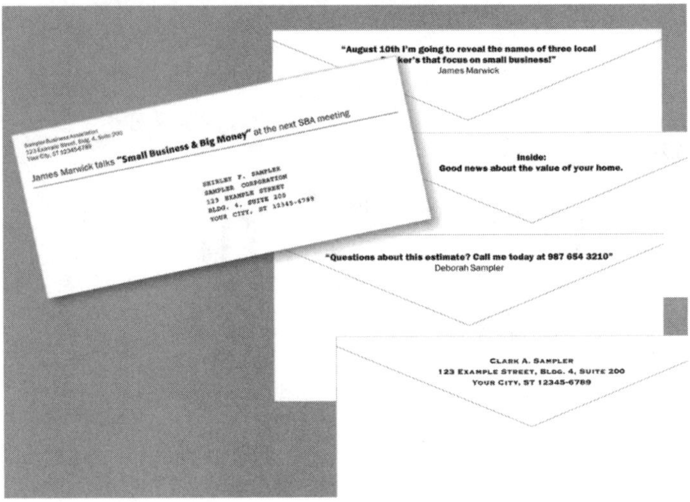


| | |
|---|---|
| SIZE | 9.5W x 4.125H |
| PAGES | 5 |
| FOLD | — |
| STOCK | — |
| BINDING | — |

## 179
## Business Reply Card

Used to create a direct response business reply card. Allows permit holders to receive mail back from customers by paying the US Postal Service postage and a handling charge for each piece returned. Apply for a permit number from local post office, apply permit number, position Facing Identification Mark (FIM) within shaded area at top of layout and Zip+4 barcode for bottom shaded area. Have mailing piece artwork approved by postal service to confirm compliance with postal regulations.

| | |
|---|---|
| SIZE | 6W x 4.25H |
| PAGES | 1 |
| FOLD | — |
| STOCK | 12pt card |
| BINDING | — |

| | |
|---|---|
| SIZE | 8.875W x 3.875H |
| PAGES | 1 |
| FOLD | — |
| STOCK | 65# uncoated cover |
| BINDING | — |

## 180
## Business Reply Mail

Used to create a direct response business reply envelope. Allows permit holders to receive mail back from customers by paying the US Postal Service postage and a handling charge for each piece returned. Apply for a permit number from local post office, apply permit number, position Facing Identification Mark (FIM) within shaded area at top of layout and Zip+4 barcode for bottom shaded area. Have mailing piece artwork approved by postal service to confirm compliance with postal regulations.

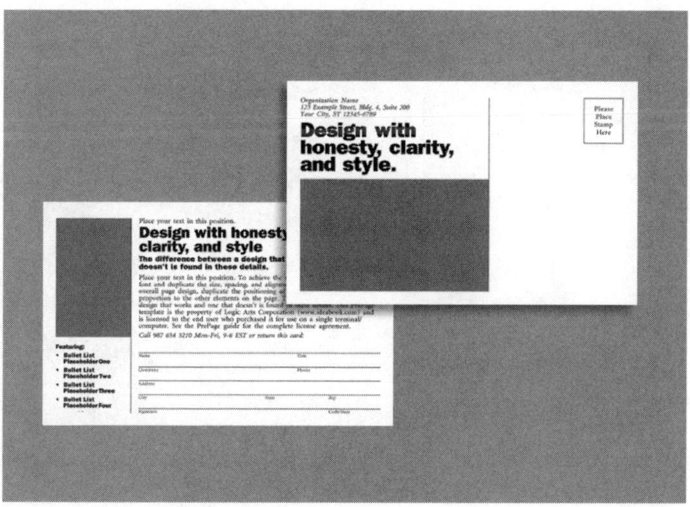


| | |
|---|---|
| SIZE | 5.5W x 3.5H |
| PAGES | 2 |
| FOLD | — |
| STOCK | 12pt card |
| BINDING | — |

## 181
## Card Deck Order Postcard 1

Used to create a direct mail card deck postcard. Have mailing piece artwork approved by postal service to confirm compliance with postal regulations. Page 1: front with space for address; page 2: back with order form.

## 182
## Card Deck Product Postcard 2

Used to create a direct mail card deck postcard. Have mailing piece artwork approved by postal service to confirm compliance with postal regulations. Page 1: front with space for address; page 2: back.

| | |
|---|---|
| SIZE | 6W x 4H |
| PAGES | 2 |
| FOLD | — |
| STOCK | 12pt card |
| BINDING | — |

## 183
## Coupon Mailer

Used to create a mailer with a built-in coupon. Page 1, panel 1 (top): coupon; panel 2: back cover; panel 3: cover; page 2, panels 1-2: text spread one. Substitute photograph or illustration for placeholder.

| | |
|---|---|
| SIZE | 6W x 11H (flat); 6W x 4H (finished) |
| PAGES | 2 |
| FOLD | letter-fold |
| STOCK | 65# uncoated cover |
| BINDING | — |

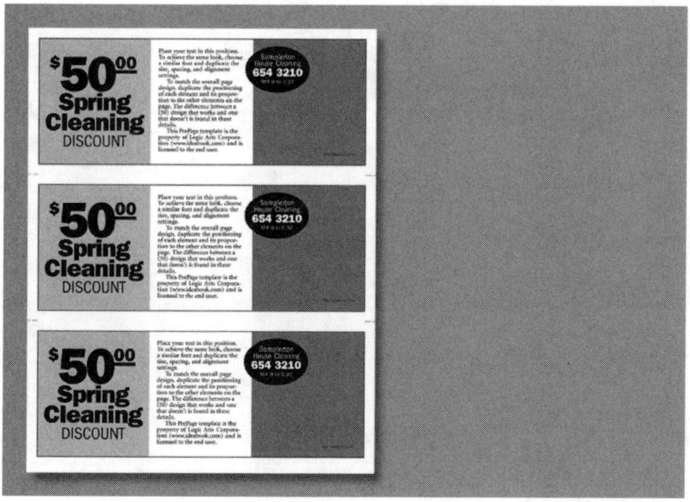


## 184
## Coupon Page

Used to create a discount coupon. Three per page.

SIZE 8.5W x 11H (flat); 8.5W x 3.625H (trimmed)
PAGES 1
FOLD —
STOCK 60# uncoated text
BINDING —

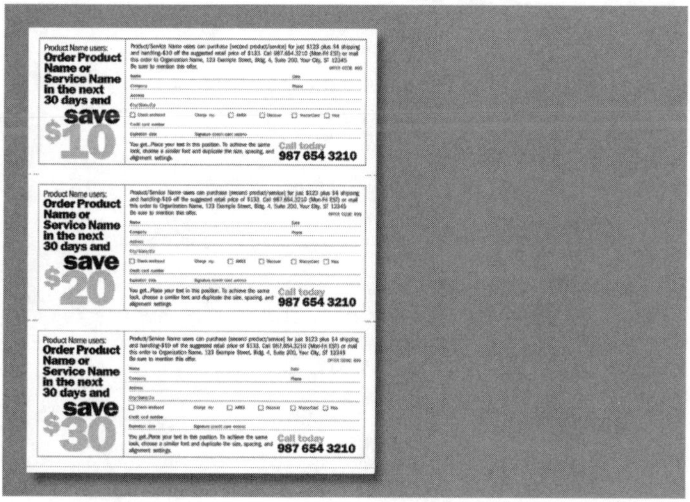


## 185
## Order Coupon

Used to create a discount coupon with an attached order form. Three per page.

SIZE 8.5W x 11H (flat); 8.5W x 3.625H (trimmed)
PAGES 1
FOLD —
STOCK 60# uncoated text
BINDING —

## 186
## Coupon Letter 1

Used to create a direct mail letter with a response coupon.

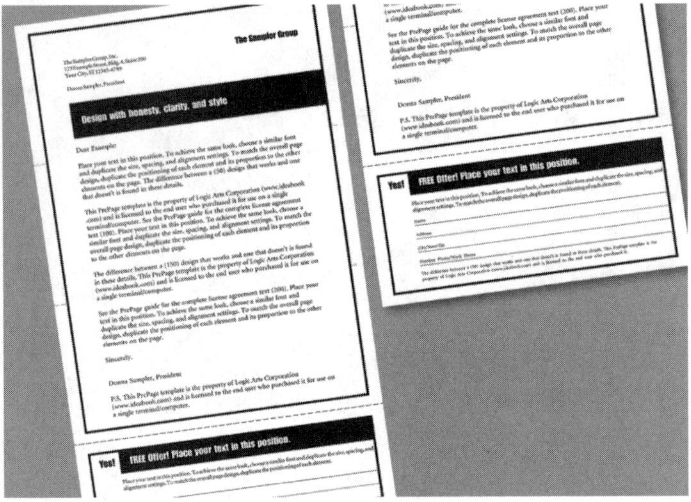

| | |
|---|---|
| SIZE | 8.5W x 14H |
| PAGES | 1 |
| FOLD | double-parallel-fold |
| STOCK | 24# bond |
| BINDING | — |

## 187
## Coupon Letter 2

Used to create a direct mail letter with a response coupon. Page 1: front with response form; page 2: back.

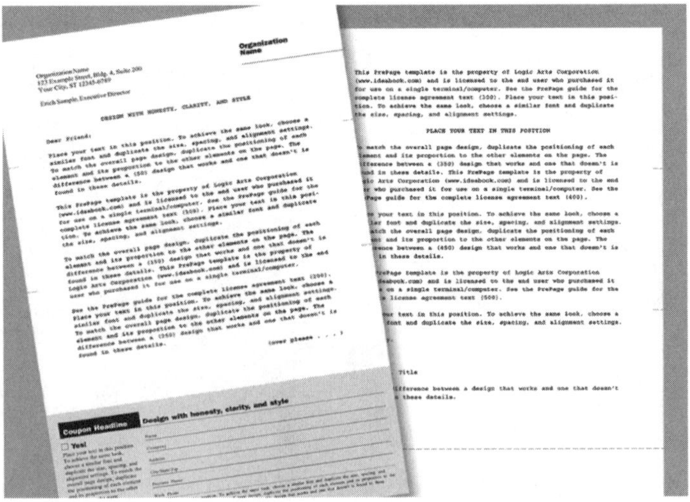

| | |
|---|---|
| SIZE | 8.5W x 14H |
| PAGES | 2 |
| FOLD | double-parallel-fold |
| STOCK | 24# bond |
| BINDING | — |

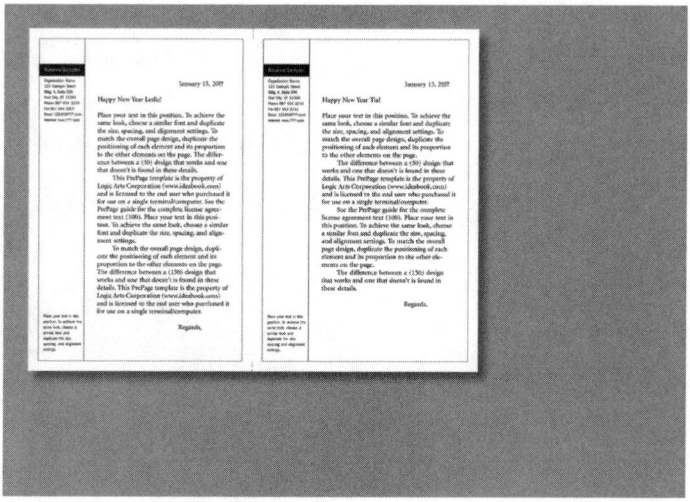

## 188
## Half Size Letter

Used to create a mini direct mail letter. Two per page.

| | |
|---|---|
| SIZE | 8.5W x 11H (flat); 5.5W x 8.5H (trimmed) |
| PAGES | 1 |
| FOLD | — |
| STOCK | 24# bond |
| BINDING | — |

## 189
## Headline Envelope

Used to create a business envelope with a headline.

| | |
|---|---|
| SIZE | 9.5W x 4.125H |
| PAGES | 1 |
| FOLD | — |
| STOCK | — |
| BINDING | — |

## 190
## Order Form–Full Page

Used to create a full-page order form for a catalog or direct-mail package.

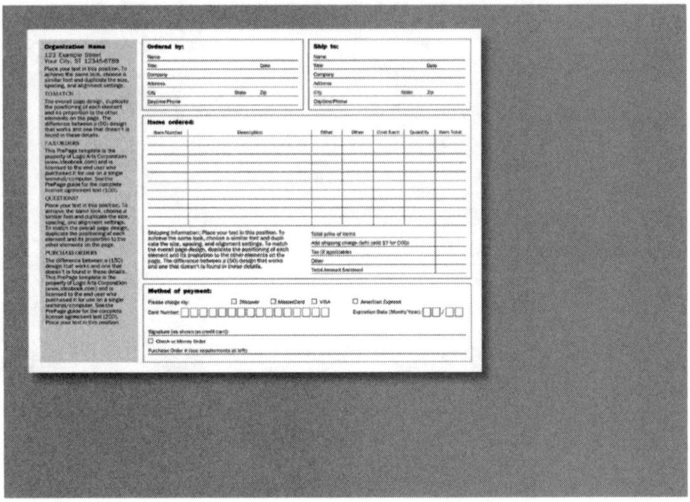

| | |
|---|---|
| SIZE | 11W x 8.5H |
| PAGES | 1 |
| FOLD | — |
| STOCK | 60# uncoated text |
| BINDING | — |

## 191
## Order Form–Half Page

Used to create a full-page order form for a catalog or direct-mail package.

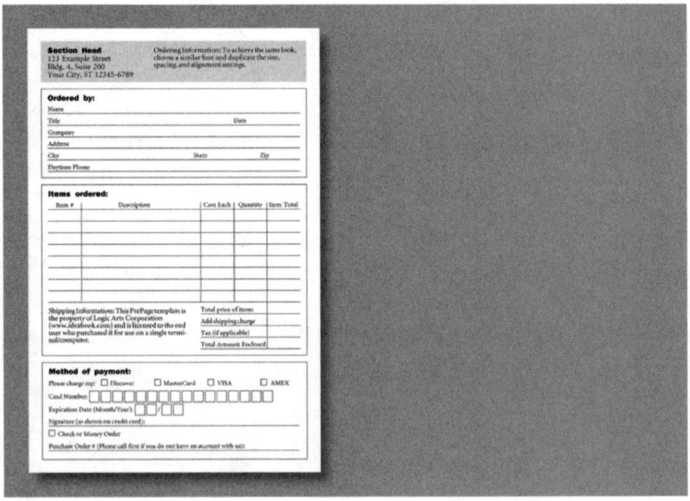

| | |
|---|---|
| SIZE | 5.5W x 8.5H |
| PAGES | 1 |
| FOLD | — |
| STOCK | 60# uncoated text |
| BINDING | — |

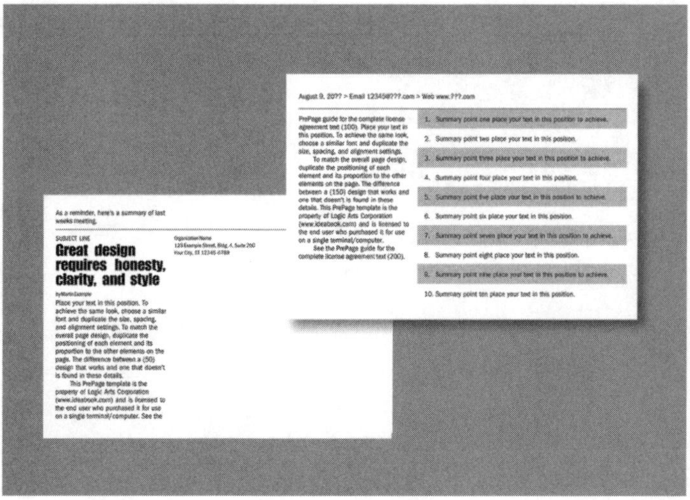


## 192
## Postcard 1

Used to create artwork for a postcard. Have mailing piece artwork approved by postal service to confirm compliance with postal regulations. Page 1: front with space for headline, text, and mailing address; page 2: back with space for a numbered list of ten items.

| | |
|---|---|
| SIZE | 6W x 4H |
| PAGES | 2 |
| FOLD | — |
| STOCK | 12pt card |
| BINDING | — |

## 193
## Postcard 2

Used to create artwork for an oversized postcard. Have mailing piece artwork approved by postal service to confirm compliance with postal regulations. Page 1: front with space for headline and illustration; page 2: back with space for illustration, text, and mailing address.

| | |
|---|---|
| SIZE | 10.5W x 5.625H |
| PAGES | 2 |
| FOLD | — |
| STOCK | 12pt card |
| BINDING | — |

## 194
## Postcard 3

Used to create artwork for a postcard. Have mailing piece artwork approved by postal service to confirm compliance with postal regulations. Page 1: front with space for illustration and mailing address; page 2: back with space for a handwritten message.

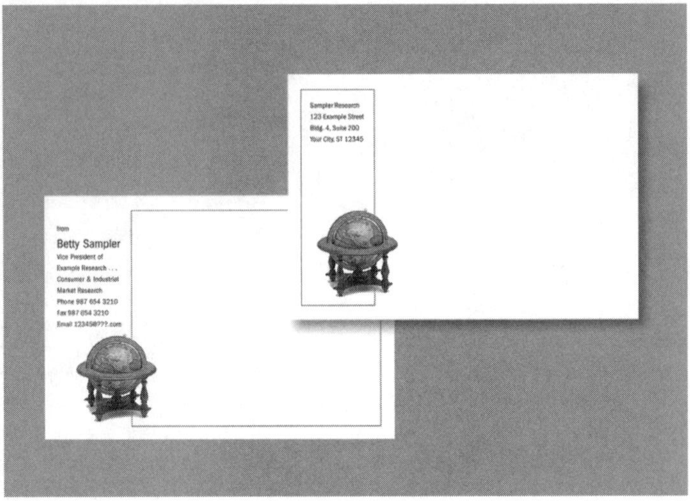


| SIZE | 6W x 4H |
|---|---|
| PAGES | 2 |
| FOLD | — |
| STOCK | 12pt card |
| BINDING | — |

## 195
## Postcard 4

Used to create artwork for an oversized postcard. Have mailing piece artwork approved by postal service to confirm compliance with postal regulations. Page 1: front with space for headline and mailing address; page 2: with space for text and illustration.

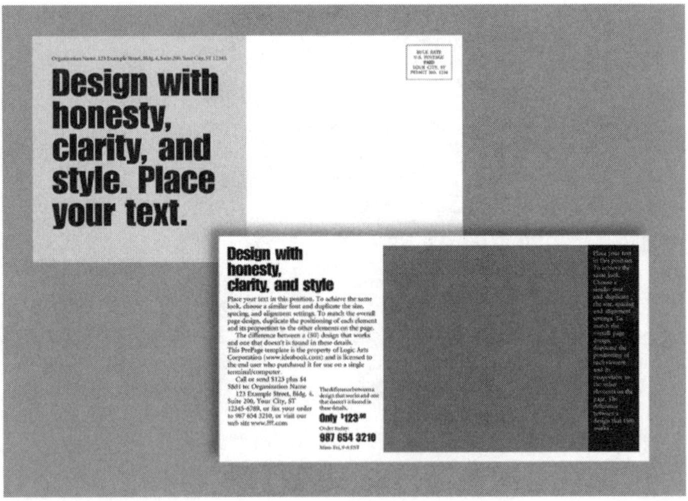


| SIZE | 10.5W x 5.625H |
|---|---|
| PAGES | 2 |
| FOLD | — |
| STOCK | 12pt card |
| BINDING | — |

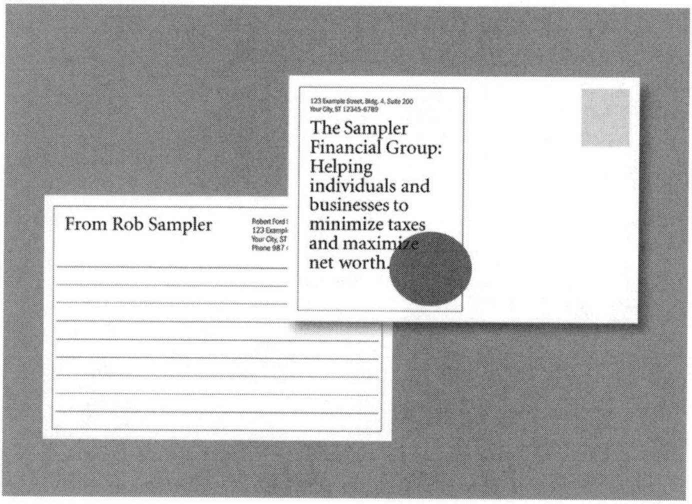


## 196
## Postcard 5

Used to create artwork for a postcard. Have mailing piece artwork approved by postal service to confirm compliance with postal regulations. Page 1: front with space for headling and mailing address; page 2: back with space for a handwritten message.

| | |
|---|---|
| SIZE | 6W x 4H |
| PAGES | 2 |
| FOLD | — |
| STOCK | 12pt card |
| BINDING | — |

## 197
## Postcard 6

Used to create artwork for a postcard. Have mailing piece artwork approved by postal service to confirm compliance with postal regulations. Page 1: front with space for headline and mailing address; page 2: back with space for a handwritten message.

| | |
|---|---|
| SIZE | 6W x 4H |
| PAGES | 2 |
| FOLD | — |
| STOCK | 12pt card r |
| BINDING | — |

## 198
## Postcard 7

Used to create artwork for a postcard. Have mailing piece artwork approved by postal service to confirm compliance with postal regulations. Page 1: front with space for headline and mailing address; page 2: back with space for headline and text.

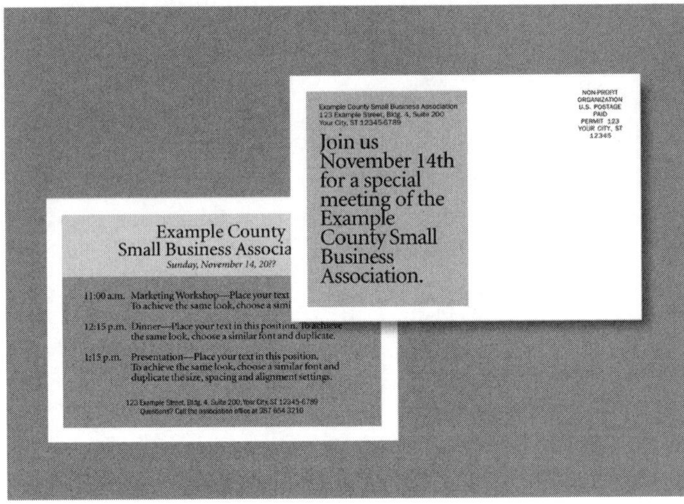


| | |
|---|---|
| SIZE | 6W x 4H |
| PAGES | 2 |
| FOLD | — |
| STOCK | 12pt card |
| BINDING | — |

## 199
## Postcard 8

Used to create artwork for a postcard. Have mailing piece artwork approved by postal service to confirm compliance with postal regulations. Page 1: front with space for text and mailing address; page 2: back with space for a handwritten message.

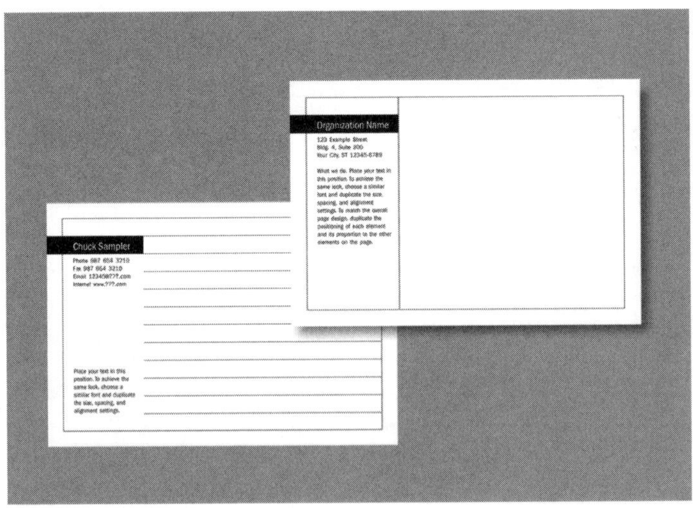


| | |
|---|---|
| SIZE | 6W x 4H |
| PAGES | 2 |
| FOLD | — |
| STOCK | 12pt card |
| BINDING | — |

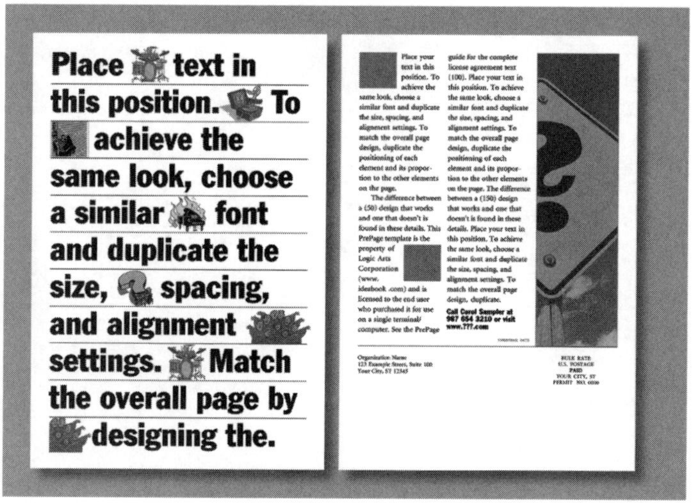


## 200
## Postcard 9

6W x 9H

Used to create artwork for an oversized postcard. Have mailing piece artwork approved by postal service to confirm compliance with postal regulations. Page 1: front with space for heading and illustrations; page 2: back with space for text, illustrations, and mailing address.

| | |
|---|---|
| SIZE | 6W x 9H |
| PAGES | 2 |
| FOLD | — |
| STOCK | 12pt card |
| BINDING | — |

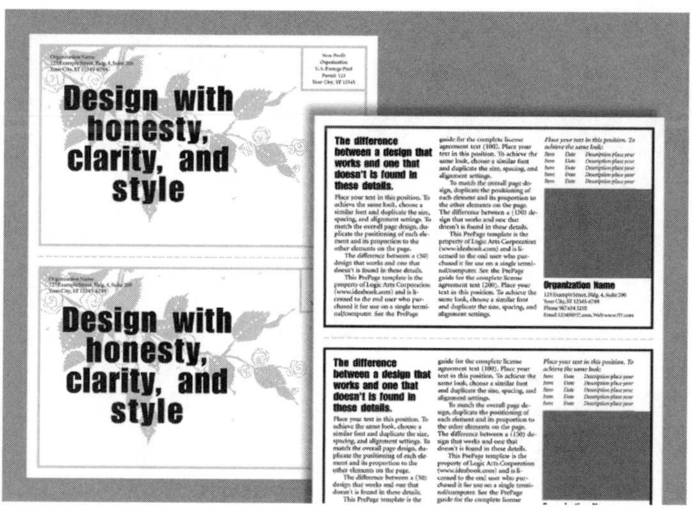


## 201
## Postcard 10

Used to create artwork for an oversized postcard. Have mailing piece artwork approved by postal service to confirm compliance with postal regulations. Two per page, page 1: front with space for text and mailing address; page 2: back with space for a headline, text, and illustration.

| | |
|---|---|
| SIZE | 8.5W x 5.5H |
| PAGES | 2 |
| FOLD | — |
| STOCK | 12pt card |
| BINDING | — |

## 202
## Postcard 11

Used to create artwork for a postcard. Have mailing piece artwork approved by postal service to confirm compliance with postal regulations. Page 1: front with space for multiple text points; page 2: back with space for headline, text, and mailing address.

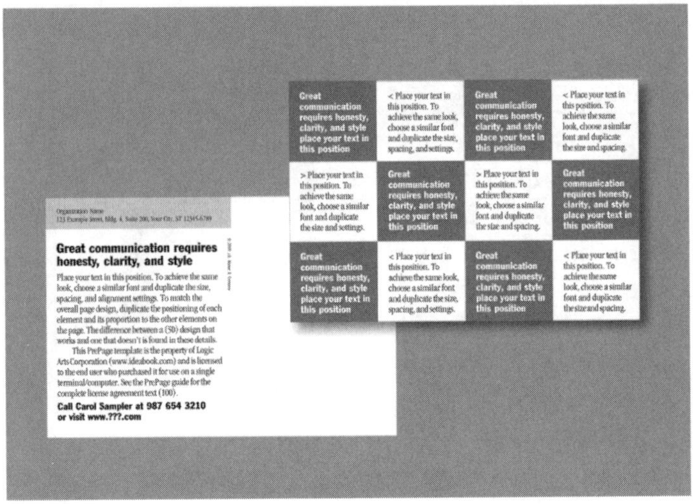


| | |
|---|---|
| SIZE | 5.875W x 4.125H |
| PAGES | 2 |
| FOLD | — |
| STOCK | 12pt card |
| BINDING | — |

## 203
## Questionnaire

Used to create a letter and a customer survey/questionnaire. Page 1: letter with space to attach a one dollar bill as incentive to respond; page 2: questionnaire.

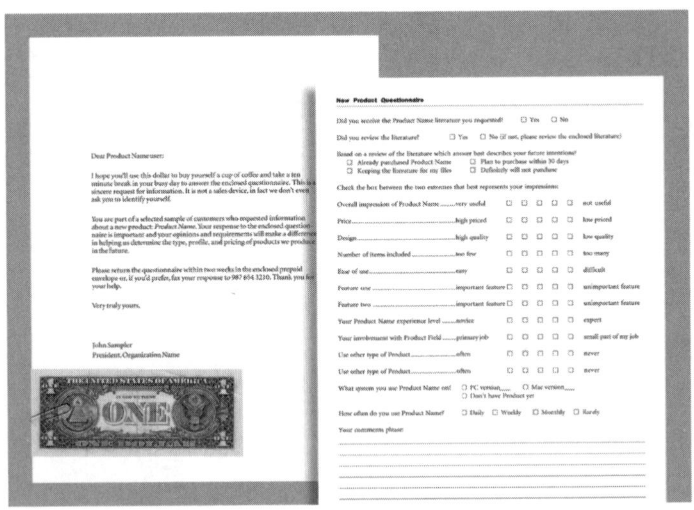

| | |
|---|---|
| SIZE | 8.5W x 11H |
| PAGES | 2 |
| FOLD | letter-fold |
| STOCK | 24# bond |
| BINDING | — |

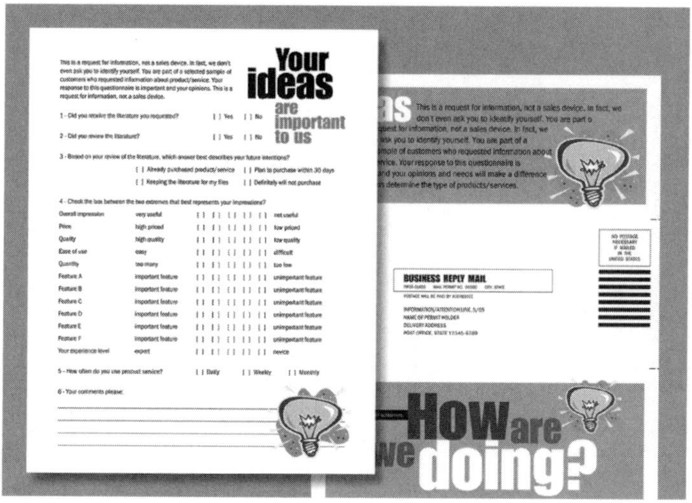


| | |
|---|---|
| SIZE | 8.5W x 11H (flat); 8.5W x 3.6875H (finished) |
| PAGES | 2 |
| FOLD | letter-fold |
| STOCK | 60# uncoated text |
| BINDING | — |

**204**
## Survey Mailer

Used to create a mailer that can be returned postage-paid by the respondent. Allows permit holders to receive mail back from customers by paying the US Postal Service postage and a handling charge for each piece returned. Apply for a permit number from local post office, apply permit number, position Facing Identification Mark (FIM) within shaded area at top of layout and Zip+4 barcode for bottom shaded area. Have mailing piece artwork approved by postal service to confirm compliance with postal regulations. Page 1: cover, page 2: questionnaire.

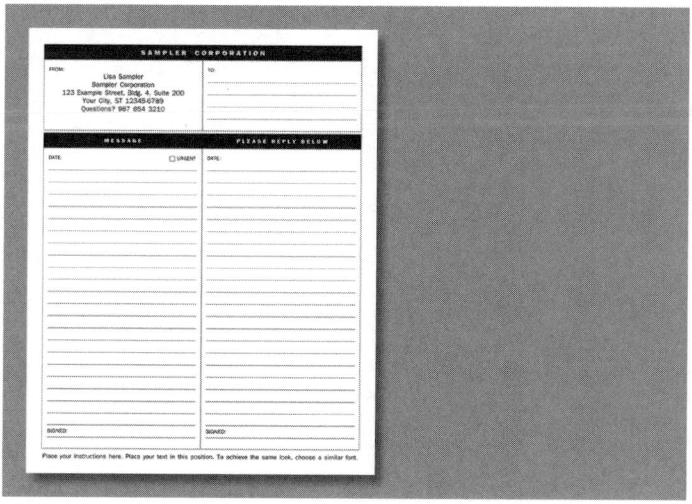


| | |
|---|---|
| SIZE | 8.5W x 11H |
| PAGES | 1 |
| FOLD | letter-fold |
| STOCK | 24# bond |
| BINDING | — |

**205**
## Two-Way-Message

Used to create a message that prompts a reply.

# Chapter 11
# Flyers

## 206
## Coloring Sheet

Used to create a kid's coloring sheet.

(NOTE: The author and publisher have used their best efforts to proof and confirm the content of the files, but you should proof and confirm information such as dates, measurements, form properties, and any other content for yourself. The author and publisher make no warranties of any kind, express or implied, with regard to that content or its accuracy.)

SIZE 11W x 8.5H
PAGES 1
FOLD —
STOCK 24# bond
BINDING —

## 207
## Conference Flyer

Used to create an all-type announcement flyer.

SIZE 8.5W x 11H
PAGES 1
FOLD —
STOCK 24# bond
BINDING —

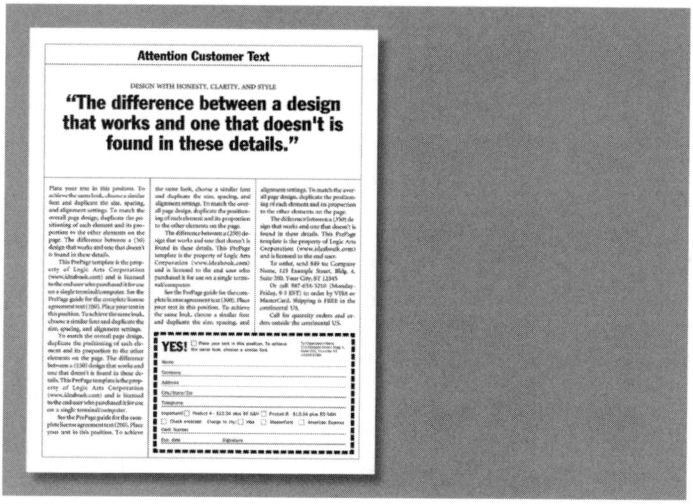


## 208
## Coupon Flyer, Large

Used to create a flyer with a response coupon.

| | |
|---|---|
| SIZE | 8.5W x 11H |
| PAGES | 1 |
| FOLD | — |
| STOCK | 24# bond |
| BINDING | — |

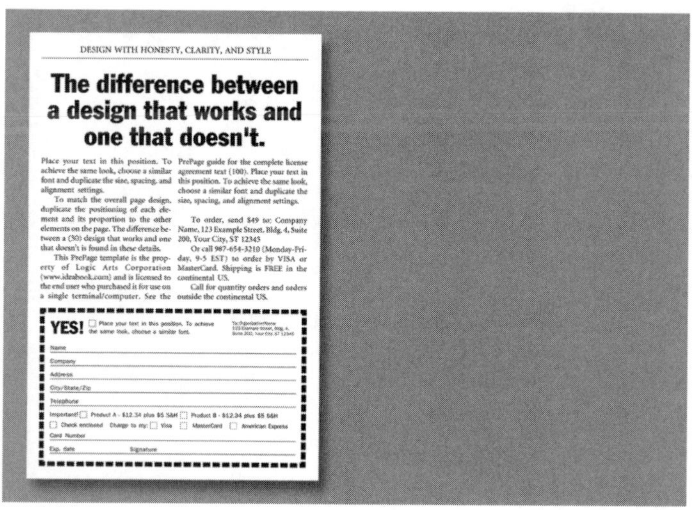


## 209
## Coupon Flyer, Small

Used to create a flyer with a response coupon.

| | |
|---|---|
| SIZE | 5.5W x 8.5H |
| PAGES | 1 |
| FOLD | — |
| STOCK | 24# bond |
| BINDING | — |

## 210
## Doorknob Hanger

Used to create a die-cut doorknob hanger (three per page) or an insert for a doorknob hanger bag (two per page). Page 1: prints on the precut sheets available through many commercial printers; page 2: trims to fit the clear door knob bags available from bag suppliers.

| | |
|---|---|
| SIZE | 8.5W x 11H (flat); Hanger: 3.5W x 8.5H (trimmed); Insert: 5.5W x 8.5H (trimmed) |
| PAGES | 2 |
| FOLD | — |
| STOCK | 100# uncoated cover |
| BINDING | — |

## 211
## Envelope Flyer

Used to print a return envelope on the reverse of any 8.5W x 11H sheet. Prompts the recipient to fold the sheet and return it by mail.

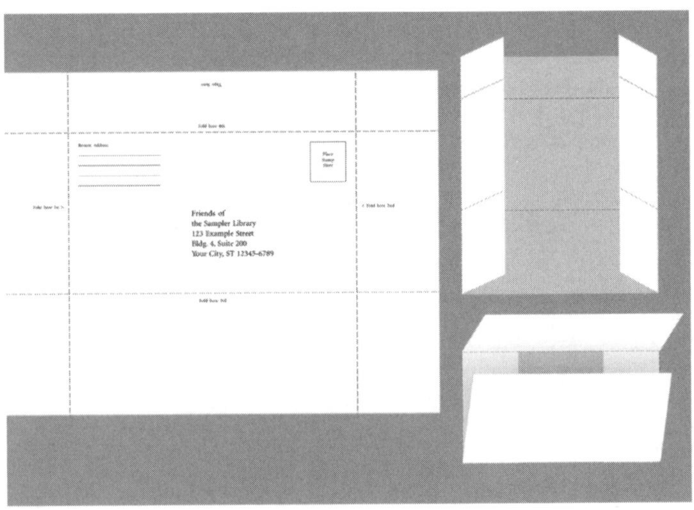


| | |
|---|---|
| SIZE | 8.5W x 11H (flat); 7W x 4H (finished) |
| PAGES | 1 |
| FOLD | custom-fold |
| STOCK | 24# bond |
| BINDING | — |

## 212
## Mini Folder Flyer

Used to create a flyer to fit a mini pocket folder (file 230).

SIZE 3.75W x 8.75H
PAGES 1
FOLD —
STOCK 100# uncoated cover
BINDING —

## 213
## In-Store Flyer

Used to promote in-store sale items.

SIZE 8.5W x 11H
PAGES 1
FOLD —
STOCK 24# bond
BINDING —

## 214
## Compact Flyer

Used to present all the basics on one side of one sheet.

| | |
|---|---|
| SIZE | 8.5W x 11H |
| PAGES | 1 |
| FOLD | — |
| STOCK | 24# bond |
| BINDING | — |

## 215
## Map Flyer, Horizontal

Used to create a map using nothing more than lines and boxes.

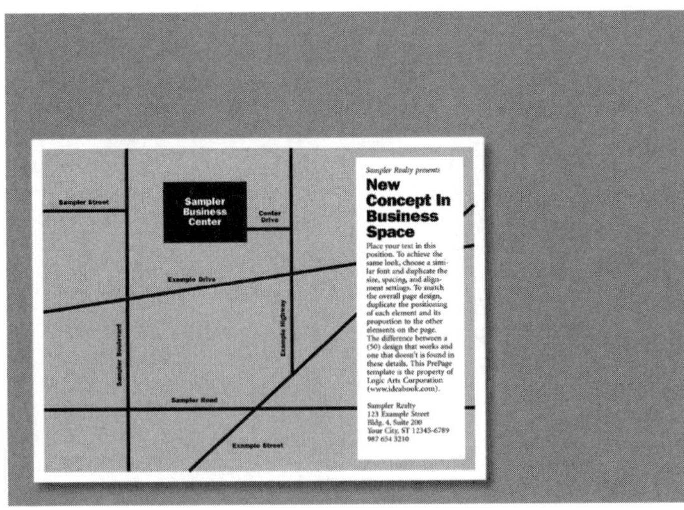


| | |
|---|---|
| SIZE | 11W x 8.5H |
| PAGES | 1 |
| FOLD | — |
| STOCK | 24# bond |
| BINDING | — |

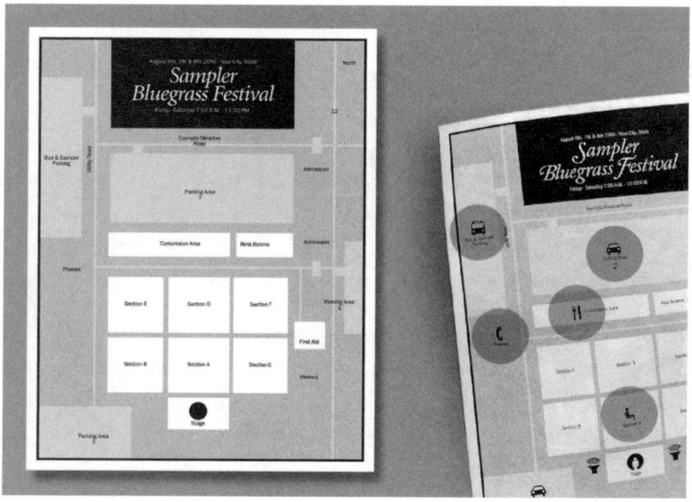


## 216
## Map Flyer, Vertical

Used to create a map using nothing more than lines and boxes.

| | |
|---|---|
| SIZE | 8.5W x 11H |
| PAGES | 1 |
| FOLD | — |
| STOCK | 24# bond |
| BINDING | — |

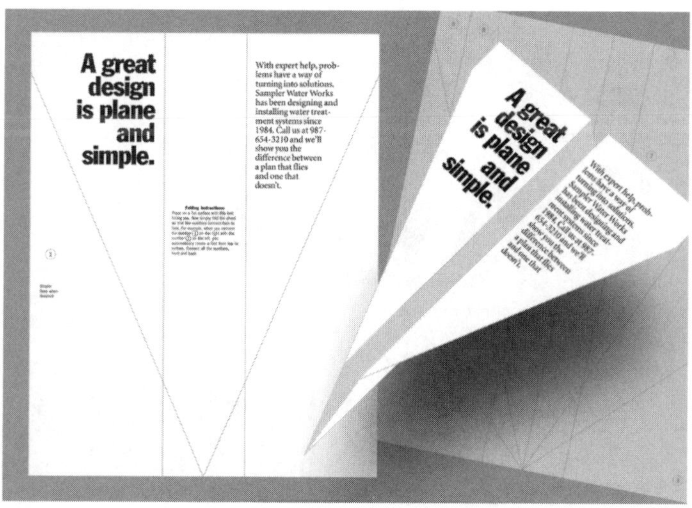


## 217
## Paper Plane Flyer

Used to create a flyer that flies. Page 1: Space for a headline, text, and instructions for using the numbers and fold marks to fold the flyer; page 2: folding lines and numbers.

| | |
|---|---|
| SIZE | 8.5W x 11H |
| PAGES | 2 |
| FOLD | — |
| STOCK | 24# bond |
| BINDING | — |

## 218
## Product Coupon Flyer

Used to create a flyer with a response coupon.

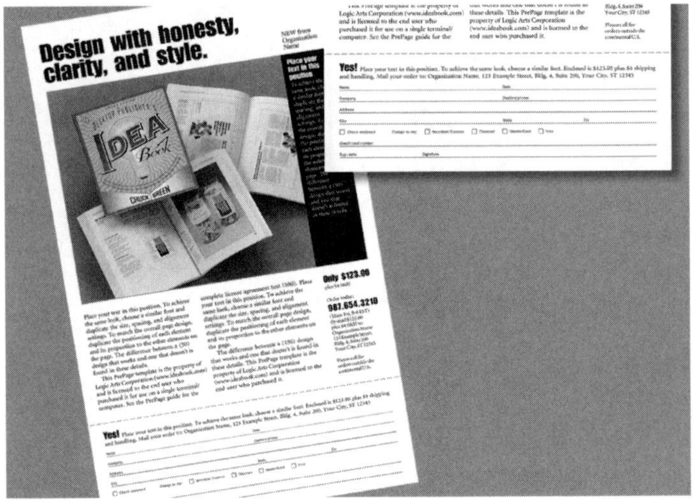


| | |
|---|---|
| SIZE | 8.5W x 14H |
| PAGES | 1 |
| FOLD | — |
| STOCK | 60# uncoated text |
| BINDING | — |

## 219
## Product Flyer

Used to create a flyer.

| | |
|---|---|
| SIZE | 8.5W x 11H |
| PAGES | 1 |
| FOLD | — |
| STOCK | 60# uncoated text |
| BINDING | — |

## 220
## Quick-Change Menu

Used to create menus that fit standard-sized acrylic frames. Page 1: large menu; page 2: small menu.

| | |
|---|---|
| SIZE | 8.5W x 11H |
| PAGES | 2 |
| FOLD | — |
| STOCK | 60# uncoated text |
| BINDING | — |

## 221
## Real Estate Flyer

Used to create a flyer with a detailed list of property attributes. Page 1: Front with space for illustration, address, and text; page 2: space for illustrations and detailed item listings.

| | |
|---|---|
| SIZE | 8.5W x 11H |
| PAGES | 2 |
| FOLD | — |
| STOCK | 60# uncoated text |
| BINDING | — |

## 222
## Telegram

Used to create a telegram-like flyer—once considered the ultimate in urgency.

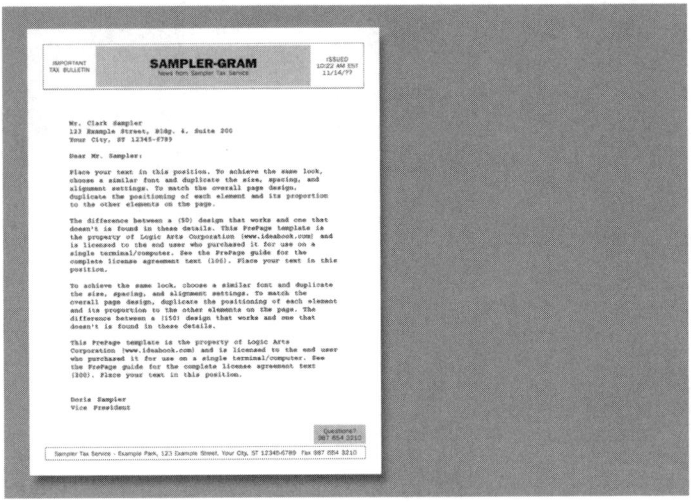

IMPORTANT TAX BULLETIN

SAMPLER-GRAM

News from Sampler Tax Service

ISSUED 10:22 AM EST 11/14/??

Mr. Clark Sampler
123 Example Street, Bldg. 4, Suite 200
Your City, ST 12345-6789

Dear Mr. Sampler:

Place your text in this position. To achieve the same look, choose a similar font and duplicate the size, spacing, and alignment settings. To match the overall page design, duplicate the positioning of each element and its proportion to the other elements on the page.

The difference between a (50) design that works and one that doesn't is found in these details. This PrePage template is the property of Logic Arts Corporation (www.ideabook.com) and is licensed to the end user who purchased it for use on a single terminal/computer. See the PrePage guide for the complete license agreement text (100). Place your text in this position.

To achieve the same look, choose a similar font and duplicate the size, spacing, and alignment settings. To match the overall page design, duplicate the positioning of each element and its proportion to the other elements on the page. The difference between a (150) design that works and one that doesn't is found in these details.

This PrePage template is the property of Logic Arts Corporation (www.ideabook.com) and is licensed to the end user who purchased it for use on a single terminal/computer. See the PrePage guide for the complete license agreement text (200). Place your text in this position.

Doris Sampler
Vice President

Questions? 987 654 3210

Sampler Tax Service - Example Park, 123 Example Street, Your City, ST 12345-6789 Fax 987 654 3210

| | |
|---|---|
| SIZE | 8.5W x 11H |
| PAGES | 1 |
| FOLD | — |
| STOCK | 24# bond |
| BINDING | — |

Chapter 12
# Folders & Binders

## 223
## Reader's Index

Used to create a reader's index—a clever alternative to using a yellow highlighter to mark the significant passages in a book, brochure, or magazine. Use the form to list the subject and page number of passages then fold on the dotted line and wrap it around the back cover.

(NOTE: The author and publisher have used their best efforts to proof and confirm the content of the files, but you should proof and confirm information such as dates, measurements, form properties, and any other content for yourself. The author and publisher make no warranties of any kind, express or implied, with regard to that content or its accuracy.)

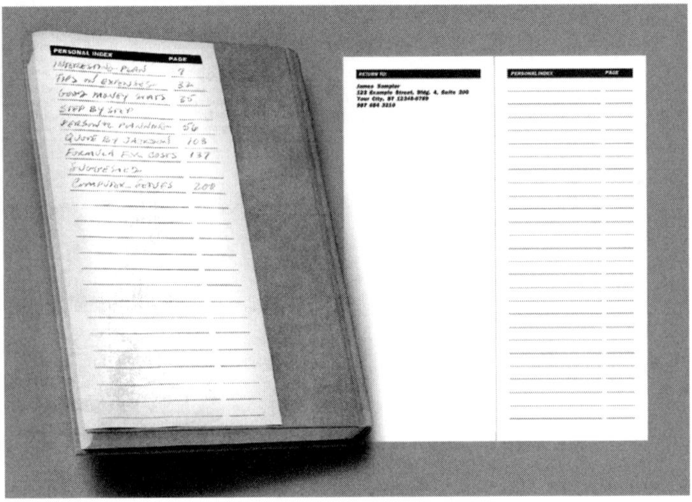


| | |
|---|---|
| SIZE | 8.5W x 11H (flat); 4.25W x 11H (finished) |
| PAGES | 1 |
| FOLD | half-fold |
| STOCK | 24# bond |
| BINDING | — |

## 224
## Brochure/Folder

Used to create a conventional pocket folder with text pages. Pocket holds loose 8.5W x 11H pages such as product sheets. Page 1: cover; pages 2–6: text; page 7: pocket; page 8: back cover.

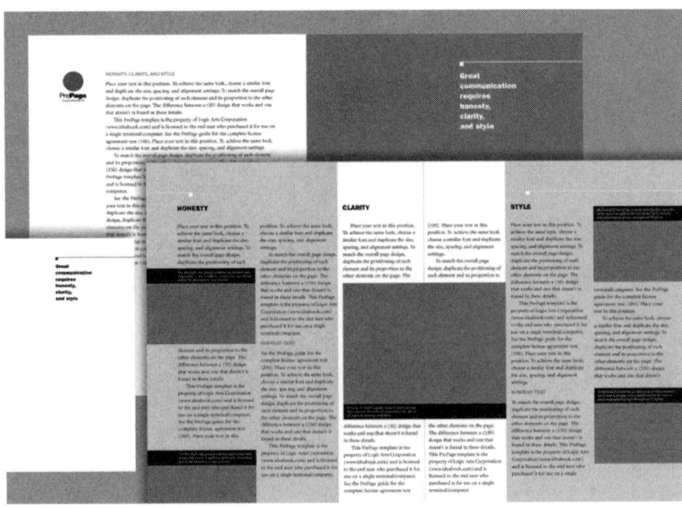


| | |
|---|---|
| SIZE | 18W x 16H (flat); 9W x 12H (finished) |
| PAGES | 8 |
| FOLD | half-fold |
| STOCK | 100# uncoated cover, 60# uncoated text |
| BINDING | saddle-stitch |

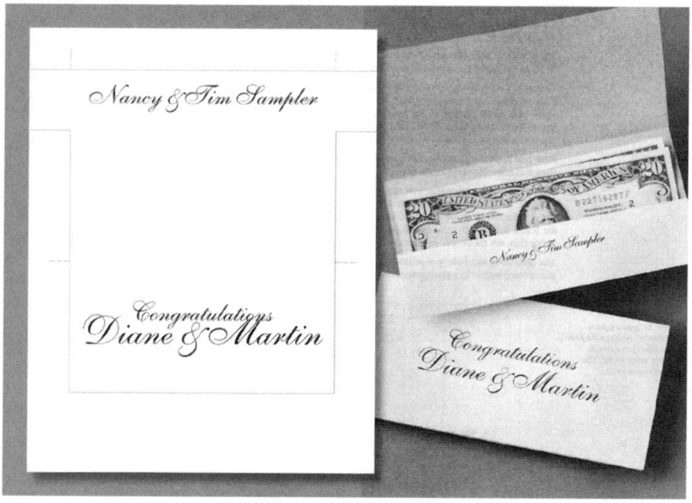


## 225
## Gift Folder

Used to create a folder for presenting currency, tickets to an event, or a gift certificate.

SIZE 6.5W x 3.25H
PAGES 1
FOLD letter-fold
STOCK 60# uncoated text
BINDING —

## 226
## Instant Binder

Used to create a two-part cover insert for a clear cover presentation ring binder. Print both sheets and trim to size. Butt sheets edge to edge and mount them on a third, heavier sheet (a rigid sheet will be easier to position once you insert it in the pocket on the ring binder). Trim the final insert .25 inch smaller than the overall size of the pocket. Page 1: top half; page 2: bottom half.

SIZE 9.5W x 11H
PAGES 2
FOLD —
STOCK 65# uncoated cover
BINDING —

## 227
## Pocket Folder 1

Used to create the front, back, and pockets of a standard-sized, die-cut pocket folder. To create your version, choose the word that best describes your profession and compose a cover definition. On the inside flap, repeat the definition.

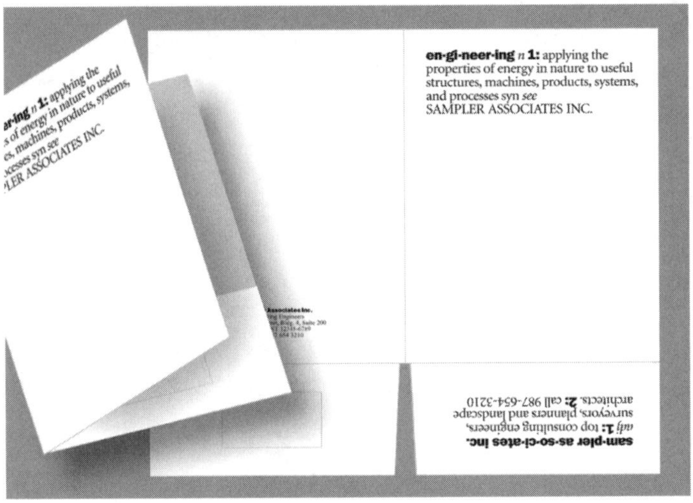


| | |
|---|---|
| SIZE | 18W x 16H (flat); 9W x 12H (finished) |
| PAGES | 1 |
| FOLD | custom-fold |
| STOCK | 100# uncoated cover |
| BINDING | — |

## 228
## Pocket Folder 2

Used to create the front, back, and pockets of a standard-sized, die-cut pocket folder.

| | |
|---|---|
| SIZE | 18W x 16H (flat); 9W x 12H (finished) |
| PAGES | 1 |
| FOLD | custom-fold |
| STOCK | 100# uncoated cover |
| BINDING | — |

## 229
## Pocket Folder 3

Used to create the front, back, and pockets of a standard-sized, die-cut pocket folder.

| | |
|---|---|
| SIZE | 18W x 16H (flat); 9W x 12H (finished) |
| PAGES | 1 |
| FOLD | custom-fold |
| STOCK | 100# uncoated cover |
| BINDING | — |

## 230
## Mini Pocket Folder

Used to create the front, back, and pockets of a mini, die-cut pocket folder. Use with Mini-Folder Flyer (file 212).

| | |
|---|---|
| SIZE | 8w x 12H (flat); 4W x 9H (finished) |
| PAGES | 1 |
| FOLD | custom-fold |
| STOCK | 100# uncoated cover |
| BINDING | — |

Chapter 13

# Labels & Tags

## 231
## 3-in-1 Mailing Label

Used to create an invoice, message, and shipping label on standard-sized sheet. Fold the finished form and insert it in an adhesive-back, clear-face envelope and attach it to the outside of package.

(NOTE: The author and publisher have used their best efforts to proof and confirm the content of the files, but you should proof and confirm information such as dates, measurements, form properties, and any other content for yourself. The author and publisher make no warranties of any kind, express or implied, with regard to that content or its accuracy.)

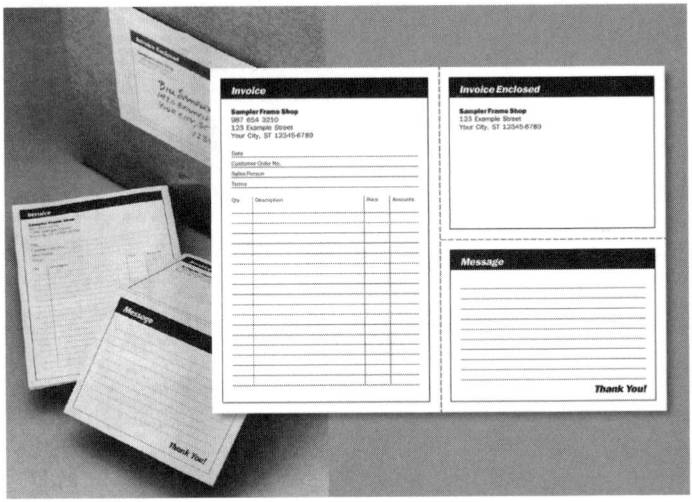


| | |
|---|---|
| SIZE | 8.5w x 11H (flat); 5.5W x 4.25H (finished) |
| PAGES | 1 |
| FOLD | french-fold |
| STOCK | 24# bond |
| BINDING | — |

## 232
## Cassette Labels

Used to print audio cassette tape labels (sized to fit Avery Laser/Ink Jet 5198). For use with cassette album (file 262).

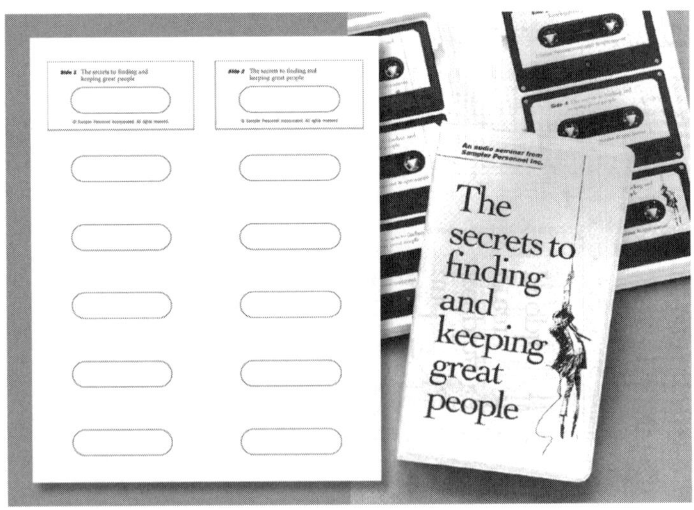


| | |
|---|---|
| SIZE | 3.5W x 1.6875H |
| PAGES | 1 |
| FOLD | — |
| STOCK | Avery Laser/Ink Jet cassette tape labels 5198 |
| BINDING | — |

**233**
**Name Tag**

Used to create a sheet of name tags. Trim them out and insert them in clear badge holders. Use the box at the bottom right to code the badges for speakers, press, exhibitors, board members, and so on.

SIZE 4W x 2.5H
PAGES 1
FOLD —
STOCK 65# uncoated cover
BINDING —

**234**
**Price Tag**

Used to create detailed pricing/information tags. Trim the tags out and insert them into clear tag holders.

SIZE 5.5W x 8.5H
PAGES 1
FOLD —
STOCK 65# uncoated cover
BINDING —

## 235
## Product Registration Card

Used to create a product or service registration and rating card. Page 1: product registration form; page 2: return address.

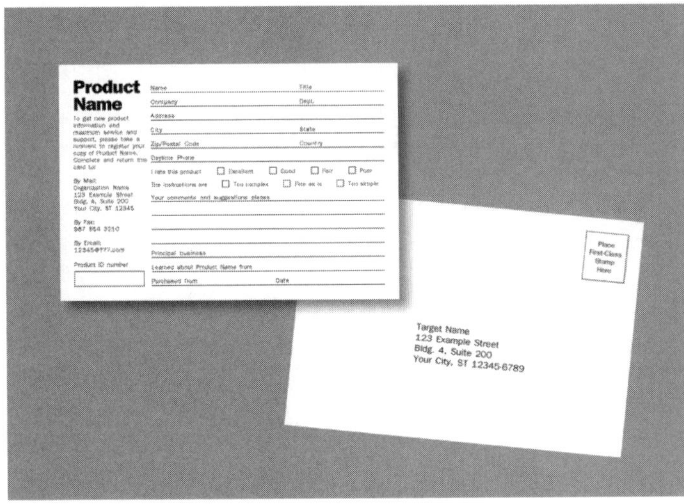


| | |
|---|---|
| SIZE | 6W x 4.25H |
| PAGES | 2 |
| FOLD | — |
| STOCK | 12pt card |
| BINDING | — |

## 236
## Shipping Label 1

Used to create custom labels. Page 1: three-up media label; page 2: four-up rush label; page 3: six-up airmail label.

| | |
|---|---|
| SIZE | 5W x 3.25H; 3.25H x 4.5W; 3W x 3H |
| PAGES | 3 |
| FOLD | — |
| STOCK | 24# bond |
| BINDING | — |

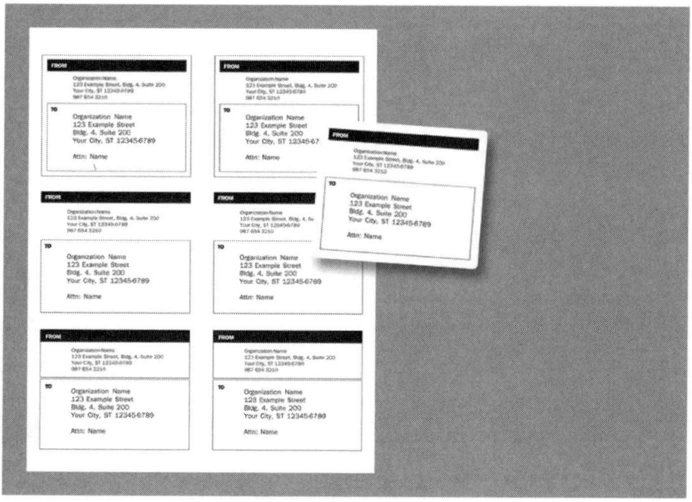


## 237
## Shipping Label 2

Used to print shipping labels (sized to fit Avery Laser/Ink Jet 5164). Three variations.

SIZE 3 1/3W x 4H
PAGES 1
FOLD —
STOCK Avery Laser/Ink Jet Label 5164
BINDING —

## 238
## Shipping Label 3

Used to print plain-paper shipping labels that are taped to packages.

SIZE 8.5W x 1.625H
PAGES 1
FOLD —
STOCK 24# bond
BINDING —

Chapter 14

# Newsletters

## 239
## Banner Newsletter

Used to create a newsletter. Features space for advertisements at the bottom of text pages. Page 1: cover; pages 2–3: text spread variation one; pages 4–5: text spread variation two; page 6: back cover. Mix and match text spreads to create multiples of 4 pages (4,8,12,16).

(NOTE: The author and publisher have used their best efforts to proof and confirm the content of the files, but you should proof and confirm information such as dates, measurements, form properties, and any other content for yourself. The author and publisher make no warranties of any kind, express or implied, with regard to that content or its accuracy.)

| | |
|---|---|
| SIZE | 17W x 11H (flat); 8.5W x 11H (finished) |
| PAGES | 6 |
| FOLD | half-fold |
| STOCK | 60# uncoated text |
| BINDING | saddle-stitch |

## 240
## Bar Postcard Newsletter

Used to create a newsletter in the form of an oversized postcard. Have mailing piece artwork approved by postal service to confirm compliance with postal regulations. Page 1: cover with space for nameplate, headlines, text, and mailing address; page 2: with space for headlines, text, and illustrations.

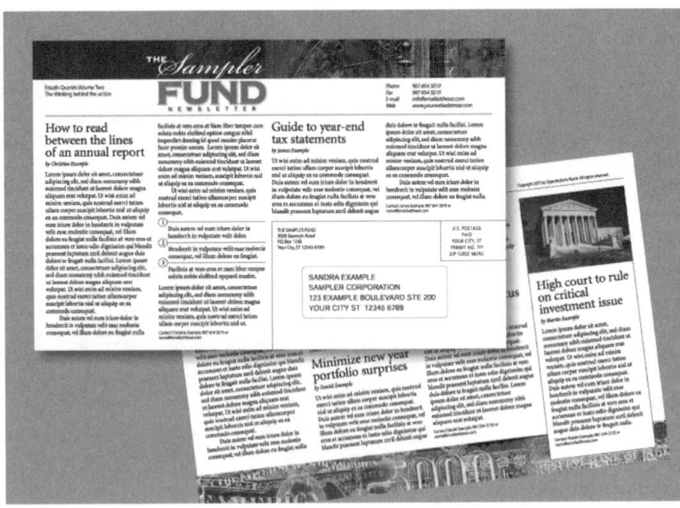


| | |
|---|---|
| SIZE | 9W x 6H |
| PAGES | 2 |
| FOLD | — |
| STOCK | 12pt card |
| BINDING | — |

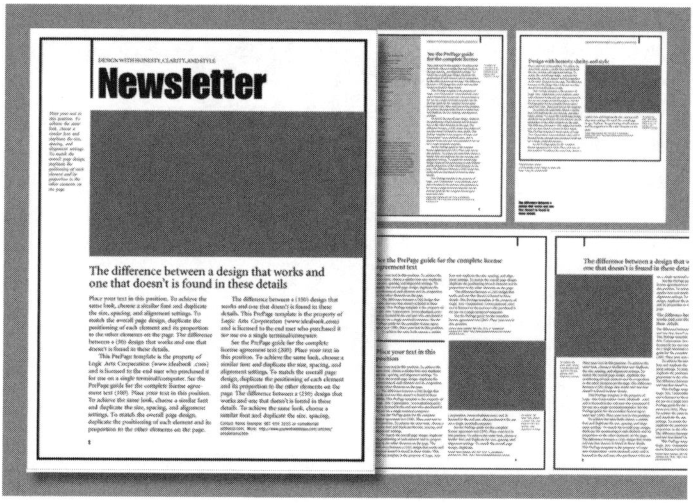


## 241 Basic Newsletter

Used to create a newsletter. Page 1: cover; pages 2–3: text spread variation one; pages 4–5: text spread variation two; page 6: back cover. Mix and match text spreads to create multiples of 4 pages (4,8,12,16). Have mailing piece artwork approved by postal service to confirm compliance with postal regulations.

| | |
|---|---|
| SIZE | 17W x 11H (flat); 8.5W x 11H (finished) |
| PAGES | 6 |
| FOLD | half-fold |
| STOCK | 60# uncoated text |
| BINDING | saddle-stitch |

## 242 Blurb Newsletter

Used to create a newsletter on legal-sized sheets to be mailed in an envelope. Page 1: cover; page 2: back cover.

| | |
|---|---|
| SIZE | 8.5W x 14H |
| PAGES | 2 |
| FOLD | accordion-fold |
| STOCK | 60# uncoated text |
| BINDING | — |

## 243
## Bulletin Newsletter

Used to create a newsletter on legal-sized sheets to be mailed in an envelope. Page 1: cover; pages 2–3: text spread variation one; page 4: text continued with a response coupon at the bottom.

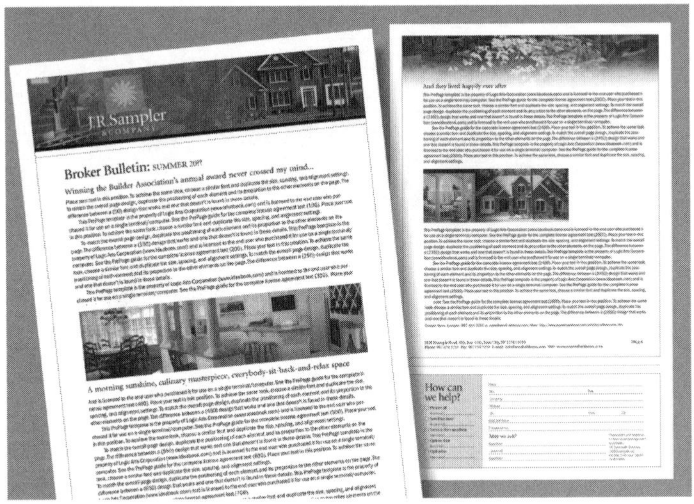


| | |
|---|---|
| SIZE | 8.5W x 14H |
| PAGES | 4 |
| FOLD | accordion-fold |
| STOCK | 60# uncoated text |
| BINDING | — |

## 244
## Calendar Newsletter

Used to create a newsletter. Features a full-page monthly event calendar. Page 1: cover; page 2: text; page 3: calendar; page 4: back cover. Add text spreads to create multiples of 4 pages (4,8,12,16). Have mailing piece artwork approved by postal service to confirm compliance with postal regulations.

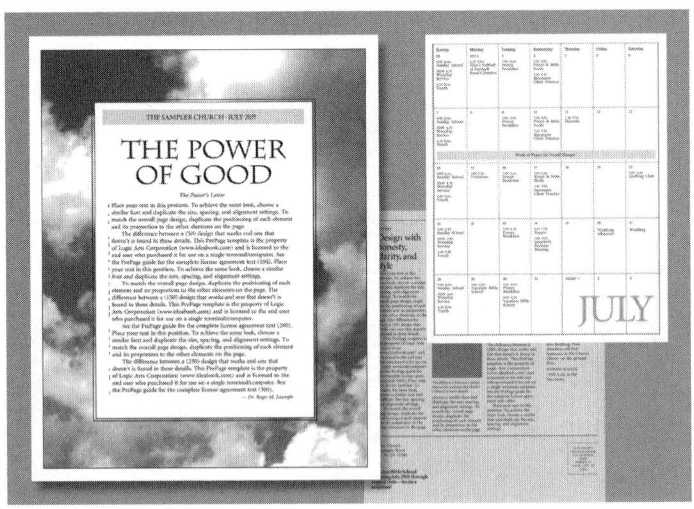


| | |
|---|---|
| SIZE | 17W x 11H (flat); 8.5W x 11H (finished) |
| PAGES | 4 |
| FOLD | half-fold |
| STOCK | 60# uncoated text |
| BINDING | saddle-stitch |

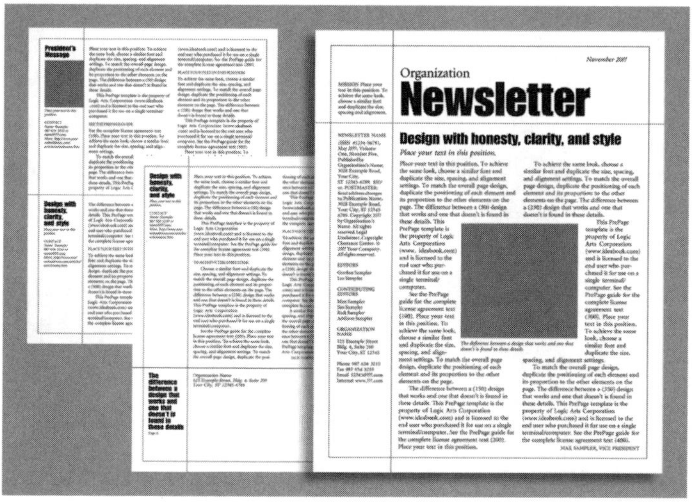


## 245 Callout Newsletter

Used to create a newsletter. Features sidebars for headlines and callouts. Page 1: cover; page 2–3: text; page 4: back cover. Add text spreads to create multiples of 4 pages (4,8,12,16). Have mailing piece artwork approved by postal service to confirm compliance with postal regulations.

| | |
|---|---|
| SIZE | 17W x 11H (flat); 8.5W x 11H (finished) |
| PAGES | 4 |
| FOLD | half-fold |
| STOCK | 60# uncoated text |
| BINDING | saddle-stitch |

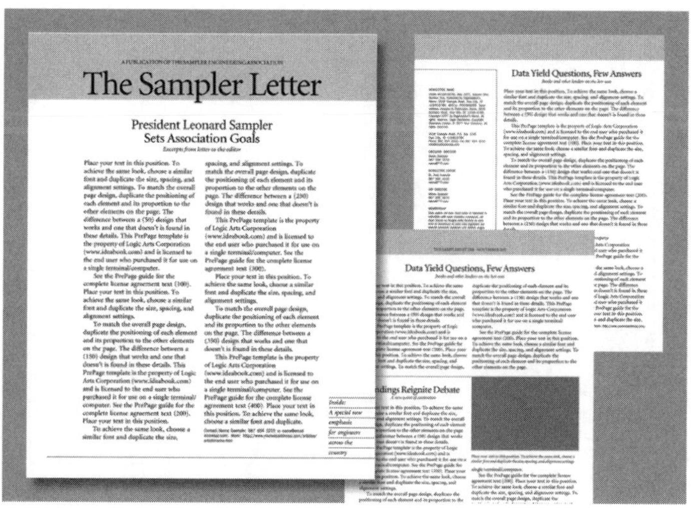


## 246 Classic Newsletter

Used to create a newsletter. Features sidebars for headlines and callouts. Page 1: cover; pages 2–3: text spread variation one; pages 4–5: text spread variation two; page 6: back cover. Mix and match text spreads to create multiples of 4 pages (4,8,12,16). Have mailing piece artwork approved by postal service to confirm compliance with postal regulations.

| | |
|---|---|
| SIZE | 17W x 11H (flat); 8.5W x 11H (finished) |
| PAGES | 6 |
| FOLD | half-fold |
| STOCK | 60# uncoated text |
| BINDING | saddle-stitch |

## 247
## Cut Quote Newsletter

Used to create a newsletter. Features quotable cut-out and response coupons. Page 1: cover with space for cut-out and mailing address; page 2: back with response coupon. Have mailing piece artwork approved by postal service to confirm compliance with postal regulations.

| | |
|---|---|
| SIZE | 8.5W x 14H (flat); 8.5W x 4.75H (finished) |
| PAGES | 2 |
| FOLD | letter-fold |
| STOCK | 60# uncoated text |
| BINDING | — |

## 248
## Easy Newsletter

Used to create a newsletter on legal-sized sheets to be mailed in an envelope. Page 1: cover; pages 2: text continued with a response coupon at the bottom.

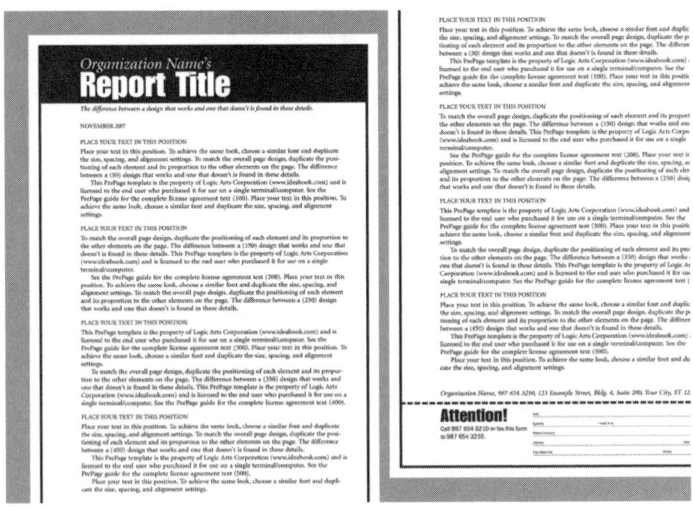


| | |
|---|---|
| SIZE | 8.5W x 14H |
| PAGES | 2 |
| FOLD | accordian-fold |
| STOCK | 60# uncoated text |
| BINDING | — |

## 249
## Element Newsletter

Used to create a newsletter. Features plug-in text and illustration elements. Page 1: cover; pages 2–3: text spread variation one; pages 4–5: text spread variation two; page 6: back cover. Mix and match text spreads to create multiples of 4 pages (4,8,12,16). Have mailing piece artwork approved by postal service to confirm compliance with postal regulations.

| | |
|---|---|
| SIZE | 17W x 11H (flat); 8.5W x 11H (finished) |
| PAGES | 6 |
| FOLD | half-fold |
| STOCK | 60# uncoated text |
| BINDING | saddle-stitch |

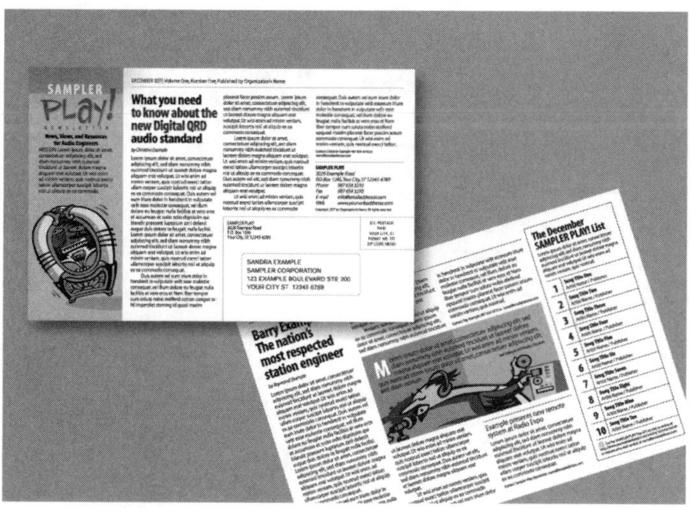


## 250
## Focus Postcard, vertical Newsletter

Used to create a newsletter in the form of an oversized postcard. Page 1: cover with space for nameplate, headlines, text, and mailing address; page 2: with space for headlines, text, and illustrations. Have mailing piece artwork approved by postal service to confirm compliance with postal regulations.

| | |
|---|---|
| SIZE | 9W x 6H |
| PAGES | 2 |
| FOLD | — |
| STOCK | 12pt card |
| BINDING | — |

## 251
## Ghosts Newsletter

Used to create a newsletter. Features a tall-thin profile with ghost gray illustrations. Page 1: cover; page 2: Contents; page 3: editor's letter; pages 4–5: text spread variation one; pages 6–7: text spread variation two; pages 8–9: text spread variation three; pages 10–11: text spread variation four; page 12: back cover. Mix and match text spreads to create multiples of 4 pages (4,8,12,16). Have mailing piece artwork approved by postal service to confirm compliance with postal regulations.

| | |
|---|---|
| SIZE | 8.5W x 11H (flat); 4.25W x 11H (finished) |
| PAGES | 12 |
| FOLD | half-fold |
| STOCK | 60# uncoated text |
| BINDING | saddle-stitch |

## 252
## Icons Newsletter

Used to create a newsletter. Features space for bold, simple illustrations. Page 1: cover; pages 2–3: text spread variation one; pages 4–5: text spread variation two; page 6: back cover. Mix and match text spreads to create multiples of 4 pages (4,8,12,16). Have mailing piece artwork approved by postal service to confirm compliance with postal regulations.

| | |
|---|---|
| SIZE | 17W x 11H (flat); 8.5W x 11H (finished) |
| PAGES | 6 |
| FOLD | half-fold |
| STOCK | 60# uncoated text |
| BINDING | saddle-stitch |

## 253 Illustrated Newsletter

Used to create a newsletter. Features space for photo/illustration combinations. Page 1: cover; page 2–3: text; page 4: back cover. Add text spreads to create multiples of 4 pages (4,8,12,16). Have mailing piece artwork approved by postal service to confirm compliance with postal regulations.

| | |
|---|---|
| SIZE | 17W x 11H (flat); 8.5W x 11H (finished) |
| PAGES | 4 |
| FOLD | half-fold |
| STOCK | 60# uncoated text |
| BINDING | saddle-stitch |

## 254 Jacket Newsletter

Used to create a newsletter wrapped in a color jacket. Page 1: jacket cover; pages 2–3: jacket text; page 4: jacket back cover with space for mailing address; page 5: newsletter cover; pages 6–8: newsletter text back cover. Add text spreads to create multiples of 4 pages (4,8,12,16). Wrap newletter in jacket and saddle stitch. Have mailing piece artwork approved by postal service to confirm compliance with postal regulations.

| | |
|---|---|
| SIZE | cover: 17W x 9.5H (flat); 8.5W x 9.5H (finished)<br>text: 17W x 11H (flat); 8.5W x 11H (finished) |
| PAGES | 8 |
| FOLD | half-fold |
| STOCK | 60# uncoated text |
| BINDING | saddle-stitch |

## 255
## Lines Newsletter

Used to create a newsletter. Features space for bold, simple illustrations. Page 1: cover; pages 2–3: text spread variation one; pages 4–5: text spread variation two; page 6: back cover. Mix and match text spreads to create multiples of 4 pages (4,8,12,16). Have mailing piece artwork approved by postal service to confirm compliance with postal regulations.

| | |
|---|---|
| SIZE | 17W x 11H (flat); 8.5W x 11H (finished) |
| PAGES | 6 |
| FOLD | half-fold |
| STOCK | 60# uncoated text |
| BINDING | saddle-stitch |

## 256
## Newspaper Newsletter

Used to create a newsletter that simulates a newspaper. Page 1: cover; page 2: back cover.

| | |
|---|---|
| SIZE | 7.5W x 3H (flat); 7.5W x 3H (finished) |
| PAGES | 4 |
| FOLD | newspaper-fold |
| STOCK | 60# uncoated text |
| BINDING | saddle-stitch |

## 257 Objects Newsletter

Used to create a newsletter. Features space for object photographic illustrations. Page 1: cover; pages 2–3: text spread variation one; pages 4–5: text spread variation two; page 6: back cover. Mix and match text spreads to create multiples of 4 pages (4,8,12,16). Have mailing piece artwork approved by postal service to confirm compliance with postal regulations.

| | |
|---|---|
| SIZE | 17W x 11H (flat); 8.5W x 11H (finished) |
| PAGES | 6 |
| FOLD | half-fold |
| STOCK | 60# uncoated text |
| BINDING | saddle-stitch |

## 258 Squares Newsletter

Used to create a newsletter. Features space for bold, simple illustrations. Page 1: cover; pages 2–3: text spread variation one; pages 4–5: text spread variation two; page 6: back cover. Mix and match text spreads to create multiples of 4 pages (4,8,12,16). Have mailing piece artwork approved by postal service to confirm compliance with postal regulations.

| | |
|---|---|
| SIZE | 17W x 11H (flat); 8.5W x 11H (finished) |
| PAGES | 6 |
| FOLD | half-fold |
| STOCK | 60# uncoated text |
| BINDING | saddle-stitch |

## 259 Strike Line Newsletter

Used to create a newsletter. Page 1: cover; pages 2–3: text spread variation one; pages 4–5: text spread variation two; page 6: back cover. Mix and match text spreads to create multiples of 4 pages (4,8,12,16). Have mailing piece artwork approved by postal service to confirm compliance with postal regulations.

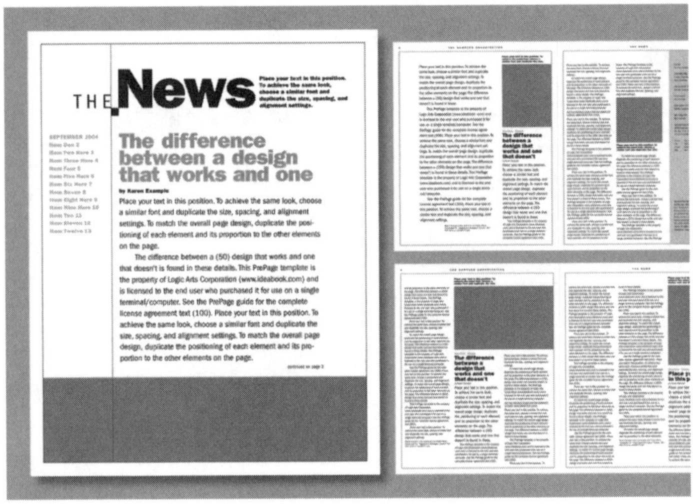


SIZE 17W x 11H (flat); 8.5W x 11H (finished)
PAGES 6
FOLD half-fold
STOCK 60# uncoated text
BINDING saddle-stitch

## 260 Tabs Newsletter

Used to create a newsletter. Features space for tabbed category headings. Page 1: cover; pages 2–3: text spread variation one; pages 4–5: text spread variation two; pages 6–7: text spread variation three; page 8: back cover. Mix and match text spreads to create multiples of 4 pages (4,8,12,16). Have mailing piece artwork approved by postal service to confirm compliance with postal regulations.

SIZE 17W x 11H (flat); 8.5W x 11H (finished)
PAGES 8
FOLD half-fold
STOCK 60# uncoated text
BINDING saddle-stitch

## 261
## Wing Newsletter

Used to create a newsletter with a peekaboo fold and a list calendar. Page 1: cover; pages 2–3: text spread; page 4: back cover with a calender list. The far-right column of the cover is folded under to reveal the photos in the far-right column of page 3.

| | |
|---|---|
| SIZE | 7.5W x 3H (flat); 7.5W x 3H (finished) |
| PAGES | 4 |
| FOLD | custom-fold |
| STOCK | 60# uncoated text |
| BINDING | — |

Chapter 15
# Packaging

## 262
## Cassette Album

Used to create artwork for a cover insert for a clear cover audio cassette album with an illustration. For use with the cassette labels (file 232).

(NOTE: The author and publisher have used their best efforts to proof and confirm the content of the files, but you should proof and confirm information such as dates, measurements, form properties, and any other content for yourself. The author and publisher make no warranties of any kind, express or implied, with regard to that content or its accuracy.)

| | |
|---|---|
| SIZE | 10.625W x 8.375H |
| PAGES | 1 |
| FOLD | custom-fold |
| STOCK | 60# uncoated text |
| BINDING | — |

## 263
## CD-ROM Label

Used to create artwork for a CD-ROM label featuring an illustration.

| | |
|---|---|
| SIZE | 116mm |
| PAGES | 1 |
| FOLD | — |
| STOCK | — |
| BINDING | — |

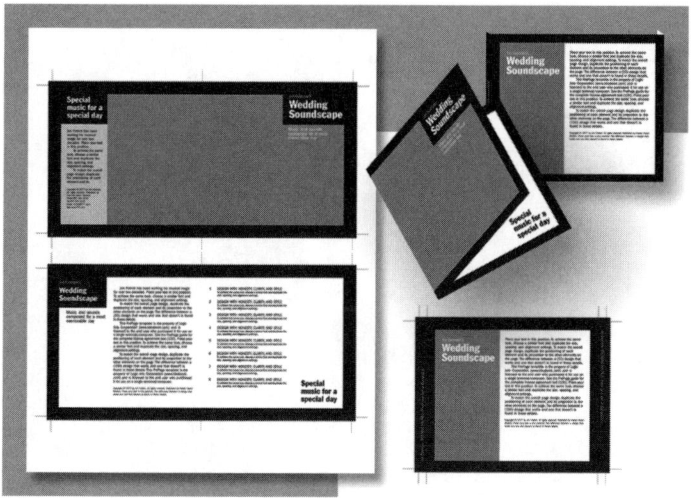


## 264
## CD-ROM Jewel Case Inserts

Used to create artwork for CD-ROM jewel case inserts. Page 1: 4-page booklet insert (top): cover; (bottom): inside; Page 2: jewel case tray insert.

| | |
|---|---|
| SIZE | cover insert: 9.5W x 4.75H (flat); 4.75W x 4.75H (finished)<br>tray insert: 5.875W x 4.625H (flat); 5.375W x 4.625H (finished) |
| PAGES | 2 |
| FOLD | cover: half-fold; tray: custom-fold |
| STOCK | 60# uncoated text |
| BINDING | — |

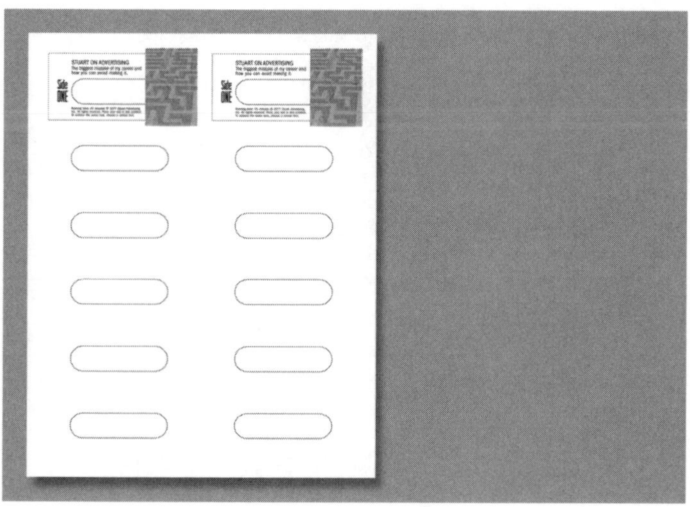


## 265
## Cassette Label

Used to print audio cassette tape labels (sized to fit Avery Laser/Ink Jet Labels 5198).

| | |
|---|---|
| SIZE | 3.5W x 1.625H |
| PAGES | 4 |
| FOLD | — |
| STOCK | Avery Laser/Ink Jet Label 5198 |
| BINDING | — |

### 266 Cassette Package 1

Used to create artwork for a cassette jewel case insert. Top: one-sided jewel case insert; bottom: cassette label.

| | |
|---|---|
| SIZE | 5.5W x 4H (flat); 2.5W x 4H (finished) |
| PAGES | 1 |
| FOLD | custom-fold |
| STOCK | 65# uncoated cover |
| BINDING | — |

### 267 Cassette Package 2

Used to create artwork for a cassette jewel case insert. Page 1: jewel case insert front; Page 2: jewel case insert back.

| | |
|---|---|
| SIZE | 4W x 4H (flat); 2.563W x 4H (finished) |
| PAGES | 1 |
| FOLD | custom-fold |
| STOCK | 65# uncoated cover |
| BINDING | — |

## 268
## Videotape Labels

Used to create artwork for video cassette labels with an illustration. Page 1: face labels; page 2: spine labels.

SIZE face: 3.0625W x 1.8125H; spine: 5.875W x 21/32H;
PAGES 2
FOLD —
STOCK Avery Laser/Ink Jet Label 5199
BINDING —

## 269
## Videotape Package

Used to create artwork for a video package insert with an illustration.

SIZE 11.5W x 8H
PAGES 1
FOLD custom-fold
STOCK 65# uncoated cover
BINDING —

**270**
**DVD Package**

Used to create inserts for Amaray® DVD packaging. Page 1: Amaray DVD case insert; page 2: Amaray DVD case booket, cover Amaray DVD case booket, inside

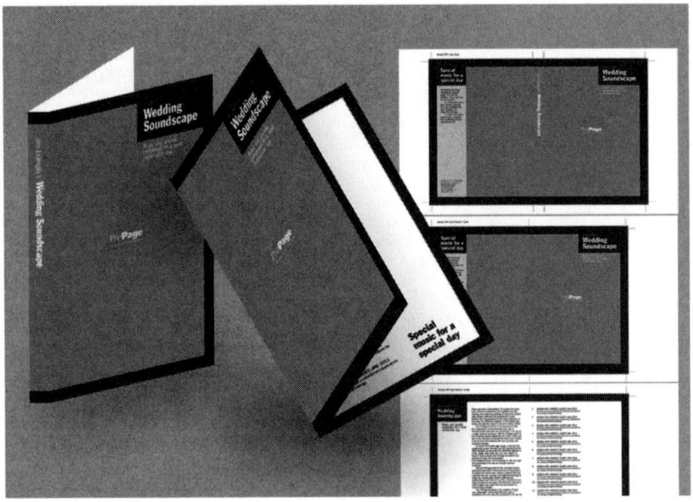


| | |
|---|---|
| SIZE | cover insert: 10.75W x 7.1875H (flat); 5.094W x 7.1875H (finished)<br>booklet insert: 9.75W x 7.3125H (flat); 4.875W x 7.3125H (finished) |
| PAGES | 3 |
| FOLD | cover insert: custom-fold; booklet insert: half-fold |
| STOCK | 65# uncoated cover |

Chapter 16

# Posters & Signs

## 271
## Bulletin Board Marketer

Used to create a sign and an attached pad of business cards for marketing your products and services on a local bulletin board. Print the backing on heavy stock and attach a pad of business-cards printed on text stock. Page 1: sign backing; page 2: business card pad.

(NOTE: The author and publisher have used their best efforts to proof and confirm the content of the files, but you should proof and confirm information such as dates, measurements, form properties, and any other content for yourself. The author and publisher make no warranties of any kind, express or implied, with regard to that content or its accuracy.)

| | |
|---|---|
| SIZE | base: 3.5W x 8.5H; card pad: 3.5W x 2H |
| PAGES | 2 |
| FOLD | — |
| STOCK | background: 65# uncoated cover; card pad: 60# uncoated text |
| BINDING | padding |

## 272
## Counter Card

Used to create an illustrated, countertop sign that fits a standard-sized 8.5 by 11 inch acrylic frame.

| | |
|---|---|
| SIZE | 8.5W x 11H |
| PAGES | 1 |
| FOLD | — |
| STOCK | 65# uncoated cover |
| BINDING | — |

## 273
## Instant Sign

Used to create illustrated signs that fit a standard-sized, wall-mounted 11 by 8.5 inch acrylic frame. Two versions.

| | |
|---|---|
| SIZE | 11W x 8.5H |
| PAGES | 2 |
| FOLD | — |
| STOCK | 65# uncoated cover |
| BINDING | — |

## 274
## Mail Art

Used to create a simple envelope featuring whatever illustrations are placed on the page. To create your version, add background images, print, trim, and fold as shown. Page 1: inside; page 2: outside.

| | |
|---|---|
| SIZE | 7.25W x 9.625H (flat); 5.75W x 4.375H (finished) |
| PAGES | 2 |
| FOLD | custom-fold |
| STOCK | 60# uncoated text |
| BINDING | — |

**275**
**Poster**
Used to create a poster.

| | |
|---|---|
| SIZE | 18W x 24H (flat) |
| PAGES | 1 |
| FOLD | — |
| STOCK | 100# text |
| BINDING | — |

**276**
**Quotations**
Used to create an inspirational quotation suitable for framing. Two versions.

| | |
|---|---|
| SIZE | large: 4.5W x 6.5H; small: 3.5W x 65H |
| PAGES | 1 |
| FOLD | — |
| STOCK | 24# bond |
| BINDING | — |

## 277
## Shelf Sign

Used to create an illustrated sign for a retail shelf. Page 1: large version; page 2: small version.

| | |
|---|---|
| SIZE | large: 5.5W x 8.5H (flat); 5.5W x 5.375H (finished)<br>small: 5.5W x 7.375H (flat); 5.5W x 4.25H (finished) |
| PAGES | 2 |
| FOLD | half-fold |
| STOCK | 65# uncoated cover |
| BINDING | — |

## 278
## Sign Pad

Used to create a countertop sign with a pad of coupons to ask the questions that sales people in a retail environment sometimes forget to ask. Print and mount it on a rigid board and attach a cardboard easel. Have coupons printed and bound as pads. Glue the final pad to the face of the sign.

| | |
|---|---|
| SIZE | base: 8.5W x 11H; pad: 5W x 3H |
| PAGES | 1 |
| FOLD | — |
| STOCK | base: 60# uncoated text; pad: 24# bond |
| BINDING | padding |

## 279
## Table Tent 1

Used to create a tabletop sign with illustrations. The page is divided into thirds, minus a flap for gluing or taping.

| | |
|---|---|
| SIZE | 11W x 8.5H |
| PAGES | 1 |
| FOLD | roll-fold |
| STOCK | 65# uncoated cover |
| BINDING | — |

## 280
## Table Tent 2

Used to create a tabletop sign as a reminder for an important event.

| | |
|---|---|
| SIZE | 4.25W x 5.5H (flat); 4.25W x 2.75H (finished) |
| PAGES | 1 |
| FOLD | half-fold |
| STOCK | 100# uncoated cover |
| BINDING | — |

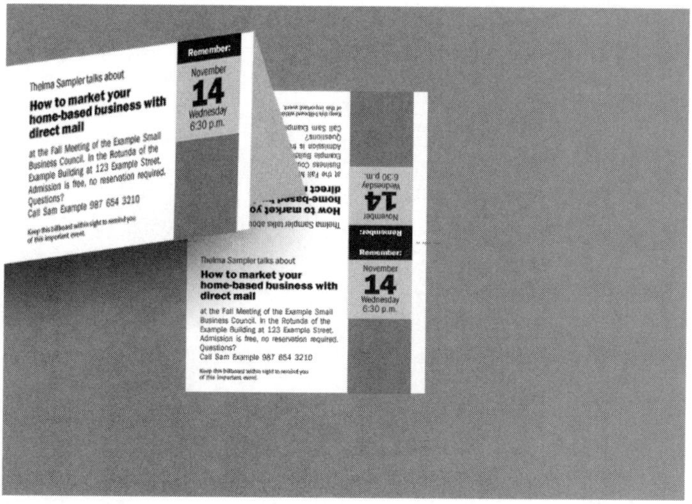


## 281
## Table Tent 3

Used to create a tabletop sign as a reminder for an important event.

| | |
|---|---|
| SIZE | 4.25W x 5.5H (flat); 4.25W x 2.75H (finished) |
| PAGES | 1 |
| FOLD | half-fold |
| STOCK | 100# uncoated cover |
| BINDING | — |

Chapter 17

# Presentations & Publicity

## 282
## Meeting Agenda

Used to create an agenda that informs and prepares your audience for a meeting. Shows the times, descriptions, and locations of a full day of activities.

(NOTE: The author and publisher have used their best efforts to proof and confirm the content of the files, but you should proof and confirm information such as dates, measurements, form properties, and any other content for yourself. The author and publisher make no warranties of any kind, express or implied, with regard to that content or its accuracy.)

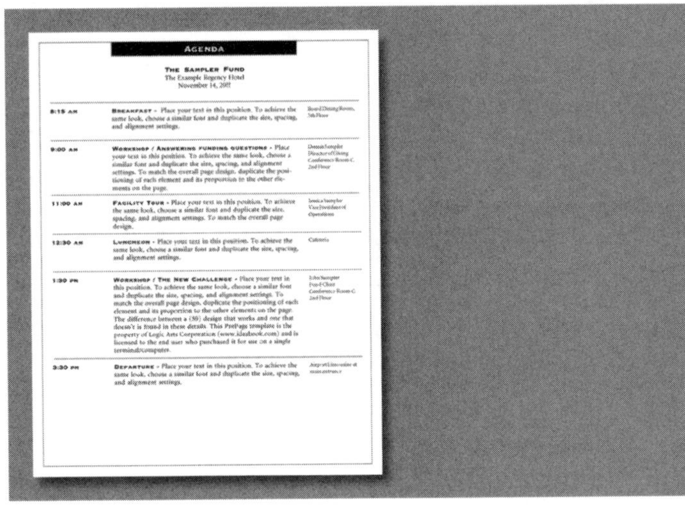


| | |
|---|---|
| SIZE | 8.5W x 11H |
| PAGES | 1 |
| FOLD | — |
| STOCK | 24# bond |
| BINDING | — |

## 283
## Multimedia Presentation

Used to create a presentation organized like a web page or as a simple template for a web site. Three versions.

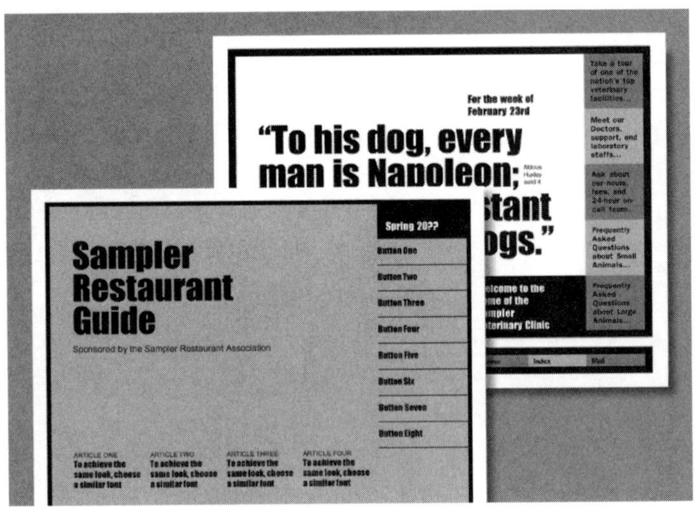


| | |
|---|---|
| SIZE | 8.5W x 11H (flat) |
| PAGES | 3 |
| FOLD | — |
| STOCK | 24# bond |
| BINDING | — |

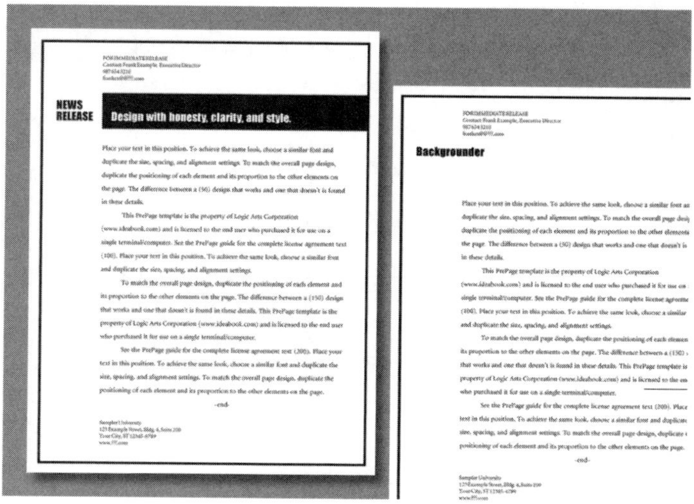


## 284
## News Release 1

8.5W x 11H
Used to create an attention-getting news release. Page 1: release; page 2: backgrounder.

| | |
|---|---|
| SIZE | 8.5W x 11H |
| PAGES | 2 |
| FOLD | — |
| STOCK | 24# bond |
| BINDING | — |

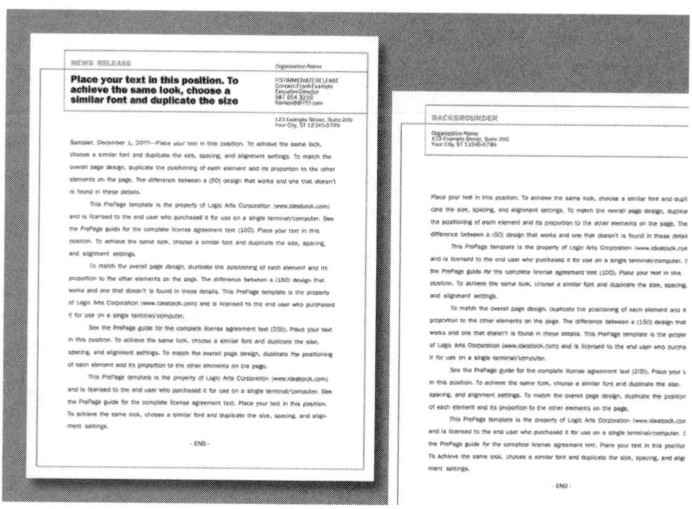


## 285
## News Release 2

Used to create an attention-getting news release. Page 1: release; page 2: backgrounder.

| | |
|---|---|
| SIZE | 8.5W x 11H |
| PAGES | 2 |
| FOLD | — |
| STOCK | 24# bond |
| BINDING | — |

## 286
## News Release 3

Used to create an attention-getting news release. Page 1: release; page 2: backgrounder.

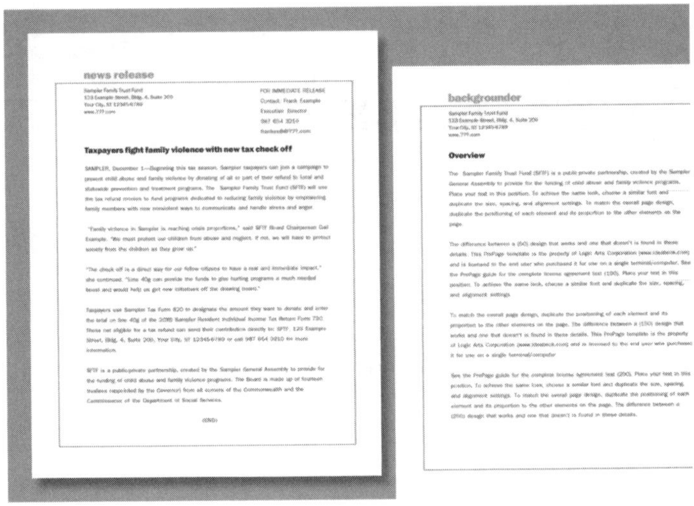


| SIZE | 8.5W x 11H |
|---|---|
| PAGES | 2 |
| FOLD | — |
| STOCK | 24# bond |
| BINDING | — |

## 287
## Overhead Transparency 1

Used to create easy, understandable overhead transparencies (sized to fit Avery Laser Transparencies 5282 or Avery Ink Jet Transparencies 5277).

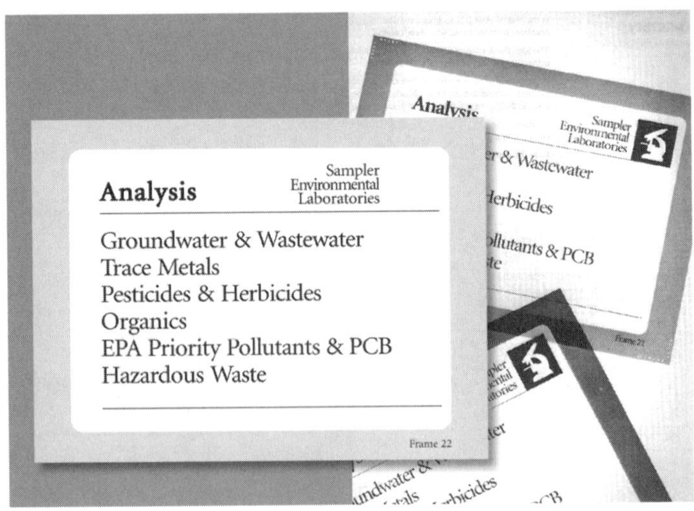


| SIZE | 11W x 8.5H |
|---|---|
| PAGES | 1 |
| FOLD | — |
| STOCK | Avery Laser Transparencies 5282; Ink Jet 5277 |
| BINDING | — |

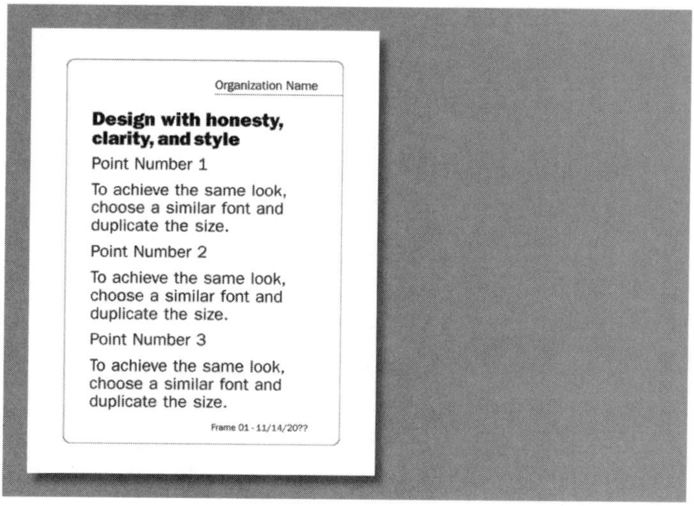


## 288 Overhead Transparency 2

Used to create easy, understandable overhead transparencies (sized to fit Avery Laser Transparencies 5282 or Avery Ink Jet Transparencies 5277).

| | |
|---|---|
| SIZE | 8.5W x 11H |
| PAGES | 1 |
| FOLD | — |
| STOCK | Avery Laser Transparencies 5282; Ink Jet 5277 |
| BINDING | — |

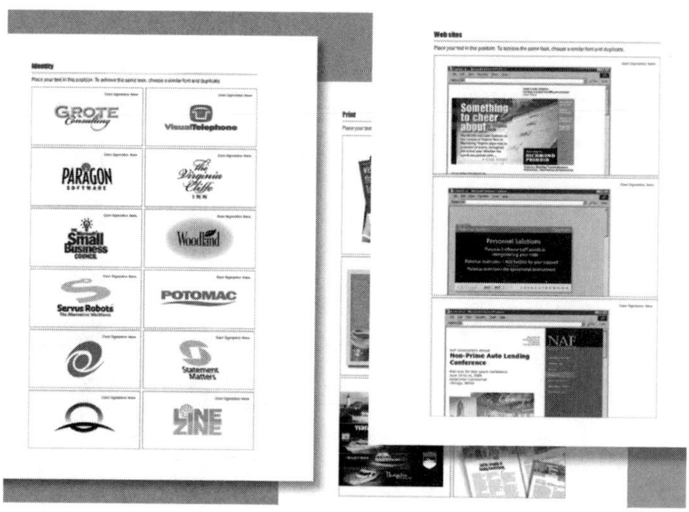


## 289 Portfolio

Used to create a printable design porfolio presention. Page 1: "Identity" page with 12 slots; page 2: "Print" page with one slot; page 3: "Print" page with two slots; page 4: "Web" page with three slots; page 5: "Print" page with four slots; page 6: "Print" page with six slots.

| | |
|---|---|
| SIZE | 8.5W x 11H |
| PAGES | 6 |
| FOLD | — |
| STOCK | 24# bond |
| BINDING | — |

## 290
## Presentation Book 1

Used to create a print presentation to a small group using an easel binder. The presentation on the left is supplemented with a column of text on the right used to assist the presenter in outlining or scripting the points that need to be made. Page 1: title page; page 2: text page.

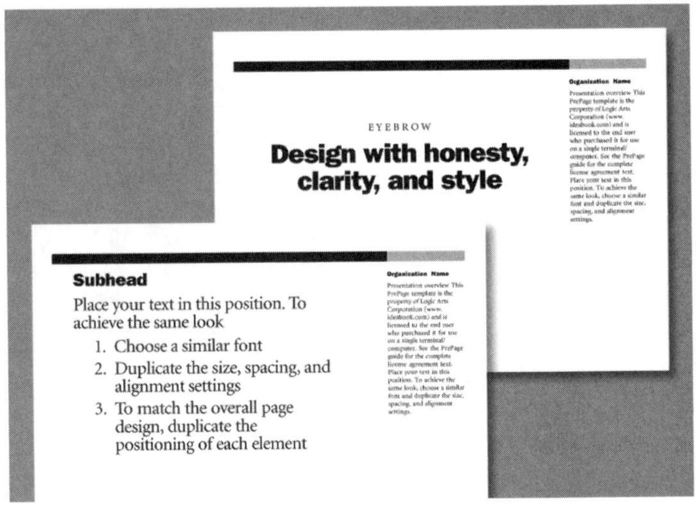


SIZE 11W x 8.5H
PAGES 2
FOLD —
STOCK 24# bond
BINDING —

## 291
## Presentation Book 2

Used to create a print presentation to a small group using an easel binder. The left-hand side of the page is used for detailed text and illustrations, the short right-hand column is used to repeat the organization's name and logo. Page 1: large text; page 2: small text.

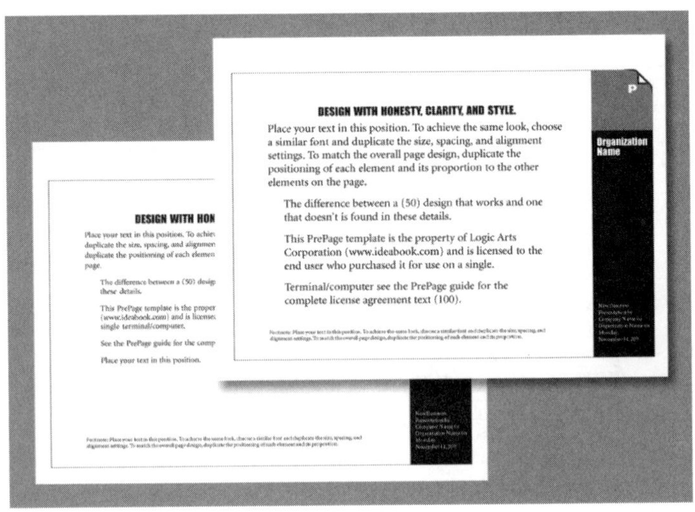


SIZE 11W x 8.5H
PAGES 2
FOLD —
STOCK 24# bond
BINDING —

## 292
## Presentation Chart

Used to create a simple, illustrated bar chart for a print presentation made to a small group using an easel binder.

| | |
|---|---|
| SIZE | 11W x 8.5H |
| PAGES | 1 |
| FOLD | — |
| STOCK | 24# bond |
| BINDING | — |

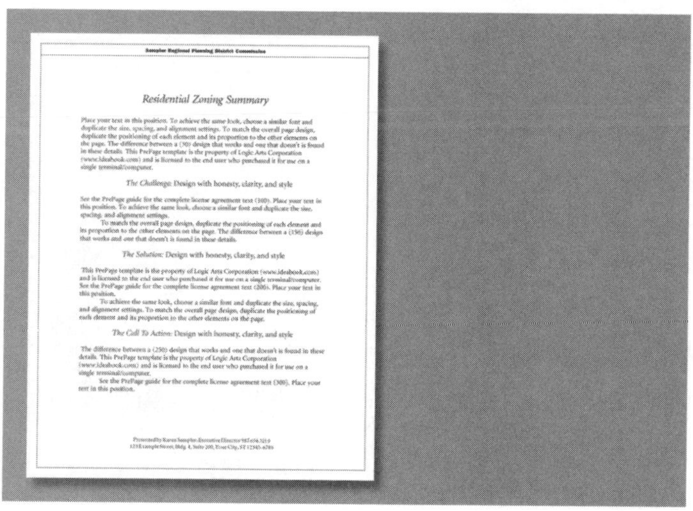


## 293
## Presentation Summary

Used to create a handout that summarizes your presentation.

| | |
|---|---|
| SIZE | 8.5W x 11H |
| PAGES | 1 |
| FOLD | — |
| STOCK | 24# bond |
| BINDING | — |

## 294
## Resume 1

Used to create an information-rich resume. This format features subheadings for objectives, education, work experience, special skills, and references.

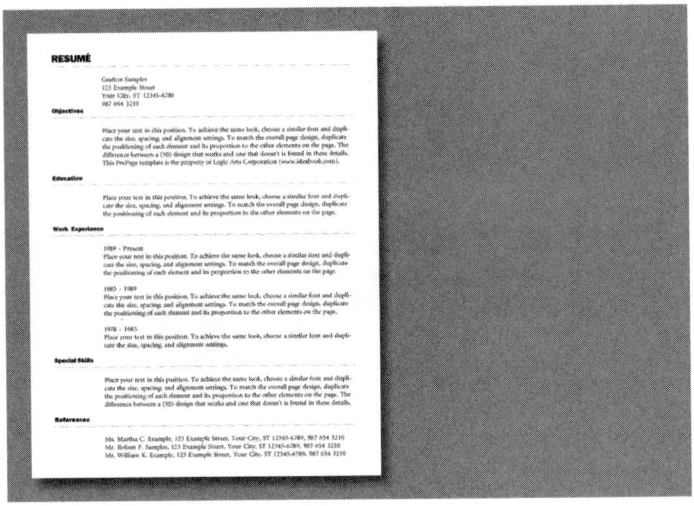


| | |
|---|---|
| SIZE | 8.5W x 11H |
| PAGES | 1 |
| FOLD | — |
| STOCK | 24# bond |
| BINDING | — |

## 295
## Resume 2

Used to create an information-rich resume. This format features subheadings for objectives, education, work experience, special skills, references, and a job title of the position being applied for.

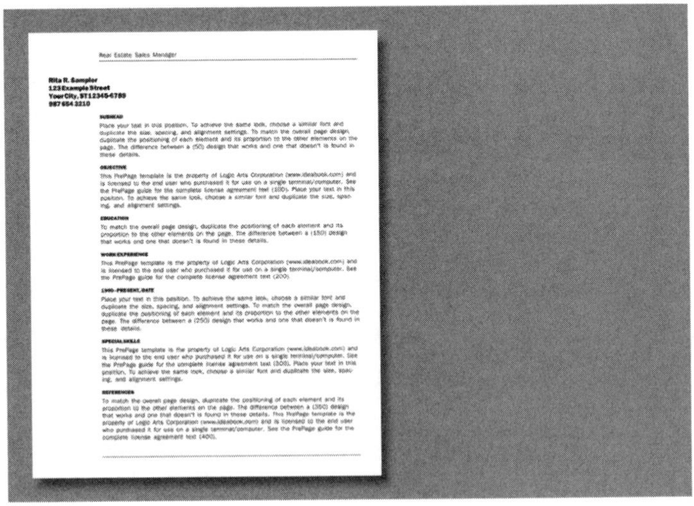


| | |
|---|---|
| SIZE | 8.5W x 11H |
| PAGES | 1 |
| FOLD | — |
| STOCK | 24# bond |
| BINDING | — |

## 296
## Family Album

Used to create a cover and caption panels for illustrating a family album. Page 1: the album cover is mounted to a second, heavier white sheet that is sized to fit a clear-cover binder; page 2: vertical caption columns; page 3: horizontal caption columns.

| | |
|---|---|
| SIZE | cover: 8.5W x 11H; large panel: 2.25W x 9H; small panel: 5W x 2H |
| PAGES | 3 |
| FOLD | — |
| STOCK | 60# text |
| BINDING | — |

Chapter 18

# Promotional Materials

## 297
## Bookmark 1

Used to create artwork for an illustrated bookmark for promoting your product or service. Page 1: large bookmark; page 2: small bookmark.

(NOTE: The author and publisher have used their best efforts to proof and confirm the content of the files, but you should proof and confirm information such as dates, measurements, form properties, and any other content for yourself. The author and publisher make no warranties of any kind, express or implied, with regard to that content or its accuracy.)

| | |
|---|---|
| SIZE | large bookmark: 2.25W x 8.5H; small bookmark: 2W x 6H (flat) |
| PAGES | 2 |
| FOLD | — |
| STOCK | 12pt card |
| BINDING | — |

## 298
## Bookmark 2

Used to create artwork for a bookmark with a table of information.

(NOTE: The author and publisher have used their best efforts to proof and confirm the content of the files, but you should proof and confirm information such as dates, measurements, form properties, and any other content for yourself. The author and publisher make no warranties of any kind, express or implied, with regard to that content or its accuracy.)

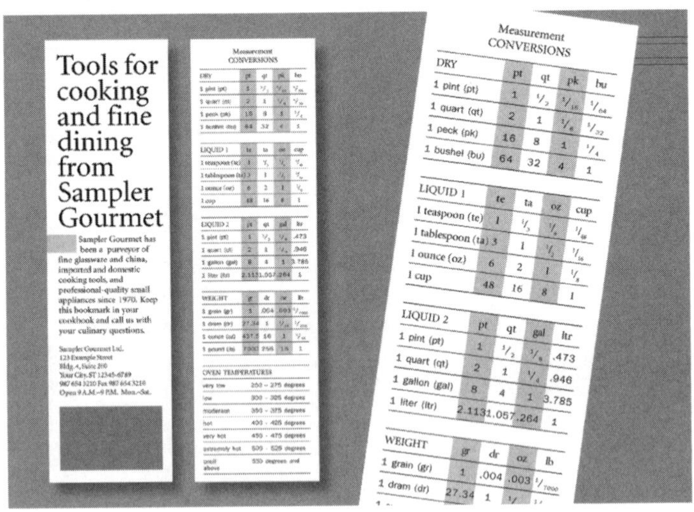


| | |
|---|---|
| SIZE | 2.375W x 8.5H |
| PAGES | 1 |
| FOLD | — |
| STOCK | 12pt card |
| BINDING | — |

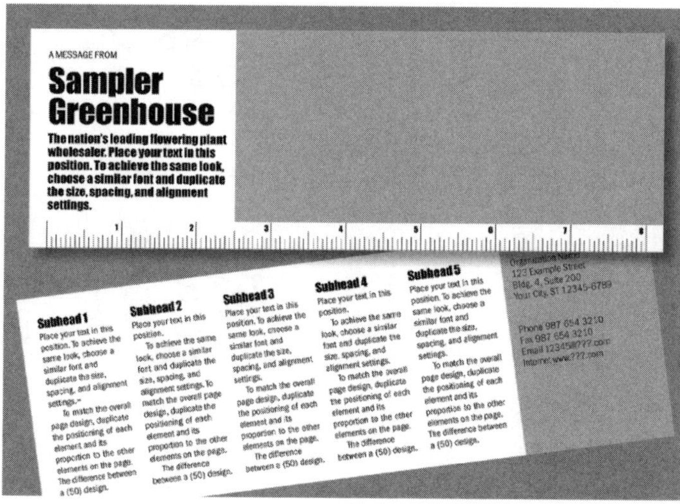


## 299 Bookmark Ruler

Used to create artwork for a bookmark with a ruler and a list of product or service attributes.

(NOTE: The author and publisher have used their best efforts to proof and confirm the content of the files, but you should proof and confirm information such as dates, measurements, form properties, and any other content for yourself. The author and publisher make no warranties of any kind, express or implied, with regard to that content or its accuracy.)

| | |
|---|---|
| SIZE | 8.5W x 3H (flat) |
| PAGES | 1 |
| FOLD | — |
| STOCK | 12pt card |
| BINDING | — |

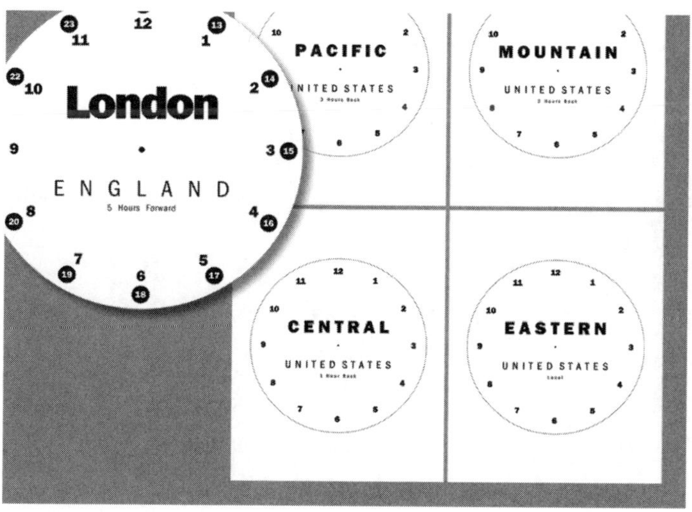


## 300 Time Zone Clock Faces

Used to create a series of clock faces that highlight time zones. The faces are sized to fit plastic battery-powered clocks found at many office supply and home products superstores. The process is easy. You disassemble the clock (most hands pull off easily) and replace the existing face with the time zone clock face. Page 1: 24 hour clock; page 2: eastern time zone; page 3: central time zone; page 4: mountain time zone; page 5: pacific time zone.

| | |
|---|---|
| SIZE | 6.875D |
| PAGES | 5 |
| FOLD | — |
| STOCK | 60# cover |
| BINDING | — |

## 301
## Coupon Money

Used to create artwork for coupons that look like money. Print stacks of coupons in dollar denominations (for example, 50 one-dollar coupons) and wrap them using the Coupon Wrappers (file 302).

| | |
|---|---|
| SIZE | 6.125W x 2.625H |
| PAGES | 1 |
| FOLD | — |
| STOCK | 24# bond |
| BINDING | — |

## 302
## Coupon Wrappers

Used to create artwork for strips used to wrap packs of coupons (file 301).

| | |
|---|---|
| SIZE | 8.5W x 1.125H |
| PAGES | 1 |
| FOLD | — |
| STOCK | 24# bond |
| BINDING | — |

## 303
## Flag

Used to create miniature flags and banners. Position a clip art flag to the right and the name of the county or state it represents to the left. Fold the flag and wrap it around a stick as shown.

| | |
|---|---|
| SIZE | 4.875W x 3.1875H |
| PAGES | 1 |
| FOLD | half-fold |
| STOCK | 60# uncoated text |
| BINDING | — |

## 304
## Gift Certificate

Used to create artwork for a product or service gift certificate. Page 1: cover; page 2: inside.

| | |
|---|---|
| SIZE | 6W x 8.5H (flat); 6W x 4.25H (finished) |
| PAGES | 2 |
| FOLD | half-fold |
| STOCK | 12pt card |
| BINDING | — |

## 305
## Idea Pad

Used to create artwork for a pad used to record ideas. Use them internally or hand them out to customers.

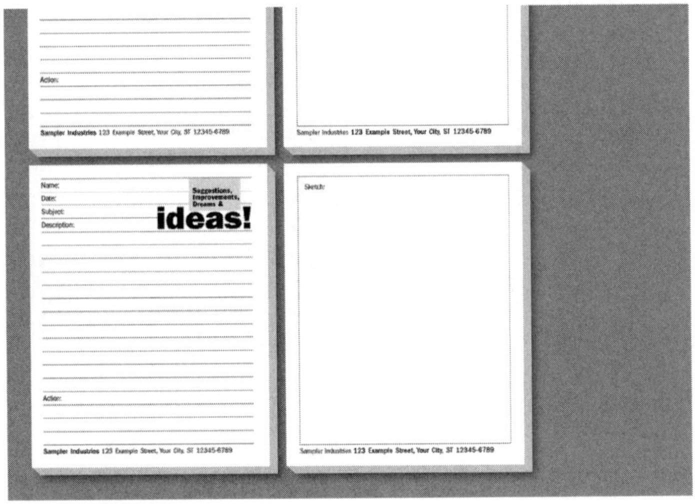


| | |
|---|---|
| SIZE | 4.25W x 5.5H |
| PAGES | 2 |
| FOLD | — |
| STOCK | 24# bond |
| BINDING | padding |

## 306
## Pads

Used to create artwork for printing illustrated promotional pads. Three versions. Page 1: lined; page 2: unlined; page 3: with illustration.

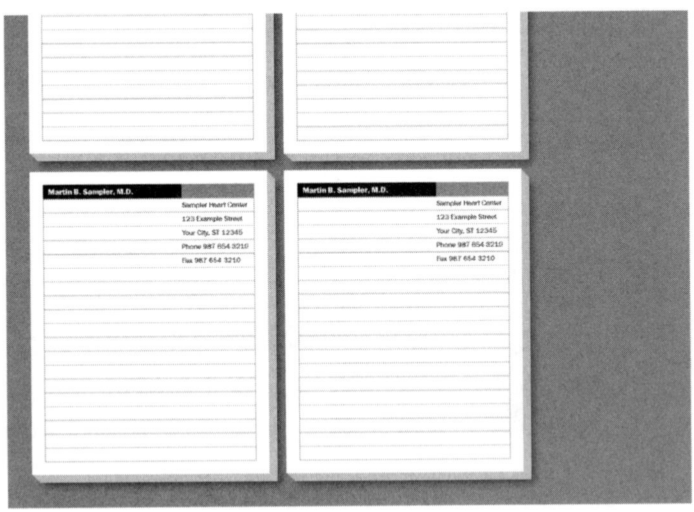


| | |
|---|---|
| SIZE | 4.25W x 5.5H |
| PAGES | 3 |
| FOLD | — |
| STOCK | 24# bond |
| BINDING | padding |

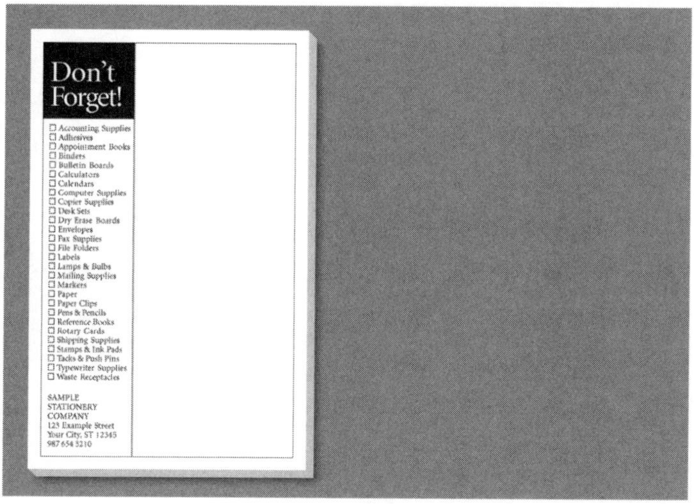


## 307
## Shopping List Pad

Used to create artwork for a promotional pad that doubles as a shopping list.

| | |
|---|---|
| SIZE | 5W x 8H |
| PAGES | 1 |
| FOLD | — |
| STOCK | 24# bond |
| BINDING | padding |

## 308
## Table Tent

Used to create a tabletop sign with an illustration. The page is divided into thirds, minus a quarter-inch flap for gluing or taping.

| | |
|---|---|
| SIZE | 8.5W x 11H (flat); 8.5W x 3.5H (finished) |
| PAGES | 1 |
| FOLD | roll-fold |
| STOCK | 65# uncoated cover |
| BINDING | — |

## 309
## Tickets

Used to create illustrated tickets for an event—with or without a name and address stub. Most printers can also perforate and number the tickets sequentially. Page 1: small; page 2: large.

| | |
|---|---|
| SIZE | large ticket: 2.75W x 8.5H; small ticket: 1.75W x 5.5H |
| PAGES | 2 |
| FOLD | — |
| STOCK | 12pt card |
| BINDING | — |

## 310
## Trading Cards

Used to create artwork for illustrated trading cards to promote hobbies, charitable organizations, schools, or businesses. Page 1, top: design based on question with answer on back; bottom: design based on interesting facts, or pictures of people, places, and things.

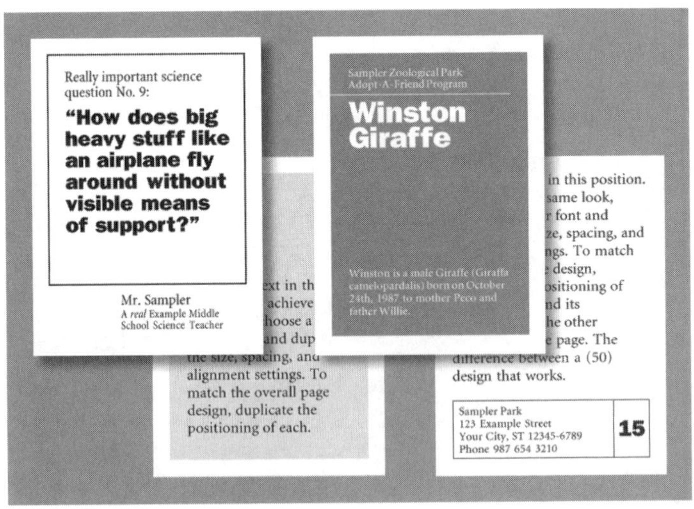


| | |
|---|---|
| SIZE | 2.5W x 3.5H |
| PAGES | 1 |
| FOLD | — |
| STOCK | 12pt card |
| BINDING | — |

Chapter 19

# Reports & Proposals

## 311
## Annual Report

Used to create artwork for an annual report. Legal requirements for an annual report and the format for how text and figures are presented varies with the type of organization publishing the report and the legal requirements. Be sure to check these before publishing the final report. Page 1: cover; page 2: contents; page 3: financial highlights; pages 4–5: section text version one; page 6–7: section text version two; pages 8–9: financial text; pages 10–11: financial figures; page 12: board of directors; page 14: back cover.

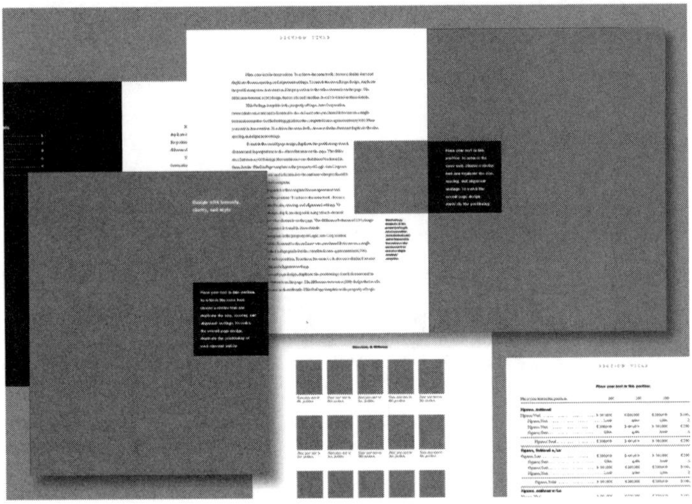

SIZE 8.5W x 17H (flat); 8.5W x 11H (finished)
PAGES 14
FOLD half-fold
STOCK cover: 100# uncoated cover; text: 60# text
BINDING saddle-stitch

## 312
## Proposal 1

Used to create a presentation of ideas in proposal form. Designed to be presented in a ring binder or presentation folder. Page 1: title page; page 2: text style; page 3: text style with chart.

(NOTE: The author and publisher have used their best efforts to proof and confirm the content of the files, but you should proof and confirm information such as dates, measurements, form properties, and any other content for yourself. The author and publisher make no warranties of any kind, express or implied, with regard to that content or its accuracy.)

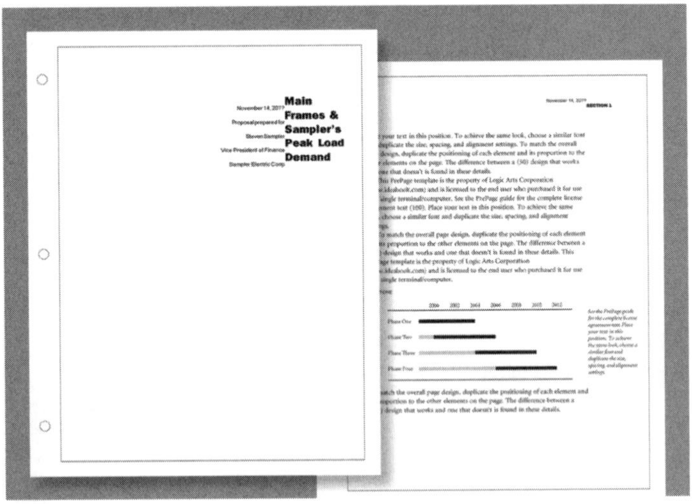


SIZE 8.5W x 11H
PAGES 3
FOLD —
STOCK 60# uncoated text
BINDING Hole punch

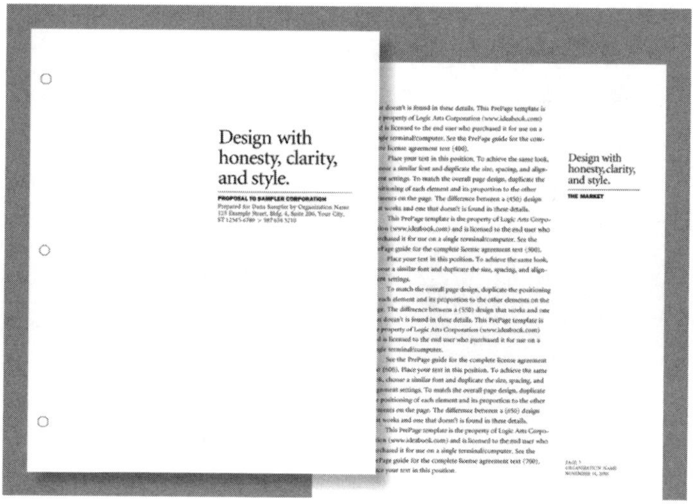


## 313
## Proposal 2

Used to create a presentation of ideas in proposal form. Designed to be presented in a ring binder or presentation folder. Page 1: cover page; pages 2–3: text style; page 4: back cover.

| | |
|---|---|
| SIZE | 8.5W x 11H |
| PAGES | 4 |
| FOLD | — |
| STOCK | 60# uncoated text |
| BINDING | Hole punch |

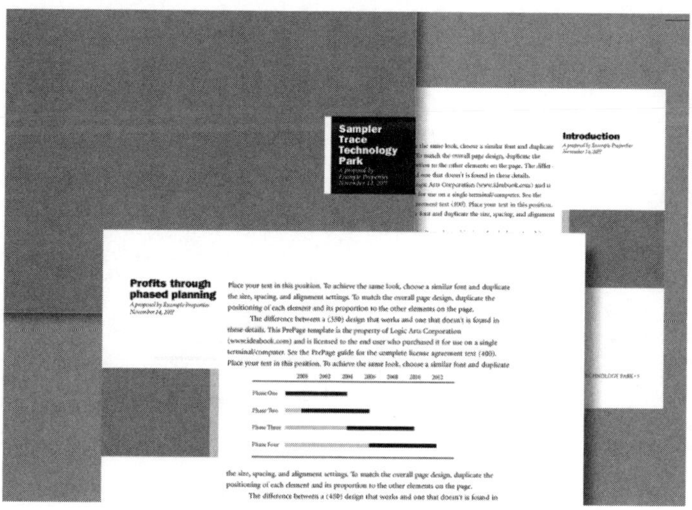


## 314
## Proposal 3

Used to create a presentation of ideas in proposal form. Designed to be presented in a ring binder or presentation folder. Page 1: cover; page 2: contents; page 3–5: text style; page 6: back cover.

| | |
|---|---|
| SIZE | 11W x 8.5H |
| PAGES | 6 |
| Fold | — |
| Stock | 60# uncoated text |
| Binding | — |

## 315
## Report

Used to create a report with sidebar titles and captions to be presented in a ring binder or presentation folder. Page 1: title page; page 2: contents; pages 3–5: text style.

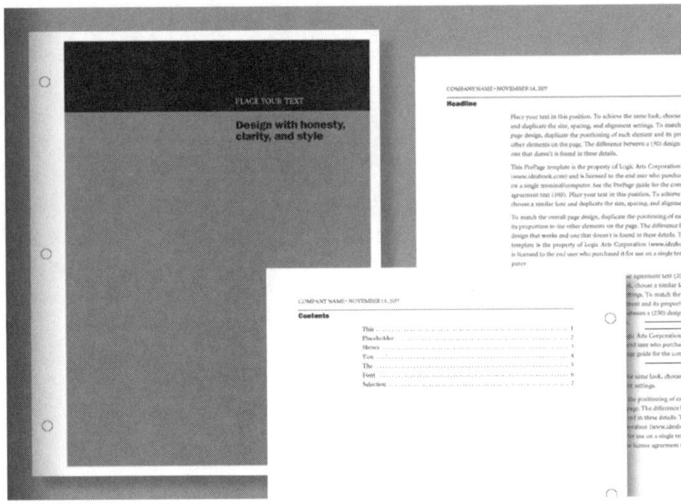


| | |
|---|---|
| SIZE | 8.5W x 11H |
| PAGES | 5 |
| FOLD | — |
| STOCK | 60# uncoated text |
| BINDING | Hole punch |

# Index

# Register your copy of The QuarkXPress Ideabook and WIN!

Register your copy of *The QuarkXPress Ideabook* and qualify to win a copy of Chuck Green's *Design it Yourself: Graphic Workshop*. PLUS, you will receive information about future books and/or editions of this book from Logic Arts. (One book awarded for every 500 registrations.)

Please complete and return your completed page or a photocopy of the page to:

Logic Arts Corp.
11475 Chickahominy
Branch Drive
Glen Allen, VA 23059

Name ______________________

Title ______________________

Department ______________________

Organization ______________________

Address ______________________

______________________

City ____________ State ____________

Zip/Postal Code ____________ Country ____________

Phone ____________ Date ____________

E-mail address ______________________

I rate this book: ☐ Excellent ☐ Good ☐ Fair ☐ Poor

The computer files are : ☐ Too complex ☐ Fine as is ☐ Too simple

Principal business ______________________

Learned about The Ideabook from ______________________

Purchased from ______________________

Date purchased ______________________

Your comments and suggestions:

Book Code: 0966958764_HB6B2407

# IMPORTANT-Read before opening the CD-ROM Package

## The QuarkXPress Ideabook/PrePage License Agreement

This is a legal agreement between you (either an individual or entity), the end user, and the publisher: Logic Arts Corporation. By opening the sealed CD-ROM package, you are agreeing to be bound by the terms of this agreement. If you do not agree to the terms of this agreement return the sealed package and the accompanying items (including this guide) to Logic Arts Corp. for a refund.

LICENSE AGREEMENT

1. GRANT OF LICENSE. Logic Arts Corp. grants you the limited right to use one (1) copy of the Logic Arts Corp. software/files (the "SOFTWARE/FILES") on a single terminal connected to a single computer. The SOFTWARE/FILES may be installed on a network server only for use by a specific individual. Additional single user versions of the SOFTWARE/FILES must be licensed from Logic Arts Corp. for use by more than one (1) user on the network.

2. COPYRIGHT. The SOFTWARE/FILES, and associated documentation are owned by Logic Arts Corp. or its suppliers and are protected by United States laws and international treaty provisions. Therefor, you must treat the SOFTWARE/FILES and documentation like any other copyrighted materials except that you may either (a) make one (1) copy of the SOFTWARE/FILES solely for backup and archival purposes, or (b) transfer the SOFTWARE/FILES to a single hard disk, provided you keep the original solely for backup or archival purposes. You may not copy the written materials accompanying the SOFTWARE/FILES.

3. OTHER RESTRICTIONS. You may not rent, lend, license, sublicense, lease, or distribute the SOFTWARE/FILES, by any means or in any form, but you may transfer the original version of the SOFTWARE/FILES and accompanying written materials on a permanent basis provided you retain no copies of the SOFTWARE/FILES and written materials and the recipient agrees in writing to the terms of this Agreement. You may not reverse engineer, decompile, or disassemble the SOFTWARE/FILES.

This agreement is governed by the laws of the Commonwealth of Virginia. If you have questions about this agreement, please contact Logic Arts Corp. at 11475 Chickahominy Branch Drive, Glen Allen, Virginia 23059 (804)266-7996.

LIMITED WARRANTY

LIMITED WARRANTY. Logic Arts Corp. grants a limited warranty only to the original licensee that (a) the SOFTWARE/FILES will perform substantially in accordance with the accompanying written documentation prepared by Logic Arts Corp. for a period of 90 days from the date of receipt by the original licensee.

CUSTOMER REMEDIES. Logic Arts Corp. entire liability and your exclusive remedy for breach of the Limited Warranty shall be at Logic Arts' option, either (a) return of the price paid by licensee solely for the SOFTWARE/FILES or (b) repair or replacement of the SOFTWARE/FILES which does not meet Logic Arts' Limited Warranty and which is returned to Logic Arts Corp. and determined by Logic Arts Corp. not to be in compliance. The Limited Warranty is void if failure of the SOFTWARE/FILES has resulted from accident, abuse, negligence, misapplication, or failure to use the SOFTWARE/FILES in accordance with the InDesign, PageMaker, or QuarkXPress / Logic Arts Corp. documentation. Any replacement SOFTWARE/FILES will be warranted for the remainder of the original warranty period or 30 days, whichever is longer.

NO OTHER WARRANTIES. LOGIC ARTS AND ITS SUPPLIERS DISCLAIM ALL OTHER WARRANTIES, BOTH EXPRESS AND IMPLIED, WITH RESPECT TO THE SOFTWARE/FILES, ITS QUALITY AND PERFORMANCE, AND THE ACCOMPANYING WRITTEN MATERIALS, INCLUDING BUT NOT LIMITED TO IMPLIED WARRANTIES OF MERCHANTABILITY AND FITNESS FOR A PARTICULAR PURPOSE. The limited Warranty specified above gives you specific legal rights. You may have others which vary from state to state. Some states do now allow limitations of duration of an implied warranty, so the above limitation may not apply to you.

LIMITATION OF LIABILITY. In no event shall Logic Arts Corp. or its Suppliers be liable for any special, indirect, consequential, exemplary, or incidental damages whatsoever (including, without limitation, damage from loss of business profits, business interruption, loss of business information, loss of goodwill, or other pecuniary loss) whether based in contract, tort, negligence, strict liability, or otherwise, arising out of the use of or inability to use the SOFTWARE/FILES, even if Logic Arts Corp. has been advised of the possibility of such damages. Because some states do not allow the exclusion or limitation of liability for consequential or incidental damages, the above limitation may not apply to you.